BRAND
TURNAROUND

BRAND TURNAROUND

HOW BRANDS GONE BAD
RETURNED TO GLORY
. . . and the Seven Game Changers That
MADE THE DIFFERENCE

KAREN POST

New York   Chicago   San Francisco   Lisbon   London   Madrid   Mexico City
Milan   New Delhi   San Juan   Seoul   Singapore   Sydney   Toronto

The McGraw·Hill Companies

1 2 3 4 5 6 7 8 9 10 DOC/DOC 1 9 8 7 6 5 4 3 2 1

ISBN   978-0-07-177528-1
MHID   0-07-177528-5

e-ISBN   978-0-07-177606-6
e-MHID   0-07-177606-0

Library of Congress Cataloging-in-Publication Data
Post, Karen
   Brand turnaround : how brands gone bad returned to glory and the 7 game changers that made the difference / by Karen Post. — 1st ed.
       p. cm.
   Includes bibliographical references and index.
   ISBN-13: 978-0-07-177528-1 (alk. paper)
   ISBN-10: 0-07-177528-5 (alk. paper)
   1. Brand name products. 2. Branding (Marketing) 3. Technological innovations—Management. I. Title
   HD69.B7P647 2012
   658.8'27—dc23   2011029498

To Denis Calabrese, Jill Griffin, Diana Marshall

My inspiring mentors and friends, without their wisdom and support this book would not be here today

Contents

Acknowledgments

A humongous and heartfelt thank you to the following people who inspired me, shared their wisdom, provided unconditional support and continue to tolerate my intense work style and unconventional ways about me.

To start with, I owe special gratitude to the CNN business reporter who phoned me more than a year ago for comments on a brand that was recalling a lot of products for the third time. After chatting with her about the brand gone bad, and if it could bounce back, the lightbulb went off. The book was born. *Gracias*, Julianne Pepitone.

My literary muses, editors, agents, and my publisher, the McGraw-Hill team, there are not enough words to show my appreciation: Donya Dickerson, Julia Baxter, Ann Pryor, Daina Penikas, Cheryl Hudson, Scott Amerman, Suzanne Rapcavage, Stephen Ingle, Ellen Schneid Coleman, Seth Godin, Mary Cucci, Kathleen Rushall, and Bill Gladstone.

And my deep gratitude to a long list of others who made this book possible.

My fabulous assistant and marketing coordinator, Lauren Angrick, who earns her title everyday as Chief Problem Solver of my companies.

I couldn't have done it without my Sherlock researchers, who found the facts, stats, and evidence for the book: Abe Sauer, and Kate Hazelwood.

My top-notch design, video, and IT team were invaluable: Kristen Friend and Barry Wallace, Andrew Ortoski, Bryan Parnell, Christian Schwier, Eric Wallace, and Austin Learner.

My sounding boards, advisors, and business partners: Diana Marshall, Jill Griffin, Denis Calabrese, Alan Weiss, James Balasco, PhD, Nancy Walker, Ron Walker, Joy Galatro, Michael Arabia, Jayne Jewell, John Connery, Laura Van Wagner, Bruce Van Wagner, Tom Schwartz, Jocelyn Ring, Carl Ring, Annette Kuntz, Kay Toolson, Ron Stewart, Kit Stewart, Michael Stewart, Chris Stewart, John Turner, John Nepute, Richard Batenburg, John Omlor, Dennis Thomas, Dr. Rebecca White, Jess English and all my colleagues from the University of Tampa, John H. Sykes College of Business Entrepreneurship Center, the University of Tampa Boards of Fellows, and Linda Olson and WAVE colleagues who provided valuable feedback, ideas, and encouragement.

My family: Cathy, JJ, Krissy, my mom and my dad who support all of my projects with unconditional love and enthusiasm.

My very first clients, who believed in me 30 years ago and gave me an opportunity to cut my teeth and do great work: Jody Larriviere and Jimmy Gossen.

My recent clients who invited me to work with their organizations and who have provided me much inspiration: Albemarle and the Earthwise team, Duchossois Group, Liberty Diversified International, Saudi Arabian Airlines, Pizza Hut (IPHFHA), Society of International Travel Executives, American Intercontinental University, Pam Iorio, The Brand Journalists Association of Nigeria, International Speakers Bureau, Leading Authorities, Five Star Speakers and Trainers, Keppler Speakers, and Marlyn Paul at Alliance Science.

My global empowerment from across the pond, who exposed me to new perspectives and cultures: João Gomes DeBrito (Johnny) Morabazza, Gerri Smith, David Taylor, Nicole Armstrong, Baptiste Houlbreque, Yousef Attiah, Neta Nwosu, Paul Maduka Okoro, Martin Lindstrom, TO/Taiwo Obe.

My tennis buddies who keep me exercising and staying on my competitive game, when I wanted to drink wine.

Introduction

You are about to learn some amazing, shocking, and sad tales about all kinds of brands. From dominant global brands to start-ups and nonprofits, from celebrities and professionals in all fields to entire countries, I've worked with all kinds of brands and witnessed the rise and fall of many.

While the details are different, all brands strive for one universal goal: to be the brand of choice. Each brand wants to be loved, respected, sustainable, and bearing meaningful fruit—profits, fame, votes, or whatever represents achievement—for its stakeholders to enjoy. One might imagine that in today's world with its multimillion-dollar budgets, rooms full of MBAs, and 47 focus groups, brands would no longer stumble. Yet they do. Why? Among the myriad reasons: no budget, no experience, no formal education, bad choices and a slew of bad luck, decisions by committee, egos the size of Texas, underfunded programs, overspending on stuff that really does not matter, inability or unwillingness to change, moving too slowly, pulling the trigger too quickly, politics, focusing on the problem and not the solution, fear of taking risks, taking too many uncalculated risks, and so on. All these things are happening right now, somewhere, and they are either building and fueling or killing and disabling the growth of those brands.

Brand Turnaround captures the churn, burn, and return to glory of more than 75 brands. Some are small; others are global leaders. Some have experienced monumental shake-ups and downturns; others have been hit with an event or situation that has caused intense public scrutiny, negative media coverage, and damage to the brand's stature. These brands span many products and services, including commercial, individual, cause-related, sports, entertainment, political, destinations, and governmental brands. Among them:

- Some were caught in a scandal, a major product recall, or a devastating accident. (We'll examine how they earned their way back to a popular and prosperous brand status.)
- Others were on the brink of disaster, experienced a brand bump, operated in troubled waters, and might have sunk at any moment. (We'll take a look at how they changed course and came back stronger than ever.)
- Still others had bit the dust and were ready for the History Channel. (We'll see how they returned from this near-death experience to become living, breathing, and back on their game.)

We'll explore both current and legacy brands to demonstrate the timeless value of some methods and to see how technology has dramatically impacted both the brands themselves and the environment in which they operate. Featured stories will include business-to-consumer, business-to-business, and nonprofit brands.

Of course, brands can change as quickly as Florida's weather. One minute it's a beautiful day; 17 minutes later a vicious storm has wiped out years of work and investment. In *Brand Turnaround*, we will study the enduring lessons these brands provide.

At the time of this writing, all the brands mentioned as turnarounds are back in their glory; however, as with all things in life, there are no guarantees about what tomorrow may bring. For updates on these brands and new case studies of brand turnarounds, visit http://www.brandturnaround.com.

What This Book Will Do for Your Brand

Brand Turnaround is not a collection of horror stories; it is your road map to a healthy, sustainable future.

By examining and analyzing the missteps and misfortunes of others, this book

- Clarifies the new opportunities and challenges that await today's brands
- Addresses how and why brands go bad, get bruised, or become broken
- Provides you with proven, pragmatic paths to brand recovery
- Inspires fresh thinking and actionable change, so your brand will succeed

The chapters are organized into two main sections. While they can be read independently to find answers to a particular problem, I recommend you read and work though all 10 chapters in sequence so that you will be able to recognize all of the phases of a brand breakdown and understand the various elements that comprise a successful turnaround.

Here's a quick tour of what's in store.

Part 1: It's a Brand-New Game

Branding fundamentals remain the same as they have always been, but many key dimensions have changed. Today, anyone (a person or a company) or anything (a product or a service) can compete as a brand. The stage is bigger than it has ever been, and the pace is faster; take your eye off the prize and you may lose it. One day a brand is on top; the next day it can be fighting for survival.

In Part 1, we look at the events that shake a brand, which can range from product recalls to poor customer preference polls; from the personal missteps or scandals that can throw a public figure off his or her game to an unsolved murder that plays havoc with an island's tourism industry.

You'll get an inside look at brands that were officially declared disasters in the public eye as well as those that experienced critical events that negatively impacted their image, consumer confidence, their stock price/valuation, or their market share.

In this part, you will find the Quick Start "Save Your Brand" Plan—an easy-to-implement checklist showing what to do when crisis hits and when you haven't got a plan in place. We will also explore the cycle of a turnaround and what you can expect once your brand returns to glory.

Ironically, some of the worst brand shake-ups have actually fueled even stronger brands. Martha Stewart returned bigger and better after her jail sentence. Her stumble humanized her in the eyes of many consumers. On her return, she landed a new and more relevant partnership with Macy's, replacing her old one with Kmart, whose brand had declined after its merger with Sears. She continues to expand her brand with successful forays into new areas, such as her recent line of pet-care products.

Each chapter reveals another facet of brands in crisis:

Chapter 1 uses four case studies to explore how commercial brands (Domino's Pizza), individual brands (Kobe Bryant), nonprofit brands (American Red Cross), and destination brands (Aruba) can repair their battered brand images, often bringing them back to even greater glory.

In Chapter 2 we investigate

- The qualifying characteristics of a "brand gone bad" or one that is fast on its way to meeting that fate
- What happens on the day the brand explodes ("That can't be *us!*")
- What to do when you are blindsided and caught without a plan, and how to create one quickly
- How to determine how vulnerable your brand is

We'll examine multiple scenarios of a brand in trouble: from the obvious disaster to the hidden symptoms of a brand doing a slow burn. This chapter is about risk management and prudent preparation.

Chapter 3 is about turning points and the moment of truth. It will help you to do these things:

- Decide when to play offense, play defense, buy time, or throw in the towel
- Determine what your real resources are and how to access the leaders, players, and support staff
- Create critical change and understand the need to sacrifice the lambs
- Evaluate the impact of disruption on your brand's culture

Brands that survive the shock, setbacks, and what seems to be imminent death not only know what to do but also are able to infuse epic transformation quickly, efficiently, and with sufficient momentum to carry on. In this chapter, we'll look at culture conversion, how to do it, and how to make sure it sticks.

Part 2: Seven Game Changers That Made the Difference

Every minute of every day, all over the world, new brands are born. The day companies or organizations open their doors for business or to further a cause, they are molding their brand and its destiny. This can happen organically or it can be thoughtfully planned and navigated.

Most brands set out to provide a product(s), solve problems, or make experiences remarkable and memorable in the hope of reaping some form of reward for their effort and investment. When successful, these actions earn brands devotion, loyalty, and respect. They make a lot of money, contribute to a better society, and, they hope, live happily ever after.

Others, such as Circuit City, Blockbuster, Washington Mutual, and Pontiac started with similar goals, but the results were very different. I originally had Charlie Sheen on this list, but the results are unknown for now. A sitcom, "Anger Management" starring Sheen, has been announced. As of this writing, no network has been named. For some, it's bankruptcy or liquidation; for others, it's a professional and personal dead end. As for Charlie Sheen, the jury is still out on this one.

This demise can stem from one monumental brand-shaking event or a series of events that alter the brand's path forward. In the public's eye, the brand often moves from a place of trust, to one of disgust. The bright, positive mental mark it once made in the mind of the market erodes quickly. Brands go bad because of real or perceived questionable actions and motives, broken promises, deception, negligent or reckless behavior, greed, and, sometimes, simply bad luck.

Today, brands operate in environments of fierce competition, media mania, market shifts, and societies with ever-changing values. Most experience their share of ups and downs, victories and defeats. One would think brands, businesses, and people isolated from serious challengers and setbacks would be on a sure track to success; quite the opposite is the case. As my favorite law of failure goes, the more one fails, the more successful one can be. Failure is in fact the best catalyst for success. You'll see this in many brand turnarounds.

Winners vs. Losers: What Makes the Difference?

When brands go bad, what separates the survivors from the big losers, the sustainable brands from the forever broken ones?

It's not what hits your brand upside the head but rather how you get back in the game that matters. In Part 2, you'll find out about the lessons learned from the trenches of business and life and how events impacted the health and sometimes the wealth of a brand. The examples are of real companies and people, their situations, and the moves that made the difference and transformed them from a place of defeat to a place of glory.

The brands we'll examine span the full spectrum of category and size. Some are individual brands; some smaller, midmarket private enterprises; and others are publicly traded and serve global markets around the world. They are all unique, have distinctive offerings, and serve diverse consumer and business segments, and yet all share a common history: one day they were popular brands in the market; the next, they were damaged and questionable in the hearts and minds of the market.

To help you apply the lessons derived from these cases to your individual situation, in each Game Changer, I identify a driving behavior or mindset, a set of questions to challenge your planning, and key takeaways to help you focus on what needs to be done. (For further help on any topic, you will find a list of resources at the back of the book.)

These lessons let you progress through a variety of brand-destroying crises and show you how to apply the best practices and breakthrough actions presented to each specific situation. At the end of each Game Changer, "turnaround takeaways" will help you focus on the actions you can take should you find yourself in a similar place.

- *Game Changer 1: Take Responsibility* (Chapter 4). Scandals, accidents, and misfortune can strike like lightning and instantly handicap even the strongest brands. The public is shocked, the media goes into a feeding frenzy, and lawyers are racking up fees. Within minutes of the news, the brand is center stage. In this lesson, I share best-case and worst-case scenarios and the elements that shifted the brand tide from crisis to composure at the height of a pivotal event.
- *Game Changer 2: Never Give Up* (Chapter 5). This chapter is dedicated to the bounce-back brands of those who have served time in prison or whom the court of public opinion has judged just as guilty as those who did—from Michael Vick, whose involvement in dog fighting and other inhumane treatment of dogs led to 18 months in jail, who re-earned his status as one of the top National Football League quarterbacks; to Martha Stewart, the Domestic Diva many love to hate; to Arianna Huffington, who survived a series of rejections to become an Internet institution. These stories address how, after suffering loss, or paying their dues to society, these people rehabilitated themselves and relaunched their careers and/or created a stronger brand.
- *Game Changer 3: Lead Strong* (Chapter 6). Here, we look at bounce-back brand leadership and the special qualities of the people behind the turnarounds. These stories address how these leaders take

responsibility for the heat and make decisions critical to the brand's future survival. This Game Changer showcases insights gleaned from the minds of the brightest leaders behind the brand, looking at triumphs as well as costly decisions that have made history and laid the groundwork for a return to full brand glory.

- *Game Changer 4: Stay Relevant* (Chapter 7). One size does not fit all in branding or brand recovery. The audiences are diverse, with different agendas and value systems. At the time of a brand-shaking event, critical voices are at the table contributing to what happens to the brand after the fall. A brand's marketplace of buyers and followers can include employees, customers, and third-party influencers. The bigger the brand is, the more complex the pool of needy and sometimes demanding stakeholders. Add to this the explosion of thousands of new segmented communication channels, and a brand in troubled waters has a huge ocean to navigate.

  Companies that have turned around the most horrific situations have consistently identified, prioritized, and crafted both strategic communications and relationship-building programs. Appeasing a diverse array of stakeholders while the company is suddenly showcased in high-profile public communication venues is one of the most difficult dances a brand team must pull off. How does a brand show sincere compassion to the Joe-Six-Pack consumer (who drives the car), while providing stockholders (who invest in you) a sense of confidence and calm, and, at the same time, not spoon-feed the plaintiff's attorneys, who are suing your butt for more money than most can imagine? We will examine the best practices to reach diverse markets.

- *Game Changer 5: Keep Improving* (Chapter 8). Constant improvement, new and different ways of doing things, and innovative changes that helped return brands to their place of glory is the theme of this chapter. No matter the exact details of what got a brand in trouble, the actions that resulted in these outcomes must change. Here you'll discover how evolving and focusing on doing things better have contributed to a brand's comeback. Whether it is a technological innovation; recycling an aspect of a former star brand; changing a product or voice; or just reinvention to keep up with change, to clean the slate and take a brand-new direction, a brand won't bounce back without real and substantial change.

* *Game Changer 6: Build Equity* (Chapter 9). It's essential to embrace honesty, authenticity, and the highest degree of brand integrity in order to build trust. This is best done by engaging all constituents, customers, employees, and partners; delivering on all promises; and staying consistent in your message. Doing so means having an open and honest dialogue with all stakeholders in good times and in bad. For businesses and brands, trust is often the defining aspect of success or failure. Once trust is lost, the consumer soon does not believe or have faith in the brand's story and defects from it. This chapter shows how successful brands create bonds with their increasingly cynical—after feeling betrayed by brands so often in recent years—consumer markets that sustain them through good times and help them survive the bad.

* *Game Changer 7: Own Your Distinction* (Chapter 10). Call it positioning, your unique attribute, or a "brain tattoo," the mental impression that consumers can't get out of their minds that sets a brand apart from the pack must be distinct, and you must own it. In the oceans of sameness and "me-too" offering economies, turnaround brands have a hold on their points of distinction, and continue to develop them. This lesson will help you clearly understand what a hardcore "blue ocean" (i.e., a new category) or compelling differentiator looks like and how distinction strategies are pivotal to the brand comeback game. We'll look at examples of turnaround brands and how their distinction—innovation, promotion, persona, and packaging—has fueled their comeback.

There is something else you need to know about turnarounds—something that can't be taught. The old adage that time heals all wounds is often true. Throughout these lessons, you will see the role patience and perseverance played in many brand bounce-backs.

It is important to keep in mind that all the bounce-back brands came to crossroads. Do leaders and staff give up or do they fight on? What impact does drinking the Kool-Aid have on staff at all levels—those on the front lines to C-level leadership? We will examine the impact that going through a comeback can have on everyone involved. Everything from a change in outward signs of confidence (e.g., posture, tone of voice, and the ability to make eye contact) to serious health issues and even suicides have resulted. Knowing what to expect and preparing for it can ease the burden and diminish the stress.

Once your brand recovers, it is essential to build on what you have learned and employ a mindset of sustainable strategies and practices. With those things in place, future brand shake-ups can be handled quickly and well and *before* another turnaround is necessary.

I've found there are some misconceptions about what a brand is and is not, so before we dive in, let's first make sure we are on the same page when we use the word *brand*.

Defining Terms: What Does *Brand* Mean?

A brand is the sum of all actions surrounding a competing entity. To use the term I coined in my first book, it is a *brain tattoo*, a mental impression that is earned through time. It is a culmination of emotional, logical, and physical attributes, characteristics, performances, assets, liabilities, and promises.

Marketing is the process; the brand is the end result.

A brand is not your name, a logo, a tagline, or the latest ad campaign. If done properly, these things are important contributors to your brand; if done poorly, they are deadly bandits who will steal your brand's life.

The brand is what the market thinks, feels, and expects when it selects one thing over another.

Strong Brands Are Vital—and Valuable—Assets

Ask an entrepreneur whose company just got acquired by another company about price. I would bet my BMW there was a brand line item in the valuation documents.

Ask a public company about the market influencing analyst reports it receives. I would bet my Rolex that, beyond earnings, there was a brand reputation in the analyst's mind.

Ask a salesperson who just scored the biggest transaction of his or her life. I would bet my Apple computer that brand credibility was an element in the selection process.

Brands on their game earn a place in the minds and hearts of the market by consistently telling their unique story, providing value, and delivering on promises that are relevant to a critical mass of buyers or consumers.

Branding in an Exploding Universe

Until recently, most business leaders believed they had figured out the basic brand game. They were on their merry way—marketing, advertising, promoting, and publicizing their brands—and then came the most monumental change to the businesses and brands that we all thought we knew so well: the Internet landed. Brands and branding morphed from a pure premium identity choice to an "any-price-point" product with a story and a promise. To complicate matters further, we not only *could* but now *had to* conduct business and build our brand message 24 hours a day, 7 days a week (24/7) and with no limits on geographical boundaries. For many, the Internet represented endless opportunity and reach, efficiency, low production costs, and a new sense of control over our brands. That feeling didn't last too long. Technological advancements added many benefits, but they also raised consumer expectations. The need for speed, a deeper customer service level, and multimedia choices presented new challenges.

Then, technology got cheaper; web engagement and functionality grew like weeds and open-source applications became the new oxygen—welcome to Web 2.0. The branding platform expanded, too. We were no longer just buying our way into consumers' worlds, pushing strategically crafted messages on them with hard-selling tactics; instead, we were having two-way conversations—listening, helping, and educating. There was a new marketing mindset:

Old Mindset	New Mindset
Sell	Help, teach
Take	Give
Push	Attract
Buy attention	Earn loyalty
Control	Let go
Talk	Listen
Transact	Experience

Brands everywhere went from brick-and-mortar offline business environments to having to earn new relationships and build stronger brand loyalty because of the new army of digital branding tools at their fingertips and at the market's.

What a difference 10 years makes! As the Internet continues to power economies and businesses, a new dimension of activity and media has sprouted. Known now as "social media" and pioneered by companies such as Friendster, Myspace, and Facebook, user-generated content has fueled this technology-driven behavior known for centuries as "socializing." Blogs, wikis, microblogging, and podcasts are just a few options in the buffet of communication choices and tools available to branders. At the start, many skeptics thought this new form of communication was purely a social pastime meant for teenagers and techno-geeks—certainly not a "for-business" movement. How wrong they were! Today, businesses, governments, religious groups, and family members are active participants in social media.

How to Gain from Our Losses

As business leaders and entrepreneurs, our first thoughts after learning that a brand has bit the dust, or is on the edge and may soon fail, often is, "Whew, I'm glad that's not me," or, "I feel their pain," or, "I wonder what really happened?" We could stop there and get on with our business, or we could gain an edge by learning from these experiences. Brand failures and meltdowns can teach us a lot. In fact, some of today's most troubled brands may even hold the secrets to future brands' successes.

Regardless of the Internet and social media, the fundamentals of branding are the same as they have always been. Cave dwellers thousands of years ago, got it. They marked their bodies, possessions, and war garb with consistent messaging: "This is who I am. This is what I stand for. Remember me." The same is true of brands today.

What is different is that the playing field has expanded, and anyone can participate. Branding is not limited to just premium-priced consumer products and entities that can buy multimillion-dollar ad campaigns and TV spots during the Super Bowl game. Any sized offering, any business venture, any organization, any destination, or any individual who competes to play can be a brand. Just pack your passion and resiliency, and be clear about your goals.

The stage is real-time, borderless, and 24/7, and it does not require an invitation to participate. Gone are the days when brands were 100 percent controlled by their owners. Today, brands are ultimately owned by the marketplace. The owners navigate and direct the story. They guide the brand's outcome with strategic behavior, consistent communication, and kept promises. To survive, however, they must retool and rethink to respond quickly and well and navigate through brand bumps and meltdowns caused by missteps and market shifts, or when something crazy "just happens" in today's crowd-sourced, collaborative branding environment.

Despite these new challenges, branding is more important than ever. A powerful and well-executed strategy is essential to achieving goals and building sustainable ventures and causes. Now, strap yourself in and get ready, because you're about to learn how to navigate a brand turnaround.

Part 1

It's a Brand New Game

Chapter 1

Mission Possible: Brands Can Turn Around

From brutal breakdowns to big, bad bumps, even the most troubled brands can get back to being on top, do a three-sixty, and turnaround. All of the brands featured in this book were once at the top of their game and then something happened. They fell from grace and lost some of their brand mojo. Faced with challenges, they figured out how to rally back. They rebuilt healthy connections and relationships with their core markets, which enabled their return to glory.

It's obvious that top brands offer meaningful advantages for their stakeholders. Whether yours is a commercial, individual, cause or nonprofit, or destination brand, being a well-regarded brand translates into some or all of the following benefits:

- *Loyalty.* Few or no defections from customers, investors, employees, or partners
- *Trust and confidence.* Less risk to buyers

3

- *Ambassadors.* Enthusiastic advocates and torch carriers singing the brand's praises
- *Protective shield.* Greater willingness to forgive and pardon missteps
- *Premium investment and price.* Perception of an added layer of value and justification of a higher price
- *Opportunities and extensions.* Natural and easier entrée into new areas

Yet there are times when none of these factors can protect a brand from falling from grace. Sometimes the problem with the brand is something the company should have been aware of but wasn't—that is, until the error was discovered by the competition. That is what happened to Persil Power, a popular laundry detergent sold under different names throughout Europe. In early 1994, Unilever introduced Persil Power with a bang and a substantial ad campaign. Within months, Unilever's archrival, Procter & Gamble (P&G), discovered that dark dyes in certain fabrics reacted badly to an ingredient used in Persil Power. In March, P&G privately warned Unilever of the problem, and Unilever ignored P&G's warning, perhaps because its own testing over the previous two years had not uncovered the problem. P&G went public with the claim. The whole affair was most famously symbolized by a pair of chewed-up boxer shorts allegedly ravaged by Persil Power. In late 1994, Unilever admitted that it had made a mistake.[1]

Sometimes the problem is something that should have been foreseen but wasn't; perhaps how a product is made. For example, in 1997, a *New York Times* article exposed oppressive working conditions and the presence of carcinogenic materials in Nike's factories in Vietnam.[2] The report was based on a report Nike had commissioned that was leaked to the *Times.* Nike responded that they had carried out an "action plan" to improve conditions and that its internal system worked in uncovering the problem. Later, Nike came under fire for using child labor in Pakistan and Cambodia also. Protests from student groups followed. In 2001, Nike admitted its responsibility.

Branding Recovery: A Full-Cycle Journey

When brands go bad, they often cycle through the following phases.

Phase 1: Brand-shaking Event or Events

Something happens, either through internal or external means, that causes a market shift, changing the brand's score from high and loved to low and questionable.

Phase 2: Market Reaction and the Brand's Reply

As a result, the environment suddenly changes and the market reacts negatively. Public opinion, once positive, turns hostile; popularity wanes or disappears; advocates and ambassadors no longer spread the word; and positive buzz evaporates. Now, these things happen to the brand:

- It is seen as a bad guy, the weak option that can't be trusted or is not needed.
- It becomes the talk of social media. It's all about the brand's bad behavior, negative situation, or circumstances.
- It gets constant negative media coverage.

During this phase, press management is critical. Often, companies hold a press conference or issue a statement shortly after a significant shake-up with their brands. Everything about this first communication is critical. That includes the spokesperson, the venue, and the message. When the situation is handled well, this step is often the opening salvo in the fight back to recovery.

Phase 3: By-products and Other Hazards That May Follow a Troubled Brand

In some cases, a company with its brand under attack handles the incident so well that the problem is soon forgotten, or its brand equity is so strong that the public quickly forgives. When this is not the case, the public and media negative sentiment continues to grow and the real burn sets in. Now, this is what the brand may face:

- Being tied in with other, sometimes more damaged brand stories and events, and being seen as equally evil
- Losing leadership position while competitors are elevated into the spotlight
- Losing significant market share
- Declining revenue
- Falling stock price or valuation
- Defecting employees and partners
- Losing brand equity

Phase 4: Road to Recovery

The road map may vary: some returns are accelerated because a bigger, more damaging event enters the news cycle and the first brand's problems recede from public memory or seem less important; others heal as a result of good planning and execution of recovery strategies and tactics.

Phase 5: Return to Glory

Even after the positive signs of a brand's recovery are evident, maintaining progress and responding to new challenges are paramount to staying on top. Without these drivers, the brand will find itself back in the mud just as quickly as it cleaned itself up.

Brands that survive a crisis move through each of these phases. Once a brand bounces back, it can experience a multitude of benefits. For the rest of this chapter, we shall examine in detail the fall and rise of commercial, nonprofit, individual, and destination brands.

Commercial Brands

Companies, big and small, own commercial brands. They are focused on business objectives and intent on profits that drop to the bottom line for stakeholders.

When the worst is over, bounce-back commercial brands often experience

- Lower customer acquisition costs (new customers arrive and defected customers return)
- Stronger revenues (sales are up)
- Stronger margins (buyers spend more per transaction)
- Organically grown advocacy (customer feedback about product, experiences, and team members is positive)
- More efficient marketing (an increase in positive media coverage and interest)
- Easier recruitment (the best talent and partners again attracted to the brand)
- Organizational pride (which flourishes and feeds brand energy)

Let's look at a specific example: Domino's Pizza.

Domino's Pizza Brand Turnaround Story

The Domino's Pizza brand represents a great slice of the American dream. What started as a very small entrepreneurial venture with big ideas is nowadays a leader in the quick-service food category. The company has been no stranger to challenges and brand shake-ups: In 1968, the company headquarters and commissary were destroyed by fire. Not long after, all of its records were lost during a conversion to a computerized system. Around this time, Domino's also ran into problems with the Internal Revenue Service (IRS) that forced its owner, Tom Monaghan, to sell his shares and—for a time—lose control of the company. Lawsuits from franchisees, creditors, and others followed. Then, in the late 1980s, it was reported that more than 20 of Domino's drivers had died in accidents, ultimately ending Domino's 30-minute delivery guarantee.[3]

The company has been up and down a few times and is now back on top delivering more than 400 million pizzas a year, which means a pizza (or at least a slice) for every man, woman, and child in the United States.

Domino's began as DomiNick's, a Michigan pizza store bought by bothers James and Tom Monaghan in 1960. The total purchase price was $500. Less than a year later, Tom traded a used Volkswagen Beetle to James in exchange for full ownership. In 1965, the shop was renamed Domino's Pizza, Inc. The first franchise opened in 1967. A plan to add one dot to the Domino's domino logo for each new store was soon abandoned because of fast growth.

In 1980, Domino's defeated a trademark infringement lawsuit by Amstar Corp., maker of Domino Sugar; at the same time, growth exploded. In 1983, the doors on the thousandth Domino's opened for business. That same year, the first international store opened in Canada. By 1997, there were 1,500 international locations. In 1998, the leader who had taken Domino's to the top, Tom Monaghan, sold 93 percent of Domino's to Bain Capital for nearly $1 billion, and retired. At the time Domino's had been losing market share in the United States—Papa John's was now number 1—but, by 2003, new management reversed this trend.[4]

By 2006, there were 8,238 Domino's stores claiming $1.4 billion in gross income. In 2009, there were 8,999 stores and global sales grew to $5.5 billion. That same year, a consumer survey by research firm Brand Keys had Domino's finishing dead last in consumer preference (tied with Chuck E. Cheese). The report monitors 79 categories and 528 brands in its annual Customer Loyalty Engagement Index. The survey pool size of 46,000 consumers includes a mix of men and women, 18 to 65 years old, drawn from the nine U.S. Census regions. Nevertheless, by 2010, the last year for which we have full data, Domino's had 9,351 stores with gross income of almost $6.3 billion.

Sources close to the situation believe that Domino's learned about the survey results by reading about them in *USA Today*. That's not a good way to start the day. The company did, however, score high on convenience and budget-friendliness. The results were a wake-up call for the brand: Domino's had become dominant, not for good food, but because it was fast and cheap—hardly a good core brand value.

As if that was not enough brand beating for one year, two employees at a Domino's store wearing Domino's uniforms uploaded a stomach-turning video to YouTube.[5] The video showed two employees sticking cheese in their noses and then putting it on a sandwich intended for customers along with other gross acts. Within hours the video went viral, and millions were exposed to this heinous act. Domino's launched its own YouTube video, assuring the public that what had occurred was an isolated incident. The employees were fired and criminally charged and convicted (although neither served jail time). Within a few days, the situation was resolved with no permanent damage to the Domino brand from the incident. But what an exercise in brand tossing! Many call it a textbook response to a crisis, while some contend the response time was not fast enough.

Finally, in early 2010, Domino's took the rebrand strategy "full-charge-ahead option," admitting that its food was not very good and promising to do better. An extensive ad campaign began with Domino's executives publicly reading letters about how disappointed consumers were in its product. It was brutally honest. The campaign titled "The Pizza Turnaround" pulled no punches. Through numerous ads and at the website www.pizzaturn around.com, Domino's used the chant "Oh Yes We Did" to point out its newfound brand honesty.

Domino's doubled down on this strategy a few months later when it released a new campaign push that built on the old one by admitting that it was up to the company to "do better," and that it was still falling short in some places. It embraced a complete all-points turnaround. Sources close to the situation report it cost Domino's two years and $2 million to reformulate its pizza and that it spent an additional $75 million on advertising.

The Domino's Brand Turnaround

The company's strategy included the following things.

Honesty and Communication. Going public and admitting that its pizza was not much better tasting than the cardboard box it came in was a bold move. In the end, this action provided insight for consumers by letting them know that Domino's knew there was a problem and was doing something about it. It also opened up numerous brand engagement opportunities, which were then leveraged into creative advertising, publicity, social chat, and continuous content online.

Product Improvement. Domino's made sure the honesty of the Pizza Turnaround campaign was backed up with action. It overhauled every part of its product, changing the crust, cheese, and sauce. It was a gutsy move for a brand that still had strong sales.

Technology Advances. Staying ahead of the pizza delivery curve, Domino's has gone high tech by facilitating online ordering via a website and phone app in some markets that allows customers to connect to their local Domino's location to order both carryout and delivery orders.

Marketing and Social Media. The new pizza and the supporting campaigns have earned Domino's a few million close friends and plenty of good buzz. They have over 27,000 Twitter followers at twitter.com/dominos and use their Twitter feed not just as a one-way communication organ to inform customers about products and deals but also to respond to customer service complaints and other brand comments. Domino's also leverages Facebook. The brand is "liked" by over three million users and makes "liking" it on Facebook rewarding by communicating special deals to its "friends." They have even created a pizza exclusively for Facebook fans in the United Kingdom called Spanish Sizzler. Its very smooth online phone app lets you not only order a pizza but also track its every move: Johnny made it; Fred is on his way to your house.

In 2011, just one year after the brave Pizza Turnaround brand initiative, Domino's announced that sales had increased sharply. It expects a full year-over-year net profit growth of 10 to 15 percent.

Cause and Nonprofit Brands

Nonprofit brands share many of the same issues as commercial ones, with additional scrutiny because their funding often comes from donations, grants, and other nonprofits.

Cause and nonprofit brand turnarounds often experience these things:

- Supporter base increases (lower cost per contribution, emergence of new supporters and reengagement of inactive patrons)
- Increased contributions (both in time and money)
- More efficient marketing (an increase in positive media coverage and interest)
- Easier recruitment of volunteers (the best talent, advocates, and partners are attracted to the brand)
- Increased organizational pride (brand energy)

Here's a specific example: the American Red Cross.

American Red Cross Brand Turnaround Story

Founded in 1881, the Red Cross was different from the beginning. In a world dominated by men, the Red Cross was founded, and presided over, by a woman. Clara Barton, the nurse hero of the Civil War, leveraged her fame to personally lead some of the Red Cross's earliest relief efforts, including the "Great Thumb Fire" in Michigan, which devastated almost a million acres. (For the curious, Great Thumb refers to the eastern part of the state which resembles a thumb). Barton's own brand put the Red Cross on the map, and soon the organization was a regular sight at disasters like the 1889 Johnstown Flood in Pennsylvania that took over 2,200 lives.

From disaster relief, the Red Cross branched out to blood donation drives and education in cardiopulmonary resuscitation (CPR). The organization's simple, bold logo has made the organization easily recognizable wherever it serves. The Red Cross grew throughout the twentieth century, and it became one of the most recognized and trusted charity brands in the world. By the twenty-first century, the Red Cross was responding to about 70,000 disasters and emergencies a year. Today the American Red Cross Biomedical Services plays a critical role in health-care systems around the world. In the United States it is the largest single supplier of blood and blood products, collecting and processing more than 40 percent of the nation's blood supply and distributing it to approximately 3,000 hospitals and transfusion centers nationwide.[6]

About 100 years after Barton led the Red Cross, another woman would lead the organization only to see the brand severely falter and lose brand trust. In the wake of the attack on New York on September 11, 2001 (9/11), the Red Cross, as usual, leaped into action. The organization and its president, Dr. Bernadine Healy, established the high-profile Liberty Fund and aggressively pushed Americans to give both blood and money to the Red Cross. The perception was that all funds donated would go to the Liberty Fund to aid the victims of 9/11.

By late October 2001, though, Healy was forced to resign.

What happened? Media organizations began reporting that not only was there no need for a Red Cross blood drive but also the Red Cross had decided to put into savings (for future terrorist attacks) much of the $564 million it had raised during the 9/11 fund drives. By early November 2001, the Red Cross found itself on the hot seat before Congress, where it was lambasted publicly and painted as an opportunist that used the 9/11 tragedy for profit.

In the course of a month, a brand once regarded as the preeminent nonprofit in American history saw its image reduced to one of a profiteering organization of scam artists. One man e-mailed the Red Cross, saying, "I am thoroughly disgusted and disappointed over your failing the families of victims from Sept. 11. I'll never contribute another penny or drop of blood." The Red Cross hurriedly announced that it would spend the entirety of the Liberty Fund on 9/11 victims. But it was too late.

Arguably they were right in not spending the money. Money at the time was not what was needed, just as blood wasn't (and the blood, if not used, would have gone to waste). It could be said that in the organization's desire to help it jumped on the bandwagon too soon and was far too specific in how it said it was going to use donations. But that did not matter. For the next few years, the Red Cross stumbled forward, trying to rediscover its identity and, more important, to rebuild the reputation of a brand 100 years in the making.

In the summer 2005, Hurricane Katrina ravaged the Gulf Coast and destroyed much of New Orleans. With so many people affected by the devastation, the Red Cross had the chance to save lives, bring families together, and rebuild its own tarnished brand. In the beginning, things seemed to be going well. But in 2006, reports surfaced about possible fraud by Red Cross contractors and volunteers, and the Red Cross was criticized for bungling elements of its response.

Long gone were the days of the untouchable Red Cross brand. With the memory of the 9/11 fiasco still in the public's mind, despite continuing catastrophic disasters, this nonprofit found itself in one of the worst economic recessions in years. As a result, in 2008, the Red Cross had a $209 million operating deficit.

The road to brand recovery would take time, fresh leadership, and major changes to its culture—not only to serve but also to operate more like a business with fiscal responsibility—in order to expand the organization's base to a new generation of volunteers and supporters. In April 2008, Gail McGovern, a former business executive with AT&T and Fidelity Investments, became president and CEO and led the charge to put the organization back on stable financial footing. The brand comeback followed.

In 2010, the earthquake in Haiti spurred Red Cross into action. In the year following the Haiti disaster, the Red Cross provided medical care for nearly 217,000 patients, cash grants and loans to help 220,000 people, latrines for 265,000 people, daily drinking water for more than 317,000 people, emergency shelter materials for more than 860,000 people, vaccinations for nearly one million people, and food for 1.3 million people for one month. In providing so much relief, Red Cross took a big step away from the tarnished image and recharged the brand as one of hope, help, and relevance.

The handling of the Haiti disaster earned the Red Cross good marks from the media, and the organization has successfully tapped into a younger, digitally connected market that has furthered the brand recovery. Time will tell if Haiti is a recovery success story for both that nation and the Red Cross.

Beyond the megadisasters, the Red Cross responds to thousands of smaller events every day in the United States and abroad. It runs the world's largest blood donor program; it trains and educates individuals and other organizations on a variety of topics, including first aid, CPR, automated external defibrillator (AED), lifeguarding, swimming, babysitting, and caregiving; and it provides needed communications and health services to U.S. Armed Forces. This is where the real work of rebuilding the brand has occurred.

The Red Cross Brand Turnaround

The organization's strategy has included the following things.

Policy Improvement. Following both the 9/11 fiasco and the Katrina criticism, the Red Cross changed its fund-raising and partnering policies to be sure that similar problems would not happen again.

Operational Improvement. As part of its efforts to restore financial stability, the organization also has streamlined and consolidated its back-end operations. Before this, the approximately 700 local American Red Cross chapters each had its own operational, banking, information technology (IT), and financial systems.

Leadership from the Business World. In addition to recruiting veteran business executive Gail McGovern as CEO, the nonprofit hired Peggy Dyer as its first chief marketing officer to oversee the development and execution of marketing strategy. The organization has also broadened its board of governors with contemporary new faces like Judy McGrath, who is the former chair and CEO of MTV Networks, a division of Viacom.

New Recurring Revenue Streams. Like many commercial organizations, the Red Cross also knew it needed to find new revenue streams that could also leverage its brand. To that end, the Red Cross is developing licensing partnerships with existing products and new ones that support a revenue model and complement its lifesaving mission.

Marketing and Social Media. Social networking has given nonprofits a powerful new avenue to further their mission, recruit volunteers, raise money, and build their brand.

The year 2010 saw continued growth in online fund-raising for nonprofit organizations. A recovering global economy, online response to disaster relief, peer-to-peer fund-raising, and the role of social media in the nonprofit sector all shaped the year. Blackbaud, a nonprofit research firm that conducts an annual *Online Giving Report*, found that online giving grew 34.5 percent in 2010 compared to 2009. Large nonprofits, with annual total fund-raising greater than $10 million, experienced the largest fund-raising increase with 55.6 percent on a year-over-year basis.[7]

The Red Cross allocates significant resources to its online and social media efforts, and its investment is paying off. The benefit goes way beyond development and fund-raising; the Red Cross uses its online activities to listen, learn, and improve all touchpoints of the organization. They monitor their social activity with Radian6, a service that helps brands listen to their markets, competitors, and influencers. Beyond the monitoring dashboard, which tracks mentions on more than 100 million social media sites, they offer an engagement console that allows a brand to coordinate internal responses to external activity by immediately updating its blogs, Twitter, and Facebook accounts all in one spot. Nonprofits can access the service for reduced rates through the company's Giving Back program.

The Red Cross is mentioned nearly 700 times a day on various social media platforms. It has more than 265,000 followers on Twitter, and the nonprofit uses the tool not only to converse but also as a real-time feed for aid needs. Facebook, YouTube, blogging, and Red Cross's website (with a page dedicated to explaining why social media is important to the Red Cross) allow an even bigger and multimedia rich story to be told about the brand with content, images, and video uploads. And if this presence hasn't reprogrammed society's expectations about the brand, check this out: a study by the Red Cross found that 74 percent of disaster victims expect response agencies to answer social media calls for help in less than an hour.

Individual Brands

Individual brands are the newest kids on the brand block; from business professionals to athletes, and from entertainers to religious, community, and political leaders, these brands are led by one person's values, style, behavior, and communications.

Here's what individual brands may experience when they turn around:

- Increased opportunities (their profile attracts business deals, other brands, and engagements)
- Increased income (they earn more)
- Positive feedback from industry and the public
- Greater exposure, features in media, on social networking sites, as well as increased number of hits by search engines
- Renewed trust, sponsors, and endorsements return

- More efficient marketing (momentum drives opportunities)
- Greater brand energy fed by greater self-esteem

Let's examine a specific example of an individual brand: Kobe Bryant.

Kobe Bryant Brand Turnaround Story

Kobe Bryant was the first superstar National Basketball Association (NBA) player to be hired straight out of high school—a practice that would become common in the years after 1996. Bryant was the winner of the 1997 All Star Game Slam Dunk Contest, and in 1998 he became the youngest All Star Game starter in history. In 1999, Bryant signed a six-year $71 million contract extension.

From the beginning, Bryant was a magnet for endorsements. Before he even touched the court, Bryant had a multimillion-dollar deal with Adidas. McDonald's and Sprite were two of his largest deals. A huge superstar by the time his Adidas deal expired, Bryant signed with Nike a five-year deal worth about $45 million. In 2000, 2001, and 2002 Kobe Bryant helped the Los Angeles Lakers to consecutive NBA championships. In 2001, Bryant married, and he and his wife's first child was born in January 2003.

At the height of his brand's popularity, Kobe Bryant was arrested for sexual assault in Colorado and accused of rape. Bryant claimed his innocence, but he admitted to cheating on his wife with his accuser. The court case would take a year, and Bryant's reputation would go from gold to mud. Prosecutors eventually dropped the charges in 2004 when the alleged victim refused to testify. The case turned into a media circus, with Bryant's name splashed over the headlines and top stories on a daily basis.

McDonald's, Sprite, and other sponsors immediately terminated relationships with Bryant. Nike maintained its contract but stopped using his image in its ads.

Although the charges were dismissed, Bryant's brand image remained low. A January 2005 Associated Press report noted that "[sales of] Bryant's No. 8 Lakers jersey—previously one of the best sellers in the world—has fallen out of the top 50." Worse yet for Brand Kobe, the quality of his play slipped too. Coach Phil Jackson once said he would not return "if Kobe Bryant is on the team next year."[8] The year 2004 would mark the first time in more than a decade that the Lakers failed to make the playoffs.

In 2005, Nike started using Kobe's image again in its advertising, but it wasn't until 2006 that Brand Kobe really started turning around. This recovery went hand in hand with his playing recovery as well, as a public display of a change in attitude. In January, Bryant hugged old teammate, Miami Heat player Shaquille O'Neal, ending a long public feud. Soon after, Bryant scored an amazing 81 points in a single game. This was just the first of numerous score-setting records. In 2007, he turned in his long-celebrated number 8 jersey for number 24, signaling to the world that he had turned a corner.

In 2008, Bryant won the Most Valuable Player (MVP) Award, and the Lakers went to the finals. Bryant's deal with Coca-Cola returned, and he was the feature player on the cover of the video game *NBA '07*. His brand recovery was aided by his place on the gold medal–winning 2008 U.S. Olympic team.

Kobe's stellar on-court performance continued to mold his return to superstar status. The Lakers, led by Kobe, won the 2009 championship and went on to win the 2010 championship, Kobe's fifth. In 2010, *Forbes* ranked Bryant only behind Tiger Woods and Michael Jordan on its list of highest paid athletes.*

History seems to favor comebacks of high-profile individual brands when the person accepts brand shake-ups head-on. Their public atonement often erases the damage their perceived sins caused and time forgives. On the other hand, Pete Rose has never recovered from having been caught gambling on baseball; in part, no doubt, because it took him 15 years to confess to his wrongdoing.[9] People did seem willing to forget—or, at least,

---

*It's worth noting that Kobe Bryant was fined $100,000 for an antigay slur he yelled at a referee. He apologized the next day, but he said he would appeal the fine. The impact on his brand is yet to be seen.

forgave—Kobe Bryant's black eye. Kobe went through the fire, but he took full responsibility for his transgression. The public expects that those in positions of status need to take *sincere* responsibility when they have violated the trust of their supporters and fans.

It will be interesting to watch how other athletes, like Tiger Woods, Barry Bonds, and even Lance Armstrong, who have recently found themselves in the glare of negative publicity, handle their problems. It is possible they will step on new landmines in the course of their journey. Barry Bonds was convicted of obstructing justice, even as a deadlocked jury resulted in the other charges relating to his alleged steroid use being dropped; and Tiger Woods is still trying to find his game. Lance Armstrong's drama will likely return to the news one day, too. All three brands should be able to bounce back; their actions will soon tell the tale.

The Kobe Bryant Brand Turnaround

This individual's strategy included the following things.

Trust and Communication. Bryant's first step toward brand recovery was to admit his transgressions. In a statement made directly to the woman who charged him, Bryant said, "I want to apologize to her for my behavior that night and for the consequences she has suffered in the past year. Although this year has been incredibly difficult for me personally, I can only imagine the pain she has had to endure. I also want to apologize to her parents and family members, and to my family and friends and supporters, and to the citizens of Eagle, Colorado."[10]

Evidence of Change. Shortly after the 2003 incident Bryant had his wife and daughters' names, an angel halo, and Psalm 27 tattooed on both his arms. In addition, he became very public about his faith and spiritual values. In 2007, after he changed his long-celebrated number 8 jersey for number 24, his jersey became the NBA's top seller in the United States, China, and Europe.

Championship Behavior On and Off the Court. Even during the high-profile hearings and media zoo that surrounded the allegations against him, Kobe came out on the court every night and outperformed 98 percent of the other players. He did what he does best: he played incredible basketball. Not only did he focus on his game and skill but he also developed into a stronger team leader. He opened up his style of play to facilitate contributions from the whole team, which after the initial change curve delivered some of the most spectacular hoop shooting, scoring, and winning in the game's history. Sports publicist Tamiko Hope described Bryant's game change as critical to his turnaround. He earned the respect of his fans, although they also understood he was human and flawed, despite the superhuman talent.

Off the court Kobe Bryant became active with a variety of U.S. and global charities. Among other things, he served as an official ambassador to the After-School All-Stars, an American nonprofit organization for after-school programs and summer camps for at-risk youth. He also created the Kobe Bryant China Fund, which partnered with the Soong Ching Ling Foundation, to raise money within China for education and health programs.

Marketing and Social Media. Like other high-performing athletes, Bryant scores major endorsement deals that can be winners for both the company's brand and the athlete's own brand. In the perfect world, the athlete earns the cash and sometimes the product; the sponsor benefits from association with the celebrity accompanied by what it hopes will be a great creative campaign; and both the celebrity's brand and the product being promoted are further fueled by the cool quality production and media exposure.

In 2008, Bryant completed a pair of videos showing him doing dangerous stunts to promote Nike's Hyperdunk shoes. The first showed Bryant jumping over a speeding Aston Martin automobile, and the second one showed Bryant with the crew of *Jackass* performers from MTV jumping over a pool of snakes. Both videos went viral, each receiving millions of views on YouTube. Bryant later hinted that the stunts were faked—actually doing them would have violated his contract with the Lakers, which prohibits him from participating in dangerous activities. This incident seems to have had no impact on his image, probably because no one was hurt and, more important, his followers—young men 18 to 35 years old—think the stunts are cool.

Kobe Bryant had adopted an alter ego, the Mamba, after a deadly snake that can raise itself four feet off the ground when threatened and is very difficult to kill. According to Bryant, "The Mamba can strike with 99 percent accuracy at maximum speed, in rapid succession. That's the kind of basketball precision I want to have."[11] To further enhance this brand and promote his Nike shoe line, he made a short film with Bruce Willis, Danny Trejo, and Kanye West which was promoted as "Kobe Bryant is *The Black Mamba.*" A couple of months after the film was released it had been viewed over three million times.

Social media and an Internet presence also have played a role in Bryant's brand rebound. His official website, www.kb24.com, reflects his champion style, and it also includes videos, news, and information about his basketball academy. At the time I write this, Bryant has had almost 73,000 followers on Twitter, and approximately 8.3 million have given a thumbs-up to his Facebook page.

Destination Brands

Destination brands dramatically impact economies, as they touch so many commerce-driving dimensions from quality of life, to tax bases, to jobs and talent recruitment.

Here's what destination brands may experience when they turn around:

- Visitor acquisition cost is lowered. (New visitors arrive and defected ones return.)
- Revenues increase. (This may also pump revenues into other businesses.)
- Profit margins can grow. (Buyers are spending more per transaction.)
- Advocacy grows organically. (Visitors report positive feedback about product, experience, and place.)
- Marketing is more efficient. (There is an increase in positive media and social network buzz.)

- Recruitment is easier. (The best talent and partners are now attracted to the brand.)
- Community pride flourishes. (This feeds into brand.)

Let's take a look at a specific example: Aruba.

Aruba Brand Turnaround Story

Aruba, a constituent country under the Kingdom of the Netherlands, is a beautiful Caribbean island that counts tourism among its top industries. Known by many as "One Happy Island," it is out of the pathway of hurricanes and generally a very safe place. The greatest number of tourists to Aruba comes from Venezuela and the United States.

For many Americans, Aruba was probably best known as the first word in the Beach Boys song "Kokomo." At least that was the case until May 30, 2005, when Natalee Holloway from Alabama disappeared during a high school trip to the island. The teenager's disappearance (which seemed to many to be a murder) became a national media sensation, with its focus on suspect Joran van der Sloot, the son of a Dutch diplomat whom police believed committed the crime but could not be convicted of it. Fox News, Dr. Phil, and even *Vanity Fair* covered the story extensively. After that, many Americans' first association to Aruba may have been "murdered teen."

Aruba's tourism industry immediately came under fire. The disappearance, never to be solved (as of this writing), was certainly tragic, but that an economy was punished so hard for an isolated incident is equally sad. The crime and the ensuing media circus drew international attention, making it seem that local politics was to blame for the poor handling of the case and possibly even a cover-up. Websites emerged that advocated a voluntary boycott of Aruba. Within a year, visits from the United States to Aruba were down 9 percent, and the small, beautiful island experienced a major business decline as a result of its internationally tarnished image.

In September 2005, a spokesperson for the Aruba Tourism Authority (ATA) told *USA Today*, "Our main priority now is, 'Let's get this [Holloway case] solved and resolved.' It's not nice for anyone involved."[12] The spokesperson was right. The main problem plaguing Aruba's public relations recovery was that it could not put an end to the case. Its reputation suffered as much from the crime itself as from its inability to convict the suspect. Aruba's image was further tarnished when van der Sloot was arrested for the murder of a young woman in Peru in 2010, to which he confessed.

Negative publicity continued to circle the destination's brand. In April 2009, Lifetime Movie Network aired *The Natalee Holloway Story*, which was viewed by a record-setting 3.2 million people, the highest in Lifetime's 11-year history. As late as 2010, the mention of Holloway's name still went hand in hand with Aruba. In 2010, NBC's Philadelphia affiliate posted the photo of a skeleton a couple had taken in Aruba while scuba diving. The headline: "Couple Snaps Skeleton Pic in Aruba: Natalee Holloway?"

Aruba is a very interesting case study: consider that cities and destinations around the world experience a much higher volume of crime, many of which are unsolved murders, yet they are rarely mentioned in the international press, let alone receive so much attention for nearly a decade. Natalee's teenage innocence, her beauty, and her parents' desperate search for justice contributed to the press's and people's fascination with the case. This high-profile crime scarred a brand, which had a dramatic economic impact.

Aruba's tourism industry is indeed showing strong signs of a return to glory. Tourism is up, and Aruba is projecting an even stronger year in 2012. Aruba is a small place, and it does not have a huge budget with which to buy back visitors like other megadestinations can. Instead, it has had to leverage grassroots means, social media, and word of mouth; most of all, it has had to deliver a wonderful and safe vacation experience. Here's how the country is doing it.

The Aruba Brand Turnaround

This destination's strategy has included the following things.

New Global Brand Identity. The Aruba Tourism Authority (ATA) created a new logo and relaunched the "One Happy Island" tagline.

Relevance. Eco-Aruba has successfully completed a $6 million eco-enhancement program; several beaches have been designated Blue Flag certified (an international program that sets environmental standards in four main areas: water quality, safety, services and facilities, education and information and environmental management).

While many Caribbean destinations lack sophisticated digital technology, Aruba is pioneering easy digital access in major hotels, and is dedicated to building relationships with friends and visitors online through its virtual community. It has jumped onto the social media bandwagon with Twitter accounts, and it boasts an impressive online community through Aruba.com (its user-friendly website) and the new Facebook Connect application. In fact, Aruba, the island of 90,000 (Facebook) friends you haven't met yet, is the first Caribbean destination to create this type of online networking community.

In 2010, Aruba began hosting an International Film Festival, where critically acclaimed films from around the world are showcased. The Aruba Tourism Authority and the Hyatt Regency, which has a resort on the island, even joined in to sponsor the film *The Greatest Movie Ever Sold,* directed by Morgan Spurlock.

Marketing. Aruba has also invested in traditional and new media. It has initiated a new advertising campaign titled "Aruba Uncovered," which will include print, TV, online, and out-of-home ads. Ian Wright, host of the travel/adventure television series *Globe Trekker,* is featured in an unscripted documentary-style film designed to reinforce the welcoming spirit of the island in an authentic, nonjaded tourist way through interaction with local Arubans.

In the next chapter we'll be taking a closer look at some of the brand killers everyone should watch out for.

Chapter 2

The Warning Is on the Label and the Clock Is Ticking

No brand is immune to a brand-shaking event. You do everything right and earn a respectable label—both on the shelves, and in the minds of the market. You also secure a spot in the moving target world, poised to be hit by any brand killer.

Brand Shake-Ups

What occurrences, behaviors, or acts of God cause a brand to go belly-up, and what will it take to return them to glory? Sadly, there is no set scientific formula for combating brand challenges. Some brands experience a major shake-up at a very high level; other slides are less dramatic—maybe only brand bumps—but both can have serious consequences that must be managed and worked through.

We can all recognize the obvious brand mishaps simply by watching the nightly news. These may be the result of many factors, including the following ones.

Accidents

The 2010 explosion at a BP oil rig and subsequent oil spill in the Gulf of Mexico will go down in history as one of the worst corporate accidents. But every day can bring unexpected catastrophes—from fires to structural collapses to contaminated food—and these can have an impact on a brand.

Product Recalls

Product recalls can happen to anyone, but Tylenol earns a triple for falling prey to product recalls at least three times—first in 1982, after cyanide-laced capsules of Extra Strength Tylenol resulted in the deaths of seven people in the Chicago area; then in 1986, when a woman died, again from cyanide-laced Tylenol, in Yonkers, New York; and last, in 2010, when the company again had to recall the pills, including children's pills, throughout the United States and elsewhere because many of them contained more of their active ingredients than they should have.

Scandals

Lance Armstrong has overcome cancer, rival cyclists, and nagging allegations of doping to become one of the world's best-paid athletes and a sought-after spokesperson. Yet, everything the seven-time Tour de France champion has created is threatened by a new opponent—a federal investigation. Philanthropic experts say his foundation, in particular, is at risk of losing future donations if its namesake, and chairman, is dragged down in controversial scandal.

Dramatic Market Shifts

Consider these dramatic market shifts: Blockbuster underestimated Netflix and the Internet-streaming delivery opportunities it represented.

Gas prices killed the Hummer, and the environmental movement will continue to challenge a multitude of brands from chemical companies to electronics makers. Such shifts happen more than you might think. Don't be caught unaware.

Poor Judgment and Bad Behavior

Eliot Spitzer, former governor of New York, was hailed as a "cleanup leader." Among other things, he went after Wall Street and prostitution rings. But he was found to be a member of a "sex for hire" club and was forced to step down as governor. We'll talk more about Spitzer in Chapter 4.

Lucky Brand jeans fell victim to its own overripe image in a trademark infringement case against Miami-based Marcel Fashion Group, which sells the GET LUCKY line of apparel. Following a five-day jury trial in the Southern District of New York, the jurors found that aggrieved plaintiff Lucky Brand had in fact stolen its luck and infringed on Marcel's GET LUCKY trademark. Branding Lucky with a permanent bad actor stamp, the jury found that Lucky had acted wantonly and awarded punitive damages of $280,000 against it.

Bad Luck and a Few Mysteries

In 2006, approximately 200 people were infected and three died after consuming fresh spinach that had been tainted with the deadly *E. coli* bacteria, which results from fecal contamination. While this situation did not spotlight a specific brand, consumers stayed away from the product once known for making you strong and healthy, fearing it could kill them.

If you think these examples have nothing to do with you, consider these scenarios. All are real possibilities and can happen to you and your brand.

- Criminal acts by management or workers
- Less-than-ethical behavior by management or workers
- Devastating weather
- Acts of terrorism

- Act of revenge by a crazy customer
- Mistakes made by partners, vendors, or affiliates
- Conspiracy by competitors, enemies, and special interest groups
- Negligence at any level of your brand

There's no question that all brands and businesses have exposure to events such as these. It seems we hear of ones like these ones daily. What's important is to make sure, if, and when your number is called, that you are ready to manage through any of these obstacles, bounce back, and not ever let the ink dry on your brand obituary.

Brand Meltdown: A Case Study

Let's all temporarily jump into a nightmare together and work through a possible "Oh, my God, the brand just exploded today" situation.

For the purpose of general risk assessment and basic context, let's consider a fictional brand and its bad day. Remember: with any brand meltdown, the magnitude and factors will vary but the principles remain the same. Later, I will share actual industry examples and solutions.

The Onset

It's a Wednesday afternoon in small-town America. There's been a horrific accident, and a local company's vehicle and driver are involved. Splashed on the local news are statistics like "five people known dead," images of the scene with a local company's branded truck (now a wreck), and crates of the company's product clearly labeled and scattered everywhere. The truck driver, a 30-year veteran is led away in handcuffs by police officers.

Earlier that day, the company made the short list for a multimillion-dollar contract with the government. And, having broken sales records, last week, it was named "business of the year" by the community and recently introduced a new ecotechnology to serve an expanding market.

This company has been in business for over 30 years, and it has built a stellar brand and reputation both locally and nationally. The founder is a very quiet, introverted guy. The company manufactures children's lunch boxes and supplies. Nothing like this accident has ever happened before.

Blindsided by the accident, the company has no crisis plan or beyond-the-brand shake-up plan in place, and as the story unravels everything gets much worse.

The Event

It turns out the 30-year veteran driver has been hiding several addictions, including gambling, pornography, and substance abuse. And he is not alone; others working at the company have shared one or more of his addictions.

Not only has the accident resulted in fatalities, but it also has led to the discovery of a child pornography ring that the driver has been running. Subsequent damaging stories break months after the initial accident. The consequences are both instant and long-term:

- The media circus is poorly managed from the start. The negative press attention spans over 12 months and becomes a national story, from the event, to the after-event, and throughout the courtroom drama.
- The company loses more than $14 million in contracts during the next two years. Three top managers leave because of stress and related investigations. The company spends more than $5 million in litigation costs and damages.
- For the next five years, the brand is synonymous with "Creepy Children's Supply Company."

In hindsight, could this brand's journey have been different? Yes. The lack of a basic plan and any awareness of "anything can happen any day" cost this company dearly. Today, all brands of any size must have a brand response and recovery plan ready to launch within hours of a shake-up and must be able to sustain it and guide it back to full-throttle brand momentum.

A plan like this is necessary and worth the investment the day your exposure exceeds your assets.

Brand Exposure, a Reality Check

While no brand can anticipate every brand bump or unexpected blow, it can lower its risk to negative consequences by operating with a clear idea of what the brand's essence is. It also needs to understand that since no one is immune to business, life, or other brand-shaking events, being prepared for all contingencies is the best policy.

A small brand has just as much exposure as a large one does; however global, public companies and their brands tend to attract more media coverage because of their vast stakeholder base, attendant fiduciary responsibilities, and their high-profile leadership.

Whatever type or size brand yours is, it should operate from three important perspectives. You and your support team or organization should do two things:

1. Have your brand essence down pat.
2. Be aware of your exposure to brand shake-ups, and have a plan ready—don't wait until you need it.

Have Your Brand Essence Down Pat

If you don't have a written document or brand framework, start with the premise that a brand's essence is built on four principles: purpose, distinction, promise, and personality. Answer the following questions about each of them and you'll have defined your brand essence.

- *Purpose.* Why is your brand here? This should include your brand's reasons for being as well as its goals.

- *Distinction.* How is your brand different from others? These are your brand's unique attributes, products, history, milestones, and the way your brand does things.
- *Promise.* What does your brand deliver that fulfills emotional needs?
- *Personality.* Think of your brand as a person. What adjectives best describe that person's characteristics and behavior style?

Knowing what your brand is will work in its favor should anything happen that adversely affects it. The opposite is also true. If you pay no attention to your brand's essence, if you don't have a clue as to what its purpose is, if you have not differentiated your brand from the others, the degree of damage that could result from a shake-up is magnified: it will be more costly, and, potentially, could destroy your brand.

Southwest Airlines is a good example of a brand with a solid foundation and clear essence. The company has done such a good job with telling the public who it is that when something happens that negatively affects it, the public is more inclined to go with it. (For more about how Southwest has done damage control, see Chapter 9.) For brands that haven't established their essence yet, any shake-up is going to be more dangerous.

Understand Your Exposure

Understanding your vulnerabilities will guide you and help build a stronger brand. In the next section, I will help you spotlight both the dangerous and more protected areas of a brand with the Brand Exposure Meter. Answer the questions below, calculate your score, and see how exposed you are.

Brand Exposure Meter. The Brand Exposure Meter is a nonscientific tool intended to highlight how likely it is that your brand will experience a brand-shaking episode, to help you focus on your preparation for the event (how you will respond and how you will change the way you are viewed), and to allow you to monitor your progress along the way.

To assess your brand exposure, answer the following questions. Add points for every exposure. Deduct points for every protective measure— core platform, brand equity, and preparedness.

Market Span

Add five (5) points for every yes answer.

1. Are you global?   YES   or   NO
2. Do you have more than 1,000 employees?   YES   or   NO
3. Are you headquartered in a major media market?   YES   or   NO
4. Do you sell to consumers vs. business buyers?   YES   or   NO

Market Interest

Add (5) points for every yes answer.

5. Does your brand have sensational and
   emotional appeal?   YES   or   NO
6. Does your product have a strong visual aspect;
   for example, can it be photographed for TV or
   print media?   YES   or   NO
7. Is your brand tied to a celebrity, high-profile
   family, or brand leader?   YES   or   NO
8. Did this personality have image problems in
   the past?   YES   or   NO
9. Are you a public company?   YES   or   NO
10. Is your brand regularly featured in media?   YES   or   NO
11. Do you have a history of bad public relations?   YES   or   NO

Defined and Documented Core Brand

Subtract one (1) point for every yes answer.

12. Does your brand operate and market from a
    defined brand essence (purpose, points of
    difference, personality, and promise)?   YES   or   NO

13. Do you present this essence on the majority of your touch points (website, advertising, in store or business graphics, etc.)?   YES or NO

14. Does your company live the brand and walk the talk; is your corporate culture aligned with your brand essence? Do people in the company share the values of the brand? (Brands that say they are on the cutting edge but act like dinosaurs are not living the brand.)   YES or NO

Brand Equity/Relationships

Subtract one (1) point for every yes answer.

15. Is your top leader respected by the media and your industry?   YES or NO

16. Does your brand have active and healthy relationships with the media?   YES or NO

17. Does your brand have active and healthy relationships with your industry groups?   YES or NO

18. Does your brand communicate to employees regularly?   YES or NO

19. Does your brand actively use social media?   YES or NO

20. Does your brand have easy access to feedback and communications points for stakeholders?   YES or NO

21. Is your brand organization marketing-centric, proactive, and visible?   YES or NO

Preparation

Subtract one (1) point for every yes answer.

22. Does your brand have a crisis communications plan in place that can be executed in a moment's notice?   YES or NO

23. Does your brand conduct mock crisis exercises
    to test your readiness?   YES   or   NO
24. Does your brand have existing relationships with
    teams of experts that work with crisis situations?   YES   or   NO

Tally your score: The higher your score, the greater your exposure is. If your score is over 50, it's high time to work on your plan. If your score is under 30, you are in a healthier place but still not immune—as no brand is.

Now, let's look at a sample plan framework.

Have a Plan Ready

It's crucial to have a plan in place for when your brand suddenly finds itself in turnaround. The Quick Start "Save Your Brand" Plan that follows will help those in immediate need put your brand back on track and form the basis—along with the seven Game Changers—for future plans once your brand has bounced back.

Each situation is different; each brand is different. In formulating your exact plan, there will be many distinct variables to consider. However, the basics are all here for you to build upon.

Quick Start "Save Your Brand" Plan. The first step is to get a handle on the brand-shaking event.

1. *Do an immediate and thorough inventory of everything that you know and can know.* Think like a reporter—answer the who, what, when, where, why, and how questions. Identify the most prevalent, brand-damaging message risks as well as your brand's strength.
2. *Do an immediate and thorough inventory of all the weapons at your disposal.* What are your assets—spokespeople, employees, third-party allies, legal services, PR, professional association(s), friendly elected officials, and so on?
3. *Assemble a multidisciplinary team.* This should include people from legal, operations, communications, leadership, and others you might need. At the same time, it is important not to compartmentalize information.

4. *Build a narrative to explain the situation and defend your brand.* Be clear about what your current position is; make sure you are aligned with your brand values and intentions. If you need more time to gather facts, state that. But also state your priorities—for example, customer safety and employee safety.

5. *Never say, "No comment," while preparing a response, even to questions you are not prepared to answer.* At the very least say something like, "We are still trying to find out the answer to that question."

6. *Respond in a timely manner to every major media contact.* By "major," I mean reporters and media venues with significant reach. In responding to reporters, follow the media and communications tips in Chapter 4. For smaller outlets, you may want to draft a simple statement and direct reporters to your website for updates.

Decide How You Will Communicate. Based on circumstances, deciding what approach to take depends on the situation, the degree of brand damage and public interest, and available resources. Taking these factors into account, you will be able to determine whether to hold a press conference, make a written and/or verbal statement, conduct a media conference call, avail yourself of some other form of communication, or use some combination of methods.

Here are some critical things you need to take into account when making these communications decisions.

1. Identify the primary spokesperson, let the person get comfortable with the statement and drill them on Q&A (questions and answers).

2. Because the situation is fluid and new facts will continue to develop or emerge, your message must constantly evolve.

3. The spokesperson must never be defensive. It's always okay to show compassion and remorse. Honesty is what people want and expect.

4. Consider daily briefings—or more frequent ones, if the situation is changing rapidly.

5. Take control of the Internet. Make sure the information on your website is kept up to date on the situation. Be certain you have a team responding to misinformation that is posted anywhere on the Web. Use aggressive search engine optimization (SEO) and posting tactics to create a "funnel" to correct information on the most relevant and targeted platforms, which may include blogs, Twitter and Facebook, and news forums.

In addition to updating the media, disseminate information about the situation far and wide; include key audiences such as employees, customers, vendors, regulators, elected officials, online community (bloggers, etc.), and other parties connected in any way to the event.

As facts unfold and the situation becomes clearer, reevaluate the spokesperson based on the challenges and opportunities presented. Many times in brand shake-ups one sector of your market is more impacted by the event than others. Is the spokesperson more technical, more compassionate, or more business oriented? The ideal brand voice is the person who can best communicate to that group.

Finally, it's important to start developing a longer-range, forward-moving action plan, set timelines, and allocate resources. The plan should include your objectives, strategies, message, stage/channels, tactics, and relationships/dialogue.

Keep in mind that, after a major brand-tarnishing event, trust must be regained, credibility restored, and, most important, your story must supersede the negative opinions and answer any questions that may have been raised. The volume must be high enough and the message suitably clear on multiple fronts. A forward-moving and solid brand recovery plan needs to address all aspects of the brand experience, from advertising to the online footprint, public relations, product, service, social media, and internal and external communications.

Ultimately, you must always be prepared for something unexpected to happen to tarnish your brand.

Chapter 3

Chains Hold You Hostage: Change Can Set You Free

Brands of all types sometimes become hostage to their own success—continuing to do what they've always done because it once worked. Sometimes their leaders are unable to recognize or understand the need for change, and they remain shackled by the past even when the market has moved on, the business climate has changed, and the competition is more intense. As you'll see, the reasons are many, and the damage those chains can do if they are not unlocked may be irrevocable.

Chains that Hold a Brand Hostage

Personal brands and business brands are each held hostage by differing kinds of chains. Each type of brand and category has a unique set of debilitating issues. The following are the most common that will block any brand's recovery. The first is for a personal brand; the second, for a business brand.

Personal Brand Chains

These are examples of personal brand chains:

- *Ego-driven decisions.* In this situation, the leader embodies personal ruler status and an "all-about-me" mindset and believes "no one can touch me or catch me, I am indispensible."
- *Lack of accountability and responsibility.* What comes into play here is the classic victim, who blames everyone and everything else for shortcomings, difficult situations, and bad results.
- *Shortcuts.* Decisions are based on whatever is easiest and fastest; there's no understanding or consideration of the long-term impact of those choices.
- *The we've-always-done it-this-way syndrome.* History—the destructive habits of the past—is embraced instead of recognizing the need for change.
- *Denial of consequences and penalties.* Here, one's head is planted firmly in the sand; there's the belief that everything is "just fine" or the present situation is merely a blip and everything will be okay if "we just ride out the storm."
- *The love-me syndrome.* This person-brand needs acceptance and submits to peer and influencer pressure and conformity.

Chains are perceived to be better than the change choice because

- There is *less risk*—certainty is perceived in the status quo.
- There is *less cost*—change is expensive.
- There is *less pain*—it's easier, faster, and much more comfortable.

Business Brand Chains

These are examples of business brand chains:

- *Soft leadership and leadership teams.* Leaders are afraid to make decisions, and they compromise brand values in an effort to please everyone.

- *Denial of reality.* Leaders refuse to recognize that a problem exists until it is far more difficult or too late to repair the damage.
- *Peace trumping progress.* There's a tendency to submit to market and influencer pressure and bureaucracy.
- *Fear of leading.* Leaders prefer to follow instead of pioneering new ground.
- *Lack of accountability and responsibility.* Leaders blame others and/or economic environment for bad results.
- *The don't-rock-the-boat mentality.* Innovation and high achievement aren't encouraged, which breeds organizational complacency and mediocrity.
- *The we've-always-done-it-this-way syndrome.* History and traditional ways of doing things are embraced instead of recognizing the need for change.
- *Shortsightedness.* Leaders view branding, marketing, and training as expenses instead of as asset-building investments.

Chains are perceived to be better than the change choice because

- There is *less risk*—certainty is perceived in the status quo.
- There is *less cost*—change is expensive.
- There is *less pain*—it's easier, faster, and way more comfortable.

Wherever these chains keep brands—circling the status quo or digging a deeper hole—change is what moves brands back into their glory.

Damaged Brands Need Change

Even if a brand is not guilty of anything, the fact that perceptions about the brand, its reputation, and image are in question indicates that a transformation is needed. The degree of change warranted is unique to every brand turnaround situation. Some brands in trouble require only potent marketing, communication, and a name change, as was the case with ValuJet; others like Children's Hospital of Orange County (CHOC), California, needed a complete brand overhaul, including significant transformations to its culture, leadership, finances, human resources, operations, and marketing.

ValuJet/AirTran Brand Turnaround Story

Founded in 1992, ValuJet was one of many low-cost carriers that thrived in the 1990s. On May 11, 1996, a ValuJet plane crashed in the Florida Everglades,[1] killing 110 passengers. In June 1996, the Federal Aviation Administration (FAA) grounded the brand's whole fleet. For a brand that already had seen its name in the news for safety problems, this was rock bottom.

To combat its image and get people flying it again, ValuJet's marketing department tried to offer free tickets, but the airline couldn't even give seats away.[2]

After what had happened, it was no surprise that ValuJet's business suffered; it reported a loss of more than $50 million. In July 1997, ValuJet announced a merger with Airways Corporation's AirTran Airways (since 2011, part of Southwest Airlines). Bucking convention, ValuJet took the smaller partner's name. It was a masterful bit of public relations magic; in a stroke it erased the sullied ValuJet name. The former senior vice president of marketing at ValuJet, commenting on the name change in *USA Today*, said, "We became the poster child for all things you don't want to think about with respect to air travel. . . . For this company to have any long-term success, we had to change our name."[3]

The name change was widely reported, so consumers knew it was the same brand, but the negative image did not seem to follow it. At the time, one traveler commented, "I think it's a good idea that they change their name. . . . It sounds like a cheap name, and it doesn't represent them at all because they treat you really well."[4]

Children's Hospital of Orange County Brand Turnaround Story

In 1996, Children's Hospital of Orange County (CHOC) was in danger of financial and brand failure, losing $48 million between 1997 and 1999. Hospital officials feared the hospital might be forced to close. In a 2007 interview with *Smart Business*, Kim Cripe, president and CEO of CHOC, said the hospital is now thriving.[5] That year, the hospital took a plan to its board to build a new patient tower—one with a $510 million price tag.

Their troubles started when CHOC was hit by a change to the reimbursement scheme for hospitals mandated by California's Medicaid insurance program to serve the indigent population. The change directed patients to other hospitals and reduced CHOC's market share and damaged the brand. The hospital under CEO Cripe's leadership took drastic measures to cut costs, while focusing on differentiating the hospital. The brand identity, marketing, and communications evolved around a heightened and distinct position of being the region's health-care leader, the first to provide more than 20 high-value, high-tech services along with a best-of-class, highly specialized medical team.

This hospitalwide plan required putting a new management team together, replacing all 13 members of the hospital's senior management over the course of 18 months. The new members came armed with strong financial skills, business development, and experience in marketing and human resources. With the new team in place and implementation of improvement on all aspects of the hospital, by 2000 CHOC recovered and was into the black. Revenues rebounded to $377 million that year, and the brand was back and strong. Since 1998, CHOC has enjoyed admissions growth of 124 percent, and CHOC and its sister property, CHOC at Mission, combined, are ranked as the seventeenth busiest children's hospital in the United States. The hospital was named by *US News & World Report* as one of the Best Children's Hospitals for 2010–2011.[6]

What It Takes to Create Real Change

Change is difficult, especially when a brand is in trouble. Change is associated with uncertainty, and often before the pleasure and rewards show up, there can be pain. But, it is also the axis to all progress, innovation, development, and improvement. It is the critical point for growth.

Overcoming Resistance to Change

To invite change into your organization or life, you must understand how the human mind and change work. Chip Heath and Dan Heath, coauthors of *Switch*, studied change both from a personal and business standpoint. Their discoveries confirm that "most people hate change," although those naysayers have a funny way of showing it. Every iPhone sold serves as counterevidence. So does every text message sent, every corporate merger finalized, and every aluminum can recycled. So do the biggest changes in most of our lives: getting married, having kids, and so on. (If people hate change, then having a child seems like an awfully dumb decision.)

It puzzled the Heaths that some huge changes, like marriage, came joyously, while some trivial changes, like changing the color of the couple's bedroom, met fierce resistance. They learned that people have two separate "systems" in their brains—a rational system and an emotional system. The rational system is more thoughtful and logical and is focused on planning. The emotional system, on the other hand, is impulsive and instinctual. The Heath brothers' conclusion: most significant change comes from a balance between our rational and emotional motivations.

I recently met Dr. James A. Belasco, change expert and author of *Seize Tomorrow, Start Today* on a trip to Saudi Arabia. We were both speakers invited to address a major conference for Saudi Arabian Airlines (SAA). My segment covered branding, and Jim's was on transforming company cultures.

The conference theme embodied change. Saudi Arabian Airlines, however, is a very traditional company, and getting it to think in a new way about its brand, communications, core values, and the changing global business traveler was a challenge.

The Saudi airline has been around for more than 60 years, and it has experienced strong growth during that time, but now it is losing market share to smaller, low-cost regional carriers. To compete in new market, SAA knows it has to make some significant changes to its internal and external branding, customer experience, and communications efforts. A couple of years ago, under Yousef Attiah, the vice president of Marketing and Product Management for Saudi Arabian Airlines, it started working with Honour, a branding firm based in the United Kingdom that specializes in the travel, transportation, and hospitality sector. At the time of the conference, the group had facilitated changes to the customer experience: the airport environments, airplane interiors, uniforms, amenities, and other important customer touchpoints that successfully leveraged the core values and distinct attributes of the airline.

The goal of the conference was to move SAA to the next big step: internal changes and changes to the brand's corporate culture.

I spent five days in Jeddah, Saudi Arabia, with Dr. Belasco, making history as the first woman to address the conference of more than 300 marketing and customer service personnel. Jim broke ground, too, introducing many ideas that were foreign to their world of business and customer experience. After hearing his talk on transformation, I asked Jim why he thought change was so difficult.

Jim has worked with start-ups and Fortune 500 companies for almost 50 years. I asked him why he thought change implementation, especially as it concerns turnaround brands, is so difficult.

Jim explained: "To get companies to think in new and different ways requires different leadership thinking. Many leaders all want to order change as if it were fast food from a roadside chain. They don't have the slightest clue of what's required to 'turn a brand around.' They also don't have the staying power to do so, even if they are supposed to benefit from short-term incentive plans (paying for quarterly and annual results); these run counter to what's needed to create a lasting turnaround. It takes time and many people to turn a company around in the long term, and companies are not willing to wait for the results that change can bring to their brand."

Understanding what *really* motivates your team is critical, without it real change is unlikely. One of the most recognized thought leaders on change, creative productivity, and life is Daniel Pink. In his latest book, *Drive,* he addresses the essence of what motivates people, which is essential if change is going to occur.[7]

Pink believes everything we think we know about what motivates people is wrong and cites scientific studies showing that, for example, the carrot-and-stick method can actually reduce production of creative solutions to problems and change.

What motivates people after their basic survival needs are met (food, sex, shelter, and so on) is the ability to grow and develop and to realize their fullest potential.

According to Pink, there are three drivers that motivate teams to produce and change:

- *Autonomy.* The more people have control over their lives, the happier they are. Self-determination is the path to engagement.
- *Mastery.* We are wired to want to be better at what we do. The mastery of something is its own reward.
- *Purpose.* We are happiest when we are working for something larger than ourselves.

It is helpful to keep the motivators in mind when implementing change for your brand.

Implementing Transformational Change

Cali Ressler and Jody Thompson, former human resource professionals at Best Buy and coauthors of *Why Work Sucks and How to Fix It,*[8] created the Results-Only Work Environment (ROWE) and put this theory into practice.

Their focus is on a management strategy whereby employees and teams are evaluated on performance, not presence. In a ROWE, people focus on results and *only* results—increasing the organization's performance while creating the right climate for people to manage change and all the demands in their lives—including work.

In our interview, Cali and Jody said that leaders in companies pose the biggest challenge to implement major changes in their culture. Organizations want to implement technical changes—easy, Band-Aid solutions—that they call "transformational" changes, but they're not transformational at all. They're flavor-of-the-month hoaxes. Real culture change involves adaptive solutions that get under people's skin—that actually cause people to question (and ultimately change) their belief system. "When we implement ROWE in companies, we always say we're comforting the disturbed and disturbing the comforted. The 'comforted' are the leaders who think things are operating just fine and that they have all the answers. They have a very hard time understanding that they need to change their belief system from Time + Physical Presence = Results to just Results = Results."

Cali and Jody's strategy for overcoming challenges that deal with human nature is adaptive. They rip the rug out from under people and let them sit in their discomfort. They guide them to discovery and provide tools for getting to the other side, but it's up to the people to do the hard work. This is the only way they will buy into the change that's happening. So many organizations put processes in place to stop the discomfort once it starts to occur. That's a big mistake; people *need* to feel that discomfort in order to *want* to find a new way.

After the big, bad brand shake-up event or market shift there are clear challenges and patterns to creating change as a brand cycles through to its return to glory.

Change must

- Be identified with a strong, meaningful purpose
- Be prioritized based on importance and investment

▪ Not be forgotten after it makes its debut; reinforcement, recognition, and relevant rewards must be carried on to brand and change ambassadors

As organizations, companies, and individuals look to change, they often stumble on these three challenges.

The "I-Want-to-Change-It-All" Syndrome

Changing everything is rarely a good idea. I call this crazy syndrome "changeitis." It's a common ailment among companies that have too much money, and it is a knee-jerk response. Instead of carefully thinking through where the real issues are and identifying what type of change is really needed, companies bring in new leadership, and everything is put on auto-pilot to change, so the new person or team can prove his/her/their worth. Companies exhibit these tendencies every day.

There is a balance of change that should happen in a turnaround. Before making any changes, it's important to do these things:

▪ Examine the core reasons and behaviors that contributed to the brand's fall
▪ Conduct research on what you believe should change with the intended audiences
▪ Only then, make the changes, but your due diligence must support these premises

How to Decide What Needs to Change

Authentic brands are derived from core values of the brand. Jim Collins, author of many great books including *Good to Great, Built to Last* and *How the Mighty Fall*,[9] brings an intriguing perspective to change. Change is good—but first, know what should never change. Ephemeral practices can change, people can change, processes can change, product strategy can change, but core values of the brand should not.

Start by asking yourself these questions:

- What are the brand's core values? Diversity? Creativity? Integrity? Fun? Tradition? Innovation?
- How do they show up in your current brand? Or don't they show up enough?
- What changes will make a positive difference to further the presence of your brand's core values?
- What should never be changed because it anchors your brand's beliefs and values?

The Impact of Size on Change

Size on both sides of the resource coin can be a detriment to the noblest plans. There is no perfect organization when it comes to implementing change. Small companies have fewer people and processes to transform, but usually they also have fewer resources as well. Large organizations have money and people but many layers of bureaucracy, offices everywhere, and stables full of dinosaurs. Big or small, they both have their challenges.

If you are a small company, ask yourself: If money were no object, what would the solutions look like? Then, ask yourself: How can I do the same thing for less? In many cases, you can accomplish the same thing in a different way, one that you can afford. You've just got to think big first and then scale it down.

If you are a large company and have lots of cash and people, what would the solutions look like if you had only 10 percent of those resources? In many cases these less costly, smaller ideas can be implemented more quickly than bigger, more expensive ideas. And sometimes time is of the essence. At other times, starting out with a smaller, less costly idea allows thinking to be more creative, and you can scale the idea up to fit your company's needs. You've just got to think in a frugal, entrepreneurial mindset and then scale it up.

Ultimately, size doesn't really matter. Whether a brand crumbles on a fast track, like Robert Downey Jr. in the 1990s, or over decades of decline and decay, like the city of Detroit once did, or from a series of bad events as happened to Xerox, brand recovery and turnaround takes time and the ability to adapt and change.

Change in brand turnaround is critical and by far the most difficult to achieve. Most people—the public, employees, and influencers—resist change. Others just loathe the idea that someone is trying to change them. The brands that fail are the ones that never fully welcome change and instead allow the chains of bad habits and fear to hold them hostage.

When a Rising Star Falls

Individual brands, professional brands, leadership brands, and celebrity brands can rise to world fame in a few hours with the right YouTube video or a couple of interviews on national media. Look at Susan Boyle, the woman with the angelic voice discovered on *Britain's Got Talent*. Since her professional launch and brand birth, she has made history, breaking sales records with her debut compact disk and sellout concert tours around the globe.

That lightning speed also goes in the other direction. Just as fast as these brands can rise to fame, they can fall from it and end up in the brand trash can. Ted Williams, branded "the homeless man with the golden voice," was discovered by a reporter and propelled to fame. Perhaps too much happened too quickly for Williams, though, because soon he was involved in a scandal. One day he's on top of the world, the next week he's headed to rehab.

What follows are three examples of brands that broke the chains of defeat and found and implemented the change needed for brand recovery.

Robert Downey Jr. Brand Turnaround Story

Robert Downey Jr., the son of a director father and actress mother, started acting at age five. His breakthrough role was as a cocaine addict in *Less Than Zero*, a role that would come to seem prescient a few years later. In 1992, though, Downey won an Oscar nomination for his portrayal of Charlie Chaplin in *Chaplin*. As an actor, he had arrived.

Unfortunately, Downey, the addict, arrived a few years later. From the mid-1990s to 2001, Downey was arrested many times. Numerous trips to rehabilitation—and jail—were followed by even more over-the-top, drug-fueled escapades. At one point, Downey told a judge, "It's like I have a loaded gun in my mouth and my finger's on the trigger, and I like the taste of the gunmetal."[10]

After almost a year confined to a substance abuse facility, Downey started over with a role on the TV show *Ally McBeal.* Downey again succumbed to addiction and was arrested once again. He lost his role in the high-profile film *America's Sweethearts* and countless other opportunities. Woody Allen wanted to hire him, but no company would insure the actor. This was the bottom.

Downey's comeback started with him lip-synching in a video for Elton John's "I Want Love." A friend posted Downey's insurance bond so that he could land the role in *The Singing Detective,* a small-budget film based on a BBC TV series. Ironically, that friend was Mel Gibson, who would soon face his own substance-abuse-fueled catastrophe from which his brand has yet to recover. Downey, however, moved on to larger independent films, gladly taking supporting roles.

Much has been made of Oprah Winfrey's ability to put a brand on the map, but what she is even better at is revitalizing a brand that has fallen. In November 2004 Downey went before the queen of daytime television to promote his debut CD, *The Futurist.* On *The Oprah Winfrey Show* he admitted that he had a problem and that overcoming it was the most difficult thing he'd ever faced. In 2005, Downey married a film producer, and he credits her with helping him stay straight.

To say that Downey was an unconventional choice to be the new Iron Man is an understatement. Initial reactions to the 2006 announcement were grim. The success of the *Iron Man* movie upon its release in 2008 thrust Downey into the spotlight and confirmed the rehabilitation of the actor's brand. Soon after he was offered the high-profile role of Sherlock Holmes, which went on to win him many professional accolades, including the Golden

Globe for Best Actor in a Motion Picture, Musical, or Comedy from the Hollywood Foreign Press Association. But this time, critics and insiders were going on not only about his "genius" but also about his "work ethic."

In 2009, Downey was nominated for an Academy Award for best supporting actor for his comic role in *Tropic Thunder*. That same year he was in the top five of *People* magazine's "Sexiest Man Alive" survey. Downey's career continues to rise to this day.

How Downey Did It

So how did this brilliant actor-turned-addict turn his brand back around? It began with turning his life around.

Downey has been drug-free since July 2003, which he credits to his family, therapy, meditation, 12-step recovery programs, yoga, and the practice of Wing Chun Kung Fu. He then had to earn back the respect of those who might hire him. When he learned of the opportunity for *Iron Man*, a screen test was required. Downey welcomed the opportunity. (He'd had to prove his talents and compete for the Chaplin role; he would do it again for this one.)

Downey's turnaround is also about the journey that led him to where he should be. He has spoken openly about his past and the fact that even in his darkest days he had a strong drive to survive as well as ambition. Finally, one day in 2003, those drives got the upper hand, and at a Burger King on the Pacific Coast Highway, he threw all his drugs into the ocean and decided he was done with that life.

Sure, Downey had to decide that he'd had enough of jail, rehab, and the public humiliation that accompanied that lifestyle, but he also discovered that when he regained the passion to act and perform without the need for drugs, his roles became bigger and his brand reemerged. Finally, the blockbuster movie *Iron Man*—with its parallel plot line of genius, extreme, near-death experience, and moment of truth—gave him the platform and the international audience that erased the tarnish to his brand.

Today, his brand turnaround success is apparent: Downey's net worth is estimated at $50 million.[11] He earned $500,000 for the first *Iron Man*; now that the brand is back, his fee for *Iron Man 2* was $10 million.[12] The admiration of his fans is evident by the multitude of websites around his work and accomplishments, several biographies, and a dance card full of new, big roles.

The Downey brand turned around because Downey did these things:

- *He ate crow and got back to doing what he did best.* Downey has never downplayed his history of bad choices and criminal behavior. His transparency, self-deprecation, and honesty about his life make his brand even more appealing to his fans. The human element of redemption is a strong bond with the public.
- *He aligned his brand with his role.* It's likely no coincidence that the *Iron Man* character Tony Stark and Downey's real-life persona have so much in common. From being down to coming back up, the hero in it all was Downey's brand, which experienced a rebirth into superstardom with this movie.
- *He kept his eye on the prize.* Downey's role in *Iron Man* was a risk for all concerned. It wasn't just another movie; it was one with a huge production budget, massive promotion, and potentially a mass global audience. The magnitude of a major franchise opportunity was what Downey needed to relaunch his career and brand.
- *He pushed through every day; surrender was not an option.* Hitting bottom for Downey was a gift. Reflecting on himself, re-sorting his priorities, and finding his ambition and the competitive hero within himself gave him new understanding. From that point there was only one place to go: up. Downey knows that the demons that earned him his orange suit and criminal record have not left the planet. Every day is a work in progress to stay clean, centered, and on his game.

Just as Robert Downey Jr. seemed untouchable at the time of his first Oscar nomination, before his ultimately short-lived downfall, a brand turnaround can happen to anyone or anything.

No Place Is Immune

Look at the city of Detroit. It has been around since 1701, when it was known as French-Canadian Fort Ponchartrain du Détroit. In the eighteenth and nineteenth centuries the city's proximity to transport waterways made it an industrial powerhouse. Through the mid-1960s Detroit was the glowing city on the hill in America, the home of the Big Three automakers and Motown.

Competition, Crime, and Complacency Almost Killed Detroit

Detroit's population peaked in 1950 at 1.85 million. As things got worse in subsequent years, many fled the city limits to the suburbs, and the city's tax base disappeared. From 1950 and through 1990, the city lost at least 150,000 people every decade. Since that time, the population has continued to decline.

Perhaps the first signs of the decline of the Detroit brand came with the race riots of 1967. Then, the fuel crisis of the 1970s slaughtered U.S. carmakers. The 1980s saw a crack epidemic. Crime skyrocketed, and the city's very name became a punch line for stories about urban despair and decline. By 2000, businesses were fleeing Detroit too.

Detroit Mayor Kwame Kilpatrick helped cement Detroit's negative image. Elected in 2001 at just 31 years old, the Detroit native would go on to become the face of Detroit, scarred by greed and graft. During Kilpatrick's two terms, there seemed to be no end to the scandals. In 2002, Kilpatrick is alleged to have hosted a party of strippers at the mayor's official residence. In 2003, one of the strippers from the party was gunned down. The investigation was mired in controversy, particularly when the lead detective was removed from the case for expressing his belief that the hit was done by a Detroit cop.

Repeatedly during his two terms, the mayor's office transferred payments to friends and cronies in amounts just under the $25,000 limit—to avoid city council scrutiny. Kilpatrick also funneled state grant money to his family and committed tax fraud. In 2007, Kilpatrick was caught having an affair with his chief of staff. In 2008, text messages between Kilpatrick and his chief of staff further revealed their affair. They also revealed that the two conspired to remove a police deputy chief from duty. Kilpatrick defiantly refused to resign. Later in 2008, Kilpatrick was charged with obstruction of justice and perjury. He pled guilty and resigned from office.[13]

To further add to Detroit's problems, the uninvited guest known as the 2009 recession punched Detroit in the stomach again. The Big Three automakers were on the verge of demise, and the third, Ford, was weakened. By 2010, to many the word *Detroit* had become synonymous with the worst city in America.

Detroit Brand Turnaround Story

In 2011, a new mayor was elected. Mayor Dave Bing, a former National Basketball Association (NBA) All-Star and successful steel entrepreneur, brought renewed energy and a "we-can-come-back" spirit to the city. Bing claimed, "When I was elected, I thought I knew what was going on. But I got here and found out . . . things were way worse than I ever imagined."[14] Nonetheless, he was determined to turn the city around. Bing is no stranger to change or challenge. His 47-year career as an athlete, business owner, and leader attests to that.

Collaborative Change Is Driving Detroit Back on Track. New leadership alone, however, cannot transform a city's brand. Detroit, like most big-city brands, has many stakeholders, agendas, and interests, from tourism to hospitality to economic development. For a brand to truly turn around, all have to work together and tell their story. A brand is the sum of all its actions, promises, touchpoints, and the opinions and influence derived from the market.

Change had to happen, or Detroit would never erase its "America's most miserable city"[15] brand.

Change had to happen if Detroit was to have a future of opportunity and prosperity. Brand Detroit's recovery, just as its fall, will be tied to the economy. That means the Big Three automakers. And that's happening. In January 2011 Ford, General Motors (GM), and Chrysler all reported sales increases.[16] More important, U.S. automakers are again seen as providing quality, innovative products with distinctive brand images. From new, attractive designs to hybrids and electric cars of the future, the Big Three are regaining their positive reputation.

As a destination brand, Detroit has had to break the chains of despair, deal with uncontrollable market conditions, and handle the constant negative battering by the media, which meant that collaborative planning and change were needed. As part of its turnaround, the city has amped up its cultural events and music and art venues in an effort to change the perception of what the city offers visitors.

Rebranding efforts have come from multiple constituents. Government leaders, the business community, the tourism and convention associations, and its citizens will have to embrace a new story, and all will have to commit to walking the talk and being proud ambassadors together.

Five years ago the official transformation in Detroit's brand started. As is true of most cities, there are common goals but diverse and competing priorities, agendas, and interests—for example, local life vs. business, and visitors and conventions tax bases vs. corporate recruitment. The challenge has been to develop one story that can be told by all, that benefits all, and that truly changes the perceptions of this tarnished town.

The Detroit brand is turning around because Detroit has done the following things:

- *It has obtained funding.* The Detroit Metro Convention and Visitors Bureau (DMCVB) is the only organization that invests significant dollars in promoting the city of Detroit and the tricounty area known as "The D." Leveraging the billions of dollars of capital investment made by many private and public entities for capital investment in casinos and upscale hotels, a revamped art museum, and a redeveloped riverfront, the DMCVB led the brand change charge.

- *It assembled a new team to drive the program and take advantage of this momentum.* Chris Baum was hired as Senior Vice President, Sales & Marketing for DMCVB. Armed with marketing, branding, and sales insight, this 30-plus-years hospitality veteran knew that understanding and being relevant to new markets was necessary, but, more important, he had to figure out how to bring all the stakeholders together to support the changes. This meant not only communicating a new brand story through tactics such as advertising and promotion but also living it by changing attitudes—instilling pride in and ownership of what the city stands for.

- *It's defined a clear position.* For years, Detroit's position was driven by the auto industry, and it was blurry at best. DMCVB began the process with a major research undertaking. The research found that younger people (21 to 34)—and those who think young—thought Detroit was a cool American city that hadn't sold out. In focus groups, Gen X and Y members thought Detroit was "gritty," meaning hip and authentic,[17] while many traditional Boomers also thought Detroit was "gritty," meaning dirty and deteriorating.[18]

  The brand positioning they settled on in Detroit is "Where Cool Comes From," and with the Shelby Mustang, the Detroit Institute of Arts, three Vegas-style casinos, Kid Rock and Eminem, and the Redwings and Tigers, the city had the cast and the characters lined up to start telling the new Detroit story.

- *It's focused on support from all community segments.* As the new guy driving the new brand change, Chris Baum and his team saw several areas where Detroit had major credibility and horsepower when compared with other cities. They also knew it would take careful rebrand development and execution with all stakeholders participating.

From the outset, political and business leaders, current customers, hoteliers, and other travel industry leaders were invited to the planning sessions, where they could share their ideas and observations. This decision proved to be a wise one, as the final brand strategy evolved, major changes were introduced, and community support was a key transforming energy.

■ *It's concentrated on attributes, not slogans.* The new branding effort has focused on five attributes—cars, culture, gaming, music, and sports—rather than a slogan. Slogans have been notoriously unsuccessful in the travel business, with Las Vegas, which spent over $100 million to build the "What happens here. . ." campaign a rare exception.[19] Detroit has also invested in a new brand mark that incorporated a new "D" design and the five brand attributes, which they pair with various creative headlines and tags for different market segments.

The New Brand Is Starting to Shine. Detroit is a place of triumphs, a city of struggles, and a metropolis with enough imagination to power the nation. The car claims center stage. The music runs deep. Sports are pursued with a passion. The culture is cooking. Trace cool to its source and sooner or later you find your way to Detroit. Few other great American cities put out so much vibrant style. Whether you are from a big city or small, Detroit wants you to know it has something you can't get back home.

The introduction of the new Detroit positioning has been critical to its success, as has been the brand positioning that has had to be lived by all stakeholders and not something shoved willy-nilly onto every touchpoint of literal text. After all, when you are a city where cool comes from, you can't tout that fact yourself, or you will not seem to be cool at all.

Detroit had its own set of folks who were not in the ring of support. For many years, Detroit was a punching bag for the media. The city did have some bad neighborhoods, like every major city in America does, but lazy reporting kept perpetuating the myths about crime rates and other negatives, so Detroit knew it had to take an assertive, offensive approach with the new brand story if they were going to change the conversation. The communications team worked proactively to place stories in key influential media such as the *Wall Street Journal*, the *New York Times*, *USA Today*, and the major TV networks—and it worked.

While the branding team at DMCVB didn't work hand-in-hand with the Big Three—Ford, GM, and Chrysler—on the new city brand (they have their own priorities and challenges), there does seem to be a natural synergy and story shared among the voices coming out of Detroit. There is a definite tone of pride, community values, and spirit—isn't that what great branding is all about?

While the DMCVB has led the major media and positioning brand program, the government, civic leadership, the business communities, the Big Three auto players, economic development groups, and the citizens have all contributed to the turnaround. Great brands are not about a campaign, but they are the sum of the total experience, the communication, and the story that sticks in the minds of the market.

Since the resurrection of Detroit's brand, meeting and convention planners, who previously wouldn't have even considered booking in Detroit, have signed contracts in record numbers. Regional tourism is rebounding well and, when the directors of Mensa (the IQ society) booked their annual meeting in the city, it further spawned smart buzz about the destination, earning it an award for the quirky campaign called "Who's the Genius Who Picked Detroit?" All proof that a well-thought-out program, with sound strategic positioning and collaboration from all stakeholders, can change perceptions and turn a brand around.

Detroit also leads the nation in "urban agriculture." The empty and abandoned lots, formerly urban blights, are being filled with lush plants and farmed. To facilitate this, the city is changing zoning regulations to accommodate the urban green boom. Kathryn Lynch Underwood, a city planner, told the *Christian Science Monitor* in May 2010, "My personal hope is that the model that we roll out benefits as many people across the board in a city that really needs people to be employed and engaged in meaningful work."

Downtown Detroit is getting a facelift too, thanks to $110 million in federal stimulus package money. The beautification efforts and demolition of old and abandoned buildings has even spawned a Detroit Revitalization Tour, another good brand experience touchpoint. The city is also spending more on public art, which draws artists and generates ancillary benefits and revenues.

To cap off a city in full recovery, Chrysler's 2011 Super Bowl spot gave the city and the recovering car brand a solid, emotional brand boost. The spot themed "Imported from Detroit" featured Eminem, a Detroit native, along with other hometown heroes.

Chrysler CEO Sergio Marchionne told *Forbes* magazine that Eminem "was not an easy choice," acknowledging that the rapper posed some risks. But in the end, Eminem turned out to be the perfect spokesperson for Detroit, for Chrysler, and its hell-and-back journey. Eminem and the commercial made a memorable impression on millions of minds around the globe. The spot was well received by the media and fans alike, creating immense viral buzz that remains very alive on the Internet today with more than 10 million views in the first 30 days after the game.

A Recovery in Progress. Detroit's brand is not completely out of the woods. The full recovery will continue to be a work in progress. As I write this chapter, the national media announced Detroit's latest census reports showed a 25 percent drop in residents during the past decade, which is not good. The mayor is appealing the numbers, because this data can significantly impact federal funding and other legal provisions from which Detroit benefits.

However, most experts seem to agree that the city's population has probably bottomed out, so it's the perfect time to consolidate neighborhoods and start repurposing the vacant land. It's also important to remember that there still are 4.5 million people in Metro Detroit, so there are plenty of young prospects who will move back into the city when they have the affordable housing—and cool neighborhoods from which to choose. That's already happening for Detroit, but a few major developments will turn a stream into a deluge. As cited in *Crain's Detroit Business*, Whole Foods is looking to open its first market in the city of Detroit.[20]

As a destination, the city that continues to rebound, the brand will require the unified efforts of many brand ambassadors, leaders, and stakeholders to continue to carry the reinvented Detroit torch. As a local economy and community, Detroit will need to stay committed to right-sizing and making tough decisions to continue to improve its quality, efficiency, and productivity to maintain its tax base and its momentum.

DMCVB cites the following as essential to creating brand Detroit's change and turnaround:

- *Research.* Detroit invested in comprehensive research, before any changes were planned. This not only provided market insight for the brand planning team but also later became an evidence tool to empower change with stakeholders.
- *A clear positioning platform.* Without clear positioning, you will waste a lot of time and resources. Detroit's position was a direct result of the research it had done, which was a key driver in the city's journey back.
- *Early collaboration and engagement.* Early collaboration and dialogue with stakeholders have paid off.
- *Making change in small bits.* Big is not best when making change. Implementation of change is best in small, tailored, and frequent bits.
- *Customization.* One size does not fit all. Introducing and executing a new brand story to diverse segments must be customized and made relevant to each segment.

DMCVB took a different creative approach to their TV advertising, which was aimed at regional tourists in places like Cleveland and Columbus, Ohio than they did to their trade media, which focused on meeting and convention print advertising and the specialized campaign they developed for the Film Detroit division.

The TV spots showed young people receiving videos on their smart phones from friends having a great time in "The D" while they were stuck back home watching a "chick flick" with their girlfriend or on a crummy blind date. The award-winning meetings campaign used clever, self-deprecating headlines like "Detroit gets good PR. Finally." to announce new convention wins (like the Public Relations Society of America's Annual Meeting) with the goal of encouraging other convention decision-makers to take a look at Detroit. For the hip Hollywood crowd, the message was "Detroit: We're Cheap and Easy," which highlighted Detroit's aggressive incentives and free assistance, combined with very hip art direction. All were true to the "Detroit is where cool comes from" theme, but each was custom tailored to a unique audience for maximum return on investment.

- *Empathy.* Understanding all the stakeholders' goals and making the new brand story applicable to their needs is vital. Some of the strongest brand traction has come in the area of recruiting great new talent to move to the city. For example, DMCVB created a hip and positive media guide to the region for Super Bowl XL that incorporated the new "D" brand. It did such a great job showcasing Southeast Michigan's unique assets that local corporations began asking if they could use the publication in their recruiting efforts. The DMCVB commenced selling the guide with customized covers at cost to local corporations, like Ilitch Holdings, owners of Little Caesar's Pizza, the Fox Theater, Olympia Entertainment, and the Detroit Tigers and Detroit Red Wings.
- *Simplicity and accessibility.* Branding tools must be simple, easy to access, and use. To accompany its "cool" positioning, Detroit is branding itself with an industrial looking D, and a "Detroit: Cars, Culture, Gaming, Music, Sports" focus. The logo is simple enough that any company can use it in their own advertising and branding

efforts. Making it even simpler to adopt are Detroit suggestions for how to use and implement the logo.

When Organizations Need to Change

Corporations, nonprofits, and products are no different from celebrity or destination crack-ups—even the mightiest can fall from grace. Brand meltdowns and shake-ups can happen in a second, like a lightning strike. The biggest difference is that business and nonprofit entity brands often have built significant brand equity over a long period of time with more resources and complex stakeholders.

Xerox Brand Turnaround Story

It's the dream of a brand to grow so powerful and dominant that its name becomes a verb describing the very thing its product does. Such is the case with Xerox. That may not have happened if it kept its original name, "The Haloid Photographic Company." Founded in 1906, it was not until 1961 that the company would come to be known as simply "Xerox."

The brand's first hit was the Xerox 914 photocopier, which in 1961 created revenue topping $60 million. By 1965, that number increased to $500 million. Through the 1980s, Xerox's cutting-edge technology kept the brand at the top of its industry.

Scandal, Fraud, and Accidents Combine to Nearly Destroy a Brand. From 1997 to 2002, Xerox was caught in a number of accounting fraud scandals. In 2001, Xerox paid a $10 million fine to the Securities and Exchange Commission (SEC) for overstating its earnings by $3 billion.[21] This shake-up along with sales channel reorganization and digital innovation challenges continued to plague the brand. And it didn't shop there.

The symbolic low point for the Xerox brand came on November 3, 1999, when a disgruntled employee opened fire in a Xerox office in Hawaii and killed seven people.[22] The state of Xerox was grim: It had no cash, was

$17.1 billion in debt,[23] and, in 2000, the stock had gone from $63.69 a share to $4.43. Change had to happen; Xerox was on the brink of bankruptcy and time was running out.

How Xerox Did It

So how did this global, debt-ridden corporation, days away from extinction in 2000 find its way back to glory? The answer is strong leadership and a team willing to change.

Xerox's turnaround was largely led by Anne Mulcahy, who was appointed president in May 2000, CEO in August 2001, and chairman in January 2002. She launched an aggressive plan that returned the company to full-year profitability by the end of 2002, while decreasing debt, increasing cash, continuing investments in research and development, and fueling the rebirth of a new, healthy brand.

Anne Mulcahy, who started selling copiers approximately 34 years earlier, later earned a variety of management positions in marketing, operations, and worldwide human resources. Taking over at Xerox's lowest point, her leadership has been chronicled as one of the greatest financial and brand turnarounds in business history. As cited in *Money* magazine, by keeping the company steadfastly focused on customers and employees, she was able to lead Xerox away from the brink of collapse to become one of the world's most profitable and innovative technology and service enterprises.[24]

A company's financial and mental health, culture, reputation, and bottom line all filter the brand impression that's left in markets' minds. So it's no surprise to see how Xerox's business success and brand are joined at the hip.

Embracing an "Environment of Crisis" Propelled Change. When you dive into the details of Anne Mulcahy's and her team's success, you find leading, executing, and embracing major change were everywhere. She often proclaimed, when describing the key turnaround strategies, "You have to change all the time; in hiring, adaptability and flexibility are standout attributes, and crisis provides an opportunity to challenge and question everything and then make the needed changes."[25]

One of the most compelling aspects of her leadership and transformation of Xerox is her background and passion for human resources and marketing. She clearly understood that the impact of change on the business and brand is an emotional process, and that compassion and empathy are critical in securing the loyalty of employees, customers, and partners, especially in tough times.

In an interview with Knowledge@Wharton,[26] she also emphasized, the role that an "environment of crisis" can play in spurring a company to change. "We took full advantage of [that environment] in terms of really getting people to think about the business differently during that time," she said. "During the very difficult days, we separated the company into two parts. There was a small set of people who worked on the issues. And then there was a large set of people whose responsibility was maintaining customer loyalty. So we 'fenced off' and insured that our customer communications were flawless, that our customers didn't feel the impact of the crisis. It became everyone's responsibility. The environment of crisis was very conducive to making significant cultural changes that are really tough to do in normal times."

What Leaders Can Learn from Xerox. Based on what happened at Xerox, it is clear that leaders *must* do the following things:

- *Listen.* Strong leaders need to make regular efforts to talk to the employee teams, customers, and partners. From individual face time with customers to town hall–style gatherings with employees, open dialogue is critical.
- *Don't overanalyze.* It's important for companies not to focus too intently on data and process. Instead, they must create clear accountability and establish well-aligned goals.

- *Have vision.* When Xerox was struggling, employees and investors wanted to know what to expect once the brand experienced a turnaround. In 2001, Anne Mulcahy's team wrote a fictional *Wall Street Journal* article, dated 2005, that detailed exactly what the company would look like.

- *Maintain commitment to research and development.* In order for Xerox to focus on its new vision, research and development were key, and the company made sure not to cut any funding in that department. She said, "I knew that there was victory that would be shallow if we solved a bankruptcy issue and wound up facing a technology drought down the road."[27]

- *Communicate.* Especially if you're a big company, people need to follow the same set of objectives, and this requires open lines of communications.

In 2008, to further communicate the fully transformed company, driven by diverse and innovative products, Xerox created a more contemporary logo. The updated word mark and graphic icon—a red sphere with a white X with three gray stripes—was meant to show how the company was closely connected with customers, employees, and shareholders in the new content-rich digital marketplace.

In 2010, Xerox continued the new brand build with a multimillion-dollar campaign called "Ready for Real Business." The campaign is one of Xerox's biggest efforts in decades and features well-known brand mascots like Procter & Gamble's Mr. Clean, Target's bull's-eye dog, and the Marriott Hotels & Resorts' bellman, to name a few of Xerox's clients.

Anne Mulcahy stepped down as CEO in 2009 when Ursula Burns, former president of Xerox Corp., was named to succeed her as chief executive officer and assumed the role of chairperson of the company on May 20, 2010. Both women worked closely as a team throughout the company's transformation.

Today, the publicly traded corporation with more than 136,000 employees (in 2011), 9,400+ patents (in 2011), and a research and development (R&D) program that invested over $700 million in 2010 alone wants you to know them as the world's leading enterprise for business process and document management.

Change Is Inevitable

Change is difficult at any time, whether you are turning a brand around or leading a successful one. Change is also inevitable because the world and everybody who lives in it are evolving every minute. Individuals, organizations, and brands that don't change will die a premature death, especially when the brand has been hit with a brand-shaking event or market threat.

All the brands discussed in this chapter have had to change or they would not be here tomorrow. Each of their situations is unique, yet each has common threads that made a difference in the change process and ultimate outcome.

Leaders who drive turnarounds must prevail in empowering diverse stakeholders and influencers into towering transformation—a process that not only feeds their value system but also is clearly aligned with the brand's objectives.

These brands, and most that bounce back from crisis to their place of glory, have done so by adhering to—and believing—the following:

- *Speed to smart solutions is not an option; it's essential.* Timely action and change are defining moments in recovery. If a brand-shaking incident happens, accept the facts and move quickly with honest, regular communication and a doable action plan. If your brand gets in trouble over time, respond promptly to even the smallest turbulence, not just to the blatant red flags. In both cases respond with strategy and with clear goals in mind.

■ *Take the pounding, and then get back to work.* It is what it is. Blame, regret, and guilt are useless activities for leaders and brand teams. Understand your stakeholders' perspectives and needs. Don't dismiss what is already working or your core values. These are where your organic power lives, and they are the strength of your brand's soul.

■ This means that every department and aspect of the brand needs to be addressed, from leadership to communications to processes, resources, and environment.

■ To effectuate change it is essential to do the following:
  ■ Know that opportunity is often disguised as crisis.
  ■ Be an excellent listener.
  ■ Communicate often and honestly with stakeholders and influencers.
  ■ Break away from the chains that got you where you are.
  ■ Don't change everything.
  ■ Understand what motivates your stakeholders.
  ■ Customize change—it is not a one-size-fits-all effort.
  ■ Create a short- and long-term plan of action that includes leadership, culture, environment, resources, processes, and communications.
  ■ Reinforce emotional values and benefits to stakeholders.
  ■ Walk the talk and live the change you want to stick.
  ■ Move with both speed and smarts; it will impact your brand's destiny.

Whether a brand crumbles on a fast track, like Robert Downey Jr., or over decades of decline and decay, like the city of Detroit, or from a series of bad events, like the Xerox Corp., brand recovery and turnaround take both time and the ability to adapt and change.

Companies, organizations, and individuals that welcome change have an advantage in brand building and brand turnaround.

Part 2

Seven Game Changers That Made the Difference

Chapter 4

Game Changer 1: Take Responsibility

To be clear, taking responsibility does not mean admitting guilt; it means showing up, leveraging media platforms—both traditional and social media—communicating in a way that is consistent with your brand, and acknowledging the situation and your commitment to finding solutions.

Nobody Likes a Crybaby: Take Responsibility

Brand turnarounds get out the message by managing media, communicating effectively, and showing a sincere and empathic focus on making things better for the market and stakeholders. The more high profile the brand, the higher the expectations are for a timely response about the issue and brand rattle.

This chapter addresses how brands show the market that they are fallible and understand their responsibilities as a public persona. This means taking actions to inform the public about the situation or correcting it, if need be, using the most effective communications available.

The media play an important role in this lesson. In this chapter, you will learn the importance of handling, working with, and leveraging journalists, news sources, and technology from the get-go—as soon as a brand goes bad and as it recovers—to shift the tide from crisis to composure during the height of a pivotal, potentially brand-shattering event.

First impressions and how the media cover your brand at the time of crisis or bad news is often a lasting brand mark—for good or ill—in the market's mind. Now, because of the Internet, postings from press conferences and key interviews associated with the breaking news can be attached to the brand for years. How a brand handles the initial communication and manages its response has been shown to be an important piece in a brand's recovery and legacy.

In Chapter 2, you learned about the Quick Start "Save Your Brand" Plan, which outlines the top-line actions most brands need to take after a brand-shaking event occurs. Now we will dig more deeply into the elements, timing, and steps real brands have taken in real situations. You'll learn about a few mistakes, but the focus will be on the smart moves that have transformed the brand and caused its turnaround.

Responsibility Example: The Tylenol Scare

In September 1982, the city of Chicago was rocked by a Tylenol scare, when it was revealed that cyanide-poisoned Tylenol capsules had killed seven people. A nationwide panic began as the Federal Bureau of Investigation (FBI) and other authorities hunted for the perpetrator. Day after day, front-page reports linked "murder" and "poison" directly to the brand name Tylenol. Sales of the dominant over-the-counter painkiller plummeted from nearly 37 percent market share before the crisis to 7 percent after.

Johnson & Johnson (J&J), the manufacturer of Tylenol, reacted immediately.[1] Within a week, Tylenol recalled over 30 million bottles of Tylenol. The brand's immediate reaction was lauded by the media. From the

Washington Post to the widely syndicated columnist, Ann Landers, commentary was positive. "Johnson & Johnson has effectively demonstrated how a major business ought to handle a disaster. What J&J executives have done is communicate the message that the company is candid, contrite and compassionate"[2] reported the *Post*; Landers' headline "Johnson & Johnson Handles Tylenol Crisis with Integrity."[3] By November, Tylenol was reintroduced in new safety-sealed containers.

Throughout the brand crisis J&J was very transparent about its efforts. Instead of trying to keep secrets, the company made all of its workings public, including how much it was spending on the recall and new packaging, a price tag that ran to more than $100 million. This assured consumers that action would continue after the recall.

J&J distributed millions of coupons to spur sales of the new safety-packaged Tylenol. By December 1982, a J&J executive claimed in the *New York Times*, "We lost 87 percent of our market. But by mid-December, our surveys show that we had gotten back 67 percent of our original market. The product is coming back faster and stronger than we ever anticipated."[4]

A year after the murders and the collapse of the drug's sales, because of J&J's fast, transparent, and honest efforts, Tylenol had recaptured a 30 percent market share, just short of where it had been before the scandal.

It's important to note, though, that lightning can strike twice. In January 2010, J&J initiated a recall of a number of its products, including Tylenol, as a result of consumer complaints of a musty odor coming from the bottles. The recalls lasted well into the year, and J&J was accused of dragging its feet. It waited 18 months from the time it received the initial complaints before acting. The Food and Drug Administration (FDA) even sent J&J a formal questionnaire asking why the company did not react sooner. Apparently, J&J had not learned from its past success about the need for a rapid response and transparency.

Time Is of the Essence: The 24/7 Media Jungle

Slow response, avoiding the topic, no comments, excuses, blame, and general lack of outreach further raise doubts and foster questions about the events and the brand.

Whether the brand is involved in a series of bad judgments, as Tiger Woods was, or in an accident, such as the BP *Deepwater Horizon* oil rig disaster, or the subject of negative publicity, such as the lawsuit filed against Taco Bell claiming the brand used just 35 percent "beef in its beef offerings," and did not meet minimum U.S. Department of Agriculture requirements, the public is often shocked and concerned, the media is in a frenzy, lawyers start racking up fees, and the companies involved need to act quickly and start building blocks of goodwill to prevent their brands from sinking deeper in the mud.

Today, brands, both big and small, are dancing in a completely new arena. The 24-hours-a-day, 7-days-a-week (24/7) news jungle has quadrupled; it now includes blogs, social networks, microsites, broadcasts, and print outlets. The coverage no longer lasts the day the event originally happened or ran, but, in many cases, it's chronicled on the web for years to come and syndicated across hundreds of other news and content sources.

The media model and environment of aggressive competition has also changed, which has created an intense need for content and constantly breaking and ever-more-sensational stories; that, in turn, is further fueled by consumers' appetite for the controversy and drama. Public participation fans the flames, as now anyone with a computer, cell phone, or camera is asked, or feels compelled, to be an official news contributor, too.

A love-hate relationship exists between the media and brands. Both need each other, and both need to be managed just as any other important relationship does. As reckless or irresponsible as the media can be (some believe), the fact remains, it does have power and still impacts public opinions around brands.

David and Goliath: The Blogger vs. Dell

When brands experience a big hit from public opinion, it is often related to a major negative event, like a product recall in Toyota's case, or sometimes it starts as a very small, isolated story by one person that resonates with a big audience and suddenly becomes a brand-pounding story, as in the case of "Dell Hell."

In June 2005, influential blogger Jeff Jarvis, founder of BuzzMachine. com,[5] posted a series of rants, coined "Dell Hell,"[6] about the Dell laptop he'd recently purchased. Jarvis's posts and sentiments spread quickly, and soon not only did public rage boil over but also major news media (including *BusinessWeek*) picked up the story just two days later; the sales and reputation of the computer industry giant began to plummet.[7]

Before the days of blogs, Dell could have dealt with a crisis at its own pace, but with today's real-time explosions of bad experiences, the company understood it had to respond in a timely fashion.

Dell started a blog of its own and made social media a key part of its response strategy. After the brand melted down, the company opened the dialogue doors, inviting people to share their ideas, pet peeves, and complaints. Dell listened and took action. It went from Dell Hell to a brand back in its glory. Jeff Jarvis—a single blogger and customer—became the catalyst for serious change.

Whether the crisis is one big event or a single customer rant that goes viral, managing the media and controlling the message outreach in a prompt, smart manner is critical to recovery. Within minutes of bad or questionable news, a brand is on center stage and can easily fall off without a carefully planned and timely response. Initial media coverage is often the first turbulence in a brand-gone-bad storm. A brand must quickly decide how to respond and start the recovery process and avoid making matters worse. Furthermore, it can't rest on its laurels; it must continue to use best practices and manage relationships with the media and other influencers.

Brands under fire are often greeted by a marketplace full of confusion and questions about what went wrong or what happened. Whether or not there is guilt, the public believes they are owed timely communication.

My colleague, Denis Calabrese, who advises brands when they are involved in a major scandal, controversy, or damaging event, recommends a timely, informed, and empathic response. He also believes the rapidness of the reply to the media is critical to the recovery process. A response soon after the event occurs and once the main facts are known can set the brand's relationship with the media and public off to the best possible start. This transparency and access show that the brand cares, is taking responsibility for the issue, and is focused on finding answers.

Think Before You Speak

As soon as the brand is shaken—before a word is spoken—it's essential to get a handle on the event and take an inventory of the situation. Making a statement without knowing all the facts—especially at a major public relations event—is a dangerous and risky move. It took some time, but then president George W. Bush and his administration learned this lesson the hard way: Standing on the deck of the USS Abraham Lincoln wearing a green flight suit and holding a white helmet, in front of a massive banner reading "Mission Accomplished," Bush told the world that "Major combat operations in Iraq have ended. In the Battle of Iraq, the United States and our allies have prevailed. And now our coalition is engaged in securing and reconstructing that country."[8] In fact, it was not until August 31, 2010 that President Obama declared an end to the combat mission in Iraq.[9] The event, which seemed like a brilliant political move at the time, the former president says he now regrets. He is certainly not the first public figure to have a prematurely positive outlook come back to haunt him. Perhaps one of the most memorable is Neville Chamberlain, the British Prime Minister, declaring on September 30, 1938, after signing an agreement with Hitler, "it is peace for our time . . ." On September 3, 1939, Neville Chamberlain announced that Britain had declared war on Germany.[10]

Know Your Audience: *Deepwater Horizon* Oil Spill

BP was criticized by the media for initially underestimating the degree of the disaster surrounding the *Deepwater Horizon* oil spill in 2010. How much oil was spilled is still being debated. Official estimates by the Flow Rate Technical Group range from 35,000 to 60,000 barrels/day (1,500,000 to 2,500,000 gallons).[11] According to the *New York Times* in April 2011, "A year afterward, assessments of the damage to the gulf, its people and their livelihoods have been varied . . ." [12] How much BP will have to pay in penalties and to the federal government is unknown as is what the possible criminal fines and restitution might be. Estimates range from the billions to tens of billions of dollars. As of April 22, 2011, BP had made a payment of $1 billion to the federal government for restoration projects.[13] Who would have thought during those early days that this accident would become the largest environmental catastrophe in U.S. history, and result in one of the most detrimental brand meltdowns?

Has BP's brand recovered? That's a complex question. BP's brand status varies among different stakeholders; as in all cases of brand recovery, perceptions are divided based on values and personal relevance of the brand to its various constituencies. In the court of public opinion, the majority does not always rule. Every brand has its own goals and critical targets. What really matters is whether what the market thinks impacts those goals. In the case of BP, it is unlikely that environmentalists will ever get over the April 20 event; they will always think BP is the devil. However, BP's brand success is not dependent on one market alone. BP is a big employer; it is also the customer of many other brands, and it plays an important role in providing energy that millions around the world consume. (In Chapter 7, we'll address how these diverse market segments actually affect a brand's recovery.)

Build Your Starting Narrative

Crafting a compelling story and telling it consistently on all touchpoints is imperative when news breaks about your brand, especially when the media have got you in the daily spotlight. No matter how tragic an event or piece of news surrounding a brand, from the onset, steps can be taken to manage the outcome and produce the most positive public opinions.

Ask yourself: What story and facts best explain the situation in a way that will defend our brand? What do we want the audience to remember? What are the top one or two messages we want to get out?

Let's take a look at a specific example: Montblanc.

Montblanc Brand Turnaround Story

This is the story of a luxury brand that took a big hit a while ago and rebounded to its former glory by responding to a major marketing backfire, by apologizing, and employing a consistent strategy of storytelling, celebrity endorsements, and partnering with one major global charity.

Montblanc is known as one of the premier, global, luxury brands. It is known for craftsmanship and elegance. In the beginning, Montblanc produced writing instruments. Today, the brand spans watches, jewelry, fragrances, and other high-end accessories. Montblanc is one of the few brands that moved up to luxury instead of down to the mass market. After it was acquired by Dunhill in 1977, Montblanc's more affordable product lines were eliminated and the brand went straight luxury.

Montblanc tightly protects its brand. For example, Montblanc will only provide replacement and repair parts if the brand itself does the repairs. This assures quality workmanship and reinforces its reputation. Price is also very controlled, and discounting is rare.

Montblanc has always been a prolific storyteller of a brand, leveraging a sophisticated literary style with legends of accomplished characters and its history with limited-edition signature products. The company introduced its first pen in 1909, and through the years Montblanc has come to represent the top of the line in branded writing instruments. But 100 years after that first pen, the brand stepped on a landmine, and its reputation took a hit.

In October 2009, Montblanc embarked on an effort to increase its profile in India, one of the new powerhouse areas of interest for luxury brands. On Gandhi's birthday, Montblanc released a limited-edition pen called the "Mahatma Gandhi."

Before the launch, Montblanc obtained formal permission from Gandhi's great-grandson in exchange for 90,000 pounds to be donated to a charity. The concept for the pen was to associate the exemplary history of this spiritual icon with the immaculate heritage of Montblanc. Around the world, Gandhi was a hero, and locally he was revered as the father of the Indian nation.

The pen carrying Gandhi's name was made of 18-carat gold and boasted a rhodium-plated nib and a saffron-colored mandarin garnet. It cost 1.1 million Indian rupees (Rs 1.1 million; about US$24,000)—a stark contrast to the humble activist, who practiced frugality, opposed luxury, and would probably not have approved any commercial use of his name, even if the money went to charity. Making the special campaign even more brazenly removed from reality, a limited edition of 241 of the handmade pens, one each to honor the number of miles Gandhi walked during his protest against the salt tax in 1930, were offered.

Montblanc's microsite for the pens announced "[t]he design pays tribute to his life and achievements. The top of the cap and cone are inspired by the spindle which Gandhi used to spin cotton—one of the symbols of Indian independence. The color white is a reference to truth and peace, while the Mandarin garnet represents the orange color that is part of the Indian flag. The nib shows the image of Mahatma Gandhi, walking with a stick. In addition, the limitation of the Mahatma Gandhi Limited Edition 3000 is symbolic for the masses of people who followed him during his fight for independence."[14]

The outrage was instantly apparent. Gandhi's followers denounced the use of his image as inappropriate, and they were appalled when billboard advertisements for the pen, which costs more than most Indians earn in a decade, loomed over some of the country's poorest slums.

Montblanc's regional director for India, Africa, and the Middle East, Oliver Goessler, told a writer for India's *Mint* newspaper, "Whatever brings Gandhi and his ideas back to mind can only be good." [15]And, demonstrating a lack of perspective or knowledge of the local culture and values, Montblanc's chief executive Lutz Bethge told the BBC, "I certainly have to say, I wouldn't have thought that people would have reacted negatively."[16]

On October 2, 2010, the *Washington Post* quoted Amit Modi, secretary of Gandhi's Sabarmati Ashram, "This pen is really funny. Gandhi would say it should be tossed in the trash or, better, sold off to pay for water and power for the poor. Gandhi would have been ashamed."[17]

Initially, to offset the backlash, Montblanc donated $145,666 to the Mahatma Gandhi Foundation. It also committed $1,000 to the foundation for each pen sold. But in February 2010 Montblanc temporarily suspended sales of the pen after the Centre for Consumer Education sued the brand on the basis of a national law prohibiting improper use of names or emblems. In March 2010, the *Financial Times* reported that the pen is still available at international stores—apparently they are still selling the initial inventory—however, they no longer advertise or promote the pen in India.

Montblanc has offered an apology for the product and insists it never intended to insult anyone. To boost its image, Montblanc has partnered with the United Nations Children's Fund (UNICEF) and many high-profile celebrities to promote the humanitarian organization's work. To date, Montblanc has given UNICEF more than $4 milion to support world education and literacy programs.

Although the Gandhi pen was a bump for the brand, Montblanc continues to tell a strong story of elegant style and craftsmanship as a premier writing instrument and accessory brand. The company invests heavily in highbrow cultural and society marketing programs. Its social media outreach extends to a dedicated presence on Facebook, YouTube, and Twitter, where it promotes community and social happenings and touts the names of its troop of celebrity ambassadors.

The Montblanc Turnaround

The brand turned around because Montblanc

- Contained bad PR by apologizing for its lack of cultural sensitivity and the offense that caused
- Contributed almost $150,000 to the Mahatma Gandhi Foundation and more than $4 million to UNICEF to support its world education and literacy programs
- Got back to what it does best, which is design, manufacture, and market fine writing instruments and luxury products, but with an increased respect for cultural differences and perceptions
- Launched other limited-edition signature lines around legendary achievers such as John Lennon, Greta Garbo, and Mark Twain
- Leveraged its profile with celebrity ambassadors and sponsoring charitable and cultural events and high-profile parties
- Created a Donation Pen Series, which honors outstanding personalities from the world of classical music—a portion of all purchases support designated art and culture funds with donations from Montblanc

Montblanc took a multifaceted approach toward containing the story of its brand's bump, choosing from among the many options available to do so. How did it decide which to utilize, though?

Select a Venue to Best Tell Your Story

Today, there are many viable options; a lot of the choice has to do with your brand's audience and the particular circumstances. You can do the following:

- Hold a press conference
- Make written and/or verbal statement(s)
- Use social media and other resources on the web
- Launch an arsenal of paid weapons (spokespeople)
- Address the situation on the air (which is easier if you have your own TV, radio, or podcast show already)

Depending on the event and magnitude of the initial brand shake-up, choose one or more of the aforementioned methods to manage your response for the best outcome as you navigate through to a full recovery. In choosing how and where to respond, be sensitive to the timing of your response(s)—consider the nature of what happened and what else is going on in the market.

Be certain to take control of the Internet. Make sure your website is up-to-date on developments that affect the situation. Sometimes it makes sense to launch a special microsite with its own web address that links to your message or public campaign. Make sure you have a team responding to misinformation that is posted anywhere on the web. Use aggressive search engine optimization and social media such as Facebook, Twitter, and blogs to leverage keywords and links to create a strong funnel to the correct information.

Now let's see how Taco Bell navigated its recovery.

Taco Bell Brand Turnaround Story

Taco Bell is no stranger to brand bumps—from lawsuits concerning labor issues in 2005, to an *E. coli* outbreak in 2006, to rats roaming in some of its New York City restaurants in 2007.

However, the company's recent handling and storytelling of the "where is the rest of the beef?" lawsuit deserves good notice. It does so not only because Taco Bell was fast in addressing the issue but also because its reaction created more news, which helped manage the story and its eventual positive outcome.

Founded in California by a 25-year-old former marine in 1962, Taco Bell was already selling franchises by 1964. By 1967, there were more than 100 Taco Bells. Today the brand is a subsidiary of Yum! Brands, Inc.

In January 2011, an Alabama law firm brought a class action suit against Taco Bell, claiming the beef the brand used was just 35 percent "beef" and did not meet minimum U.S. Department of Agriculture (USDA) requirements.

Taco Bell made a quick and beefy response. Its prompt, confident reaction to the accusation demonstrates why the brand is a little bit like the movie "The Blob"—it just absorbs any force that comes up against it and turns it around to benefit the brand.

Taco Bell had its story down. The brand struck back by taking out a full-page ad in the *USA Today*, the *Wall Street Journal*, and *New York Times*, saying, "Thank you for suing us. Here's the truth about our seasoned beef." The ad went on to claim that Taco Bell's "beef filling" was 88 percent real beef.

Instead of holding a traditional news conference, Taco Bell posted a video statement on YouTube. There, Taco Bell's president, Greg Creed, explained that the claims made against Taco Bell and its seasoned beef were absolutely false, and he assured customers that there were no secrets about the company's products.

Taco Bell also added a microsite that linked from its homepage to address any questions about the beef claims along with a fact sheet about its beef products. They also launched a multimillion-dollar TV campaign to counteract the story. And to further prove its point, it began offering its "Crunchwrap Supreme" for 88 cents, "celebrating" the fact that it contained 88 percent real beef.

Brand loyalists also jumped in to defend the brand and create buzz, which, for a brand like Taco Bell, added even more contemporary popularity. Within days, social media sites, bloggers, and high-profile comedians were telling the story.

Since the scandal the sales have been strong and Yum! Brands stock has increased about 8 percent.

Taco Bell has had the last word. Just months after all the attention and allegations, the class action lawsuit was voluntarily dropped.

Most brands would be thankful if the distraction just went away, but Taco Bell is keeping the message on the front burner. After the announcement, Taco Bell started by running full-page ads in major newspapers ripping the law firm that filed the suit: "Would it kill you to say you're sorry?" read the ad in 50-point-type headline. The ad went on to say:

> The law firm that brought false claims about our product quality and advertising integrity has voluntarily withdrawn their class action suit against Taco Bell. . . .
>
> Sure, they could have just asked us if our recipe uses real beef. Even easier, they could have gone to our Web site where the ingredients in every one of our products are listed for everyone to see. But that's not what they chose to do. . . .
>
> As for the lawyers who brought this suit: You got it wrong, and you're probably feeling pretty bad right about now. But you know what always helps? Saying to everyone, "I'm sorry." C'mon, you can do it![18]

People close to the company indicate these ads are just the beginning, and that the company plans to continue with a major brand-building campaign to turn this negative attention into a reassuring message about the quality of its food.

The Taco Bell brand rebounded because the company

- Took a prompt, confident, and strong stand on its position
- Employed a multimedia approach
- Placed the CEO firmly behind the message
- Clearly stated its story on all customer touchpoints: leveraged paid insertions, PR, content-rich social media, and search engine optimization (SEO)

- Leveraged an 88-cent-beef-product sales strategy as it reinforced the fact that the product was 88 percent beef
- Used light humor style consistent with its brand persona
- Turned up the heat after the suit was dropped and launched a new campaign focusing a hugely positive message about the brand around the idea that some silly lawyers needed to say, "We're sorry"

This last effort, both taking responsibility and making light of the whole affair, serves as a stark contrast to brands that tend to play the blame game.

Never Play the Blame Game

Increasingly, media relations around brands in trouble is being mismanaged by those I call "crybabies." The brands are on the hot seat and, instead of communicating with poise and a story that will help improve their situations, they whine, they rant, they blame, and they shed tears, and they think this will gain them sympathy.

Here are some recent classics in the crybaby genre:

- Tony Hayward, BP CEO, saying, "I'd like my life back," days after the *Deepwater Horizon* oil rig blew up and oil was spilling into the Gulf of Mexico
- BP, Transocean, and Halliburton pointing fingers, playing the blame game at congressional hearings in Washington for days during the worst environmental disaster to date in American history: the 2010 gulf oil spill
- Then South Carolina governor Mark Sanford's rambling, tearful apology in which he announced that he had spent the past five days—during which no one on his staff knew his whereabouts— "crying in Argentina," while visiting a woman with whom he was having an extramarital affair, not hiking the Appalachian Trail (as his staff said he was)

■ Charlie Sheen spewing an eight-and-a-half-minute, grandiloquent, profanity-laced tirade online a day after he was sacked from *Two and a Half Men* for erratic and unprofessional behavior

Clearly, the public's perception of these actions does not help these brands' recovery; instead, it accelerates their fall.

While these examples are of individual and corporate brands, similar responses sometimes come from the spokespeople for product brands when they get beaten up by the market. Instead of focusing on the problem, they bully the media, the Federal Communications Commission (FCC), and sometimes even their customers. (Remember Apple's initial response to "Antennagate"? The iPhone4 lost reception when it was held by the antenna band, and Apple replied to initial complaints by telling customers not to hold the phone in a way that alters the reception.)

It's certainly tempting to unleash your emotions, cast fault on someone else, and not take responsibility or be responsive, but it's usually not in the best interest of your brand.

Apologies may go a long way toward rectifying the situation and refurbishing a brand's image, but actions go further. We live in a forgiving world—simply apologizing in a sincere manner and immediately stopping the offending behavior can earn a brand a place back in glory. Notorious brands in trouble have been known to deliver attention-getting, sappy sob stories and soon return to their bad brand ways; for example:

■ Televangelist Jimmy Swaggart made a living preaching about right and wrong. In 1988, he was found soliciting sex from a prostitute[19]— not a good thing for a religious leader's image! During his now infamous "I Have Sinned" apology, Swaggart broke down in front of his congregation and the world. His emotions seemed real and believable—that is until he was caught in 1991 with another prostitute.[20]

■ Lindsay Lohan was a promising actress and brand. Her career was on a fast track; she'd starred in many blockbuster films, but then had a series of run-ins with the law, both because of and complicated by substance abuse issues. As a result, for the last couple of years, her brand has spun out of control. She's apologized to the world a few times and to a judge several times, and her mom has apologized for her, but, unfortunately, each time she seems to return to her old ways.

Acknowledge the Situation

The events that shake up brands seem to get crazier and crazier every year. Even so, handled well, they can become a small blip on the pop culture memory screen. Mismanaged, they can scar a good brand for a long time.

JetBlue, the low-cost airline, was flying high with brand loyalty and customer love until its first rough brand experience in 2007. After an epic breakdown in the airline's inadequate computer and communications system during an ice storm that affected the eastern United States left JetBlue passengers stranded across the country or sitting on tarmacs, the airline found itself at the center of nationwide media frenzy. According to the *New York Times*, other airlines had canceled "more flights earlier, sending passengers home and resuming their schedules within a day or two. But JetBlue thought the weather would break and it would be able to fly, keeping its revenue flowing and its customers happy."[21] This bad decision combined with a reservations system inadequate to handle customer calls and the airline's inability to locate many of its pilots and flight attendants and direct them to their next flights resulted in the cancelllaton of flights in and out of JFK airport. In the end, JetBlue cancelled approximately 1,000 flights over the next five days.[22]

JetBlue's founder and chief executive officer at the time, David Neeleman, responded promptly; he explained what went wrong, apologized, took responsibility, and compensated the passengers who bore the awful nightmare. Shortly after the incident, the airline introduced a passenger's bill of rights and made needed operational and policy changes, which were significant. Most would agree that JetBlue's brand was flying high again and had regained its favorable relationship with the market.

Then, in 2010, a stressed-out flight attendant, acting out his frustrations, cursed out passengers and exited the plane, beer in his hand, via an emergency slide.[23] The story was highly bizarre, of course, and the media jumped on it like flies on honey. JetBlue was back in the spotlight. This time, JetBlue took a low-key approach, which some media analysts felt was a PR time bomb ticking. Ultimately, time has shown that JetBlue made the smart move by facing the situation two days later, after they gathered all the facts.

When they did respond, they limited the distribution of their official response to their blog, ensuring social media buzz but, at the same time, avoiding making something big out of something just plain weird. JetBlue's light-hearted, self-deprecating approach to the event took the edge off the situation. By acknowledging the weirdness of the incident and avoiding the serious side, they directed social media conversation away from any safety topics that might have turned critical of the airline.

Speak Your Truth

The truth will set you free and can give your brand a boost too. Lying to the public has no upside unless you enjoy getting in trouble. With media venues paying crazy money for the smoking gun and the human desire to have 15 minutes of fame, no one can bet their secrets will be safe from the public for long. Just ask Arnold Schwarzenegger.

In 2009, David Letterman was thrown a hot potato of his own baking—and his honesty about the issue ended up saving his brand.

A late-night TV icon, David Letterman has seen his brand go from the new and quirky kid on the block to cantankerous old-timer. Since 1982, Letterman has been a staple of the late-night TV circuit and has received 67 Emmy nominations. Letterman was by no means seen as a saint before the scandal hit. His public feuding with Jay Leno over who would get the *Tonight Show* job after Johnny Carson retired was fodder for a movie and many industry stories.

On October 1, 2009, Letterman's brand would take its biggest hit. Unlike many brands in turmoil, Letterman had his own TV show on which to take responsibility and try to make amends for his actions.

"I'm glad you folks are here tonight, and I'm glad you're in such a pleasant mood. I have a little story that I would like to tell you and the home viewers as well. Do you feel like a story?" That is what Letterman said to audience applause at the beginning of his nightly monologue. Nobody knew what would come next. "This started three weeks ago . . . yesterday . . ."[24]

Letterman then described an affair he had had with an employee and the story of a man who tried to blackmail him about it. At one point he said, plainly, "I have had sex with women who work for me on this show."[25]

The audience didn't know how to react. Neither did the media. The headlines the morning after reported: "David Letterman Blackmail Shocker: Host Confesses to Affairs after Extortion Attempt."[26] Ironically, the affair brought Letterman some of his best ratings in years. The day he apologized to his wife, there was a 36 percent increase over the previous week.

As shocking as it was at the time, Letterman's direct address to his audience saved his brand. Had Letterman denied the charges or had the scandal come out in the tabloids or on the news, his image would have suffered much more. That he both broke and addressed the story gave him control and his critics nowhere to go.

Letterman's character before the scandal perfectly positioned him for a speedy recovery. The TV host is well known for personalizing his humor. For example, he often includes his mother in skits, and he brought his entire medical team onstage when he returned to the show after quintuple bypass surgery. He later lobbied Indiana, his home state, to rename a freeway "The David Letterman Bypass." Letterman's humor shines through even in philanthropy. His charity, which between 2001 and 2009 donated about $7.7 million to various organizations, is named "American Foundation for Courtesy and Grooming."

But what made the message so successful was the fact that Letterman did not crack a single joke about the affair or the blackmail. As the *Los Angeles Times* noted on October 3, "David Letterman affair is no joke."[27] The incident went on to stir debates about sex in the workplace and taking advantage of one's position. Letterman seemed to recognize this early on; by not joking about it in his apology, he proved that he was serious about it. If he had made light of the matter, it would have opened him up to character assassination. And it would have done so not only on the grounds that he was a "male chauvinist pig," who took advantage of a younger employee, but also that he was a sexist boss out of touch with reality.

In November 2010, Letterman finally posted better ratings than Jay Leno, who had returned to the *Tonight Show* after the network's disastrous decision to replace Leno with Conan O'Brien. On February 10, 2011, the *Late Show with David Letterman* reported its highest ratings of the season, and the show continues to battle it out with the *Tonight Show*. Letterman appears untouched by the scandal.

It's interesting to examine brands under fire that became chronic crybabies; they misused apologies and committed repeated offenses in basic communications on public stages. What's most strange is that many of these brands have had the resources and advisors to get it right, but it didn't work out that way. Effective communication is critical to brand turnarounds. The smallest detail can end up being a pivotal Game Changer with the media and public perception.

Select the Most Effective Voice for the Brand

When the brand is an individual, such as David Lettermen, there is only one possible spokesperson, unless the person can no longer speak. However, when the brand is a company, nonprofit, or another entity, the spokesperson designated can be crucial to the perception he or she generates as the voice of the brand.

For this reason, it is essential to identify the primary spokesperson, let the person get comfortable with the statement, and drill the person on questions and answers (Q&A). Communicating in the immediate aftermath of a crisis or brand-shaking event is not easy. Spokespersons often have to speak without the benefit of all of the information and facts, and it's an emotional time. Spokespersons don't have to be perfect to succeed. They are judged for their confidence, competence, and compassion during a difficult time. These people must never be defensive. It's always okay to show compassion and remorse. Honesty is what people want and expect.

BP's Tony Hayward was not the best choice as spokesperson for a disaster that primarily impacted the Gulf of Mexico and the United States. In addition to Hayward's continuous misstatements and the PR photo blunder showing him at sea on his sailboat during the crisis, his British accent, and arrogant-sounding tone widened the perception of a disconnect with the public.

In July 2010, a warmer, American-accented, Robert "Bob" Dudley replaced Hayward as CEO and top disaster spokesperson. Dudley, born in New York City and raised in Mississippi, was seen as a more compassionate and operationally hands-on personality than Hayward, and he quickly soothed some public tension with the brand.

The primary media spokesperson for a brand shake-up should be someone with a full grasp of the formula for communication success—that is, someone who has the knowledge and expertise to talk about the event and the brand and can compassionately address the emotional concerns of the public.

Leverage the Best Impression

The old adage "put your best foot forward" definitely applies to restoring to its glory days a brand gone bad. The difference between embracing this concept and ignoring it can be the difference between a public who forgives you and gives you time to get things right and one who kicks your brand and leaves it bleeding at the curb.

According to Albert Mehrabian, professor emeritus of psychology at the University of California, Los Angeles (UCLA), the impression you make is based on three factors:

1. *55 percent is physical.* This is what you look like—your posture, body language, and movement—eye contact (or lack thereof), expressions, clothing, and the environment—background and props.
2. *38 percent comes from the tone of voice.* This is how you sound—your volume, your vocal inflection, the speed at which you speak, when and where you pause, and your accents.
3. *7 percent is derived from the words spoken.* This is what you say, your choice of words, and your content. [28]

Here are some examples:

Words to use	Words to avoid
I believe . . .	I think . . .
I am confident . . .	I feel . . .
A challenge . . .	A problem . . .
I personally . . .	In my opinion . . .
I don't know . . .	Off the record . . .
We researched that . . .	We considered that . . .

Keep Your Message Positive

Remember, it's important to never repeat negatives. This common error can come back to haunt brands for years to come, if the media pick it up and wallpaper it everywhere.

So often individuals and spokespersons for brands will, under pressure, repeat a negative instead of citing a positive in media interviews. "This is a kiss of death," says Merrie Spaeth, a crisis management strategist who served under president Ronald Reagan as Director of Media Relations at the White House. Her PR company, Spaeth Communications, Inc., even produces an annual Bimbo Award, which recognizes the dumbest repeated negative public comments. The award is named after a young woman who was caught with a high-profile, married man, who said, "I am not a *bimbo*," which of course caused everyone to think she was. The award is a reminder that repeating negatives only reinforces the negative message and misses the opportunity to convey the right message.

Here are a few great examples from Spaeth's collection of nominations:

- "*It may be stupid, it may be negligent, but it's not corrupt,*"[29] said long-time representative Charles Rangel, as he tried to explain one of his 13 ethics violations, sending hundreds of solicitations on congressional stationary for contributions to a City University of New York (CUNY) fund for a building to be named in his honor.[30]
- "*I do not believe I wrecked his home,*" said Rielle Hunter, Senator John Edwards's mistress and mother of his daughter. She told Oprah Winfrey that posing for *GQ* in panties and a man's shirt was a "mistake," but she said she has no regrets.[31]
- "*We are not covering up anything and we are not running away from anything,*" said Toyota Motor Corp. president Akio Toyoda when U.S. safety regulators began to investigate the timeliness of the 8.5-million-car recall that resulted from reports of sudden acceleration.[32]

Know When to Fold

Timing in brands is everything. Sometimes it is best to pull out, resign, and remove your brand's presence from the public radar screen. In most cases, this should happen after owning up to the situation as New York's governor Eliot Spitzer did. Use this time to regroup, work on your recovery, or just let time cool some of the heat. You can always return.

The Spitzer Brand Turnaround Story: Stay Tuned

Eliot Spitzer was born into a New York real estate fortune. He made a name for himself as a young Harvard-grad prosecutor going after the organized crime. In 1998, he was elected New York State attorney general. He immediately made white-collar crime his obsession. Going after price fixing and investment scandals, he went after AIG in the early 2000s, when AIG was still a respected financial institution. He even sued the former chairman of the New York Stock Exchange (NYSE). In June 2004, the BBC asked, "Is no target too big for Eliot Spitzer, the Attorney General of the State of New York?"[33] as the then-prosecutor turned his sights on GlaxoSmithKline. A hero prosecutor seen as one of the few truly on the side of the people and against injustice, Spitzer was elected governor with a historically high margin of victory.

On March 12, 2008, Eliot Spitzer resigned as governor of New York completing one of the most spectacular rises and falls of a politician in recent memory. After just over a year in office, the governor had been caught patronizing a high-end prostitution service. He was "Client 9." Immediately after that, a *New York Times* op-ed piece wrote, "Gov. Eliot Spitzer did exactly the right thing on Wednesday, announcing his resignation after 14 months in office."[34]

Spitzer's immediate resignation may be what saved his brand and his career. Had he stayed in office and fought possible criminal charges, the whole sordid business would have come to overshadow his administration and taint every achievement he had.

In the years since, Spitzer has even demonstrated that he is able to laugh at himself when it comes to the prostitution scandal, something that bodes well for his brand's recovery. In June 2010, Spitzer made a quiet return to public life as the cohost of the CNN show *Parker Spitzer*, which was later retooled with Spitzer as the main host and renamed *In the Arena*. In July 2011, CNN canceled the show. Spitzer's case is largely mirrored in the TV drama *The Good Wife*, in the character played by Chris Noth, something that could help humanize him in the public's eye. Spitzer has dismissed rumors that he would again run for office, even though his protestations have not stopped the rumors. It's also been rumored that he's interested in running for mayor of New York City. One of the few true crusaders against Wall Street avarice before the 2008 meltdown, it may be as an advocate for the individual against the greed of Wall Street and the excesses of big corporations where Spitzer best has a chance to refashion his image and make a comeback. He just needs to bide his time until his name is no longer preceded by the word *disgraced*.

In light of the circumstances, Eliot Spitzer handled his initial news conference as well as anybody could:

- He took prompt action and resigned.
- He maintained his composure and calm during the scandal.
- He admitted his bad judgment and took responsibility for his behavior.
- He apologized publicly.
- He laid low and out of the spotlight for almost two years.
- He reentered the public arena with a major news network, in a professional new role.

Twenty-five Ways to "Meet the Press"

If you or your leadership team have not been professionally media trained or you find yourself making communications missteps, the following tips for managing an interview or news event will help you navigate the toughest news conference and interviews and begin the process from brand shake-up to brand glory.

1. *Be prepared.* Always write down your talking points and know what you want to cover in advance. Do a dry run with an associate.

2. *Maintain control.* Media interviews and news conferences are not passive situations.

3. *Bridge out of uncomfortable topics.* Manage attacks by changing the subject.

4. *Know as much as you can before the interview begins.* If it's a one-on-one interview, ask the reporter, in advance of the interview, what she or he is looking for.

5. *Be confident and helpful.* Share resources, data, and industry connections that help get your story out.

6. *State the things that are most important to you first.* Just as in a press release, the most important facts and message come first. Editors and producers are often on tight deadlines, and the information at the end may get cut in editing.

7. *Be concise.* Use simple words. Phrases that pay and bumper-sticker-style comments often get picked up as the sound bite or headline. These phrases should be thought through before a major media event and repeated during interviews.

8. *Avoid technical terms or acronyms.* Use words your audience understands; otherwise your message may get diluted or, worse, completely missed.

9. *Never repeat negatives.* The media and your audience will remember these, and these negatives often push your real message from your listeners' minds. Negatives are often pounced on by the media; they make great sound bites and headlines.

10. *Emphasize the positives.* These comments will just further the message you want to get out.

11. *Use the interview as you would a commercial—but don't go overboard.* Remember, interviews are platforms to get your message across.

12. *Sound authoritative, knowledgeable, and sincere.* Speak slowly and confidently; cite simple evidence that demonstrates you are an expert.

13. *Use examples and anecdotes.* Often reporters and the audience don't understand the details of your business; provide simple stories that make your message clear.

14. *Demonstrate personal commitment.* But do *not* state personal opinions. In commercial, brand-related media interviews, the spokesperson expresses the company's voice, not the spokesperson's opinions.

15. *Don't go "off the record"*—ever. As soon as you make that statement, the reporter starts reporting.

16. *Say, "I don't know. I'll find out for you."* Don't bluff when you don't know. Make sure to follow up on your promises.

17. *Thank a reporter for good coverage.* Thank-you notes go a long way.

18. *Use blind sources.* You can always allude to a reliable source without naming the individual—but only when you know you have the actual data to support the message. Citing generic industry experts, associations, or researchers may be more persuasive than blind sourcing.

19. *Don't speculate.* Doing so often just opens new cans of worms when you don't have the facts.

20. *Put the public's best interest first.* Remember that the media serve the public. Always try to address the public's concerns and focus on their best interests.

21. *Never lose your temper.* An outburst of temper will be the piece that ends up on the news, and it will not convey the image of a composed and confident leader or brand voice.

22. *Always tell the truth.* Lies or misleading information just further more questions and enhance negative opinions about the brand.

23. *Remember that good media relationships are worth their price in gold.* Take good care of them.

24. *Dress the part.* Your wardrobe can add to your credibility and enhance your believability.

25. *Make sure that even small details are on brand and on story.* Missteps can be blown up and become a big faux pas.

Turnaround Takeaways

Instead of crying, take responsibility and communicate on brand:

- Take an inventory of the situation, before you speak.
- Build your starting narrative.
- Decide what venue is best to tell your story.
- Take a stand.
- Apologize, when appropriate.
- Acknowledge the problem.
- Speak your truth.
- Select the most effective voice for your brand.
- Leverage the best impression.
- Keep the message positive.
- Manage the media, don't let the media manage you.

Chapter 5

Game Changer 2: Never Give Up

When a brand goes down, turnaround is about finding stamina, inner strength, and the will to come back. It's about reframing the story of failure to one of redemption and rebound.

Find Conviction, Beyond Conviction

As I look at brands that went bad and returned to glory, most were in very scary, dark places. They experienced mountains of rejection; others had extreme debt or were about to run out of money; some brand leaders or individual brands were sentenced to prison time and a lifetime criminal record; some felt abandoned by their stakeholders; all questioned their self-confidence and battled inner demons as well as aggressive public enemies—they were on the edge facing an uncertain future.

Too often, some in the media see these brand blow-ups as an opportunity to sell more papers or draw more viewers. The bigger the brand name, the more they trumpet the story. They'll slice and dice the story from every possible angle—sometimes long after the story is told and the brand is down. There is a tendency on the media's part to search for several smoking guns; thus, a story about an explosion at a plant, for example, might start with the explosion, but then the media targets the CEO's past, the vendor's past, other plants, and so on.

In the public's eyes, the brand has failed. It is marked as a loser, an outcast, and remains the subject of brand-slamming conversations that just keep the story alive until something more sensational makes the news. For comedians, of course, this provides fresh material for months.

Such unfortunate brands soon come to a fork in the road. It's often when leaders and individuals experience their lowest mental and emotional point. One direction leads to terminal defeat. For some, this is the easiest route. Sadly, some literally end their lives; others just fold the cards, close down, and let their failures become their legacy.

The other path is far more difficult and risky. It means finding humility, shaking off the past, doing a lot of work, reinventing themselves, and managing the emotional toll of external and internal critical voices. After all that is done, there are still no guarantees of success.

In the course of this chapter, we will examine individual brands that have lived through major setbacks. Some are famous, like Martha Stewart, the Domestic Diva; Michael Vick, a National Football League (NFL) athlete; and Arianna Huffington, a media mogul. But the same kinds of things often happen to the less famous people—executives under investigation, politicians who have hung around with the wrong crowd, media figures, community leaders caught in a domestic or other personal scandal, and even entrepreneurs and regular folks who suffer major rejection and setbacks and ultimately become a brand.

The brand turnaround stories we'll be looking at involve very serious actions with costly consequences. These brands struggled through the legal system and months of nonstop media ridicule. They battled addictions and public rejection. They lost millions, important relationships, and business partners. The good news is all of these brands had undeniable passion for their craft or talent and resilient values that transformed them back to a place of glory.

From the Big Board to the Big House

Brushes with the law are not uncommon. In fact, according to *One in 100: Behind Bars in America 2008* conducted by the Pew Charitable Trusts, 1 in 100 Americans is currently behind bars, and a greater percentage have done time at some point in their lives. The report also states that serving time reduces an individual's annual income by 40 percent.

Any legal controversy or even allegations of misbehavior or association with others in trouble can dent up a brand quickly. Business partners can bail out, endorsements may vanish, and, in some cases, no one wants to touch you with a 10-foot pole. While some brands have deserved this punishment, others have been in the wrong place at the wrong time but nevertheless have received the same opprobrium as those convicted of the crime.

New Beginnings: One Door Shuts, Another One Opens

We've all heard innumerable motivational theories that tell us that the bad stuff is really the good stuff dressed up in a Halloween costume—so long as it does not kill you. Others say it's a life and brand test that will make you a lot smarter. Most miss (or ignore) the gritty details: the extreme pain, doubt, and emotional wear and tear these dramas can have on one's soul and ultimately one's brand.

Throughout this lesson, we will look at individuals, who, while serving their time in jail, rehab, or left out in the wilderness, found deeper conviction and were resilient enough to keep their dreams alive and put their brands back on track. They survived their punishment, paid their dues, overcame their addictions, and battled back. They made changes and refreshed their image; as a result, their brands have returned to their former glory.

The Impact of Failure

Before we look at brands that have successfully turned themselves around after a big setback, major humiliation, public embarrassment, or legal scandal let's look at the definition of failure and its impact on the individual and their brand. In the book *When Smart People Fail* by Carole Hyatt and Linda Gottlieb, the authors explain failure as a judgment about a particular event. *Failure* is a word used to denote a phase; it is not a condemnation of one's character. It is not a permanent condition, nor in most cases is it a fatal flaw or a contagious social disease. Failures do not mold people or their brands; how they cope and manage these events does.

Hyatt and Gottlieb go on to describe the anatomy of failure as emotional stages that often include shock, fear, anger, blame, shame, and despair. When a person experiences a monumental brand-shattering event it can be debilitating not only to the individual's self-esteem but ultimately to his or her brand.

No matter what the situation, the way that these stages are handled has a direct impact on the individual's future brand. Resilience and the will to overcome the past and move forward are by-products of working through the complete emotional cycle that results from a high-profile failure.

Of all brand turnarounds, individual brands are usually the toughest. Psychiatrists call these events "narcissistic losses" because they can strip away every ounce of a person's self-worth. No matter how often you tell yourself, "It's not personal," for individual brands seeking to recover from a bad event, it feels *very* personal. The keys to success are to reframe or rewrite the story, rediscover what earned you brand fame and success in the first place, and not to repeat the actions that created the nightmare. To do this, you need a tough-as-steel mindset that allows you to block out and not believe what the negative critics keep repeating.

Here's an individual brand that had critics repeating a lot of negatives: Michael Vick.

Michael Vick Brand Turnaround Story

In 1999, Michael Vick was a Heisman Trophy candidate at the Virginia Technical Institute and State University (Virginia Tech), and, in 2001, he was the first overall draft pick of the Atlanta Falcons. For six years, Vick was a superstar, taking the Falcons to the playoffs twice. However, while he was seen as a team leader and excellent athlete, there were questions about his sportsmanship and temperament. Vick also had numerous run-ins with fans. In 2004, he threw a water bottle at angry fans and contended that they first threw it at him. In 2005, he was very publicly sued by a woman, who claimed he had given her herpes. The allegation noted that Vick used the name "Ron Mexico" to get her the medication she needed. While this may have harmed his reputation among some fans, others bought customized Vick number 7 Falcons jerseys with the surname "Mexico" printed on the back. (The NFL banned the sale of the jerseys on its website.) In 2008, Vick gave fans the middle finger for heckling him after a loss.

In early 2007, sports tabloids were abuzz about a water bottle Vick discarded at the airport that purportedly contained a secret compartment filled with marijuana. This was the beginning of many rumors within the sports community about the shadiness of Vick's life.

It was still a surprise later that year, however, when Vick was fingered as the leader of a heinous dog-fighting club. In August 2007, Vick pleaded guilty to the charges, and he was sentenced to 21 months in federal prison. Vick, the league's highest paid player, lost his $135 million NFL contract; his endorsements fled; he was millions of dollars in debt; he had no job; and his future was grim.

For the next several years, Vick's brand was mud. Animal rights groups, late-night talk show hosts, and people on the street all used Vick's name as a punch line to a very sad joke.

One month after being incarcerated, Michael started evaluating his life and his choices, and he started making a plan to change himself. He spent days crying and reflecting on the terrible acts he had committed and the hurtful things people were saying about him—that he was lazy, selfish, and deserved everything he got. He knew it was all true. He could not change the past, only the future. He knew his destiny was up to him.[1]

While Vick has described his prison time as the worst days of his life, he has also said he would not change anything about them. He believes that the bad choices and his incarceration will ultimately help many others.

When he was in jail he never lost hope. He claims that talking with God, remaining optimistic, and visualizing what his new life out of prison would look like helped him to get through it. He also said that on his lowest, darkest days, he experienced the greatest motivation.

Once released, Vick filed for bankruptcy. He focused his energy on his family first and getting mentally transitioned back into society. Football was put on the back burner; he took a temporary job at a construction company, while continuing to thoughtfully plan his full return as an athlete and brand.

In 2009, he rejoined the NFL as a Philadelphia Eagle. At the time, the team was criticized for the signing deal. Protestors appeared outside the Eagle's Lincoln Field with signs expressing their anti-Vick sentiment.

Vick stayed mum, played his few opportunities, and worked hard. Through it all, he remained pious, demonstrating that he had genuinely changed. But his play would cement this notion. In 2010, Vick moved into the starting quarterback position and began a string of great games. A September 2010 ABC headline reads, "Michael Vick's Rehabilitation Now Almost Complete." The turning point was November 15, 2010, when Vick passed for 300 yards and ran for 50, then passed for three touchdowns and ran for two—the first NFL player in history to do so. Soon, Vick's name was being thrown around for Most Valuable Player (MVP). The Eagles made the playoffs.

In 2011, Vick was named Associated Press Comeback Player of the Year. After the 2010–2011 season ended, the Eagles gave Vick a vote of confidence and made him its "franchise quarterback." The franchise tag allows an NFL team to select one player and prevent him from becoming a free agent once his contract expires. The tag means Vick's one-year contract will now be worth $16.4 million.

In December 2010, President Barack Obama congratulated the Eagles owner for giving Vick an opportunity for redemption. An important symbol of just how much Vick's image was rehabilitated is reflected in a statement to the *Washington Post* from Henry E. Hudson, the U.S. District Court Judge who sentenced Vick in 2007: "He's an example of how the system can work."[2]

Public accolades have continued to mount for Vick. NFL Commissioner Roger Goodell told the *New York Daily News* in a November 18, 2010, article that he was proud of Vick and sees his off the field work as inspiring to others: "My main concerns were off the field. He's done terrific off the field. . . . He's turning himself in the right direction. For that, I'm very proud of him." In a November 2010 *Meet the Press* appearance, Philadelphia mayor Michael Nutter expressed his admiration at the redemption of Vick and the positive impact his presence on and off the field has had on the city of Philadelphia. What Vick most appreciates is his acceptance by the fans. In 2011, the fans voted him into the NFL Pro Bowl.

Michael Vick will never have every fan on his side. No brand will, not even those who don't experience such a public brand meltdown as Vick's. He seems to have done an admirable job, though, of rebuilding his image and turning a bad situation into one that can have a positive impact on many.

How Vick Did It. After his second season with the Philadelphia Eagles, Vick hired French, West, Vaughan (FWV), a public relations, communications, and advertising firm, to help him build a stronger relationship with the Philadelphia community and reestablish his commitment to touching the lives of young people.

Christopher Shigas, vice president with FWV, said his firm and Vick first connected shortly after Vick signed with Philadelphia. The engagement became formal in 2011 when Vick wanted to increase his community service and outreach both locally and nationally. Although there were reports that Vick was required to do community outreach as part of his probation, Shigas said these stories were not true. Vick was investing his time and money because he was sincerely committed to having a positive impact on others and helping community groups. Vick does two to three major events every month, often driving five to six hours each way to avoid the airport drama.

The Vick brand turned around because he did these things:

- *He put first things first.* After his release from prison, Vick's priorities were focusing on family and building a support network around him. Along with his family and close friends, he credits for his success his mentor relationship with Tony Dungy, a former player and coach, who became Vick's full-time mentor beginning while Vick was still in prison.
- *He looked forward and wasn't bitter.* Vick has said that as terrible as his past was, he has no regrets. He believes that everything happens for a reason and it's up to him to turn his bad choices into meaningful messages for kids.
- *He listened to what mattered.* Vick knows there are some who will never forgive him. He can't control that. He focuses on the positive feedback and the evidence of his fan base, which continues to grow.
- *He stayed optimistic and did not lose his faith.* Vick believes attitude and mental toughness on and off the field can change outcomes.

This brand turnaround success is also due to some additional factors, including Vick's

- *Transparency and interview style.* Since Vick's release from prison, he has conducted local and national media interviews. His demeanor is soft-spoken, poised, and authentic. He answers questions and does not sound like a scripted robot. In 2010, Vick participated in a

10-part documentary for BET (Black Entertainment Television) that chronicled his rise, fall, and return.

■ *Community service.* His community work is extensive and includes both publicized and private events with the Humane Society of the United States and with many inner-city and educational programs in Philadelphia and around the United States.

■ *Outreach efforts.* Vick has more than a million fans on Facebook and more than half a million on Twitter. In addition to his social fan outreach team, Michael is a hands-on social media guy who often responds to fans and even wishes them happy birthday on Twitter. His community service and his football highlights are found on YouTube.

■ *Associations.* With whom and what a brand associates itself shows up in its image. Vick has been thoughtful and aware of the company he keeps to the things he endorses from his mentor Tony Dungy. Vick is surrounding himself with a positive circle of partners.

Now let's take a look at another individual brand that got run through the ringer: Martha Stewart.

Martha Stewart Brand Turnaround Story

Born in New Jersey in 1941, Martha Stewart is one of the ultimate "dream big" inspirations. After giving up a career as a stockbroker, Stewart started a catering business in Connecticut that would eventually become Martha Stewart Inc. In the late 1980s and early 1990s, Stewart published books about cooking, weddings, crafts, and entertaining and began a slow climb to stardom. In 1997, she formed Martha Stewart Living Omnimedia, Inc., which went public on October 19, 1999 at $18 per share; at its closing that day it was $38 a share.

Attitudes toward her and her brand, however, have been mixed. Stewart's brand was not just built on baking cookies, she stood for a lifestyle— one that many people in America didn't welcome for a variety of reasons, ranging from ideas about class to just plain jealousy.

Stewart strived for perfection, and perfection is distrusted by many. Seeing Stewart weakened by insider trading allegations, the media sprang on her because the only thing America likes better than a "Feel-Good American Dream" story is a "Destruction of the American Dream" story.

In July 2002, a *Newsweek* cover featured Stewart with the title "Martha's Mess ... An Insider Trading Scandal Tarnishes the Queen of Perfection."[3] Despite being a multimillionaire, Stewart was brought down by just $45,673. That is what her loss would have been had she not sold stock in what seemed later to be insider trading. (Although indicted on this charge, she was not convicted of it.)

On June 4, 2003, Martha Stewart was convicted of nine counts of obstruction of justice and securities fraud. She resigned as CEO and chairwoman of the brand, and on October 8, 2004, she reported to prison. Martha Stewart jokes abounded.

On March 4, 2005, Stewart "marched forth" from prison. Immediately, she was in the news for her "prison poncho." Still, the time in prison seems to have helped rehabilitate her image. With Martha Stewart brought low and humbled, people were ready to love her again. CBS even did a "how to knit Martha's prison poncho" segment. Martha was again on the cover of *Newsweek*. Only this time the headline was "Martha's Last Laugh: After Prison, She's Thinner, Wealthier & Ready for Prime Time."[4] Unfortunately, the cover created a scandal of its own when it was revealed that *Newsweek* had put Stewart's head on the body of a model—there's no indication that Stewart had anything to do with the cover.

Stewart leaped back into her brand. She rejoined her magazine and show. She expanded her licensing with national retailers. But she wisely did not pretend the incident never happened. After prison, Stewart's brand was aided with a burst of self-awareness and self-deprecating humor. After the incident, Stewart seemed to take herself much less seriously; she was willing to poke fun at herself, a quality that disarmed critics before they could even take aim. Stewart even became a regular on Conan O'Brien's show and he on hers. She allowed O'Brien to make fun of her brand; in one segment, she even had an on-air beer with him.

Basically, she re-engineered her personality without changing the consumer brand. In August 2005, Stewart debuted a new daytime show *The Martha Stewart Show*, and the marketing material promised a "sense of humor." The show became an instant success. Martha was back.

How Stewart Did It. Unlike the old Stewart brand, Martha today keeps her brand fresh by doing the unexpected. In 2006 she did a cameo on the TV show *Ugly Betty*. In 2008, a small TV network, Fine Living, developed a show mocking Stewart, called *Whatever Martha!* Not only did Stewart embrace the show, she was in on it with her daughter. Speaking about fans who might be upset by the show, she told the *New York Times*, "If they do [get upset], then they just shouldn't watch it."[5]

In 2008, the company launched a wine, Martha Stewart Vintage, and a deal with Wal-Mart to sell Martha Stewart–branded items. In 2010, she left NBC and partnered with the Hallmark Channel and ended her longtime relationship with Kmart, citing quality issues and not being able to work out a new contract that worked for both parties. Stewart merchandise can now be found in Macy's, Home Depot, and PetSmart.

Martha Stewart's brand continues to grow and change. Today Martha Stewart's Living Omnimedia is involved in three business sectors: publishing, merchandising, and broadcasting. While some financial analysts question aspects of the company's future such as her role, whether it may go private, and the overall health of publishing, there is no question that her brand, in the mind of consumers, has returned to glory. As of this writing, reports in the *Wall Street Journal* indicate that the company has retained the investment banking firm Blackstone to explore new partners, investors, and other opportunities concerning the company's future.

The Stewart brand turned around because Stewart did these things:

- *She immediately started the process of recovery.* To this day, Stewart's position has been that she did nothing wrong. Nevertheless, when she was found guilty, instead of appealing, she asked the judge if she could start serving her sentence right away. Stewart decided to surrender for prison as soon as possible, citing the need "to put this nightmare behind me, both personally and professionally." She added, "I must reclaim my good life." Stewart wanted to get past the situation and get back to work.[6]

- *She resigned as CEO and turned over the running of the company to a competent team.* After being indicted, Stewart voluntarily stepped down as CEO and chairperson of Martha Stewart Living Omnimedia, but she stayed on as chief creative officer. While she was in prison, she could not conduct business, but her team continued to secure new deals and move the company forward.

- *She turned lemons into lemon soufflé.* Martha Stewart did not throw in the dish towel at any point. She hung in there. Yes, her brand and company took a big beating during the debacle (the episode cost millions of dollars in legal fees and related business losses) and was major distraction, but Martha made the best of a bad year. Not only did her stint in jail awaken a whole new fan base, it also aroused new interests and perspectives in her. Additionally, it brought a new dimension to the conversation, and the media coverage, even when it was critical of Stewart, continued to add intrigue to her story.

- *She kept experimenting and learning.* Even though the Martha Stewart *brand* has been tagged with the image of "absolute perfection," the Martha Steward *person* always has had a strong entrepreneurial tendency to launch and learn. She's never been afraid to try new ideas, partnerships, and projects. Some have worked; other expensive experiments have ended up in the garbage. The 2005 reality series *The Apprentice: Martha Stewart* was short lived. In 2006, the company started *Blueprint*, a glossy magazine aimed at young women. The expensive venture failed within a year. While other significant partnerships, such as with Kmart and

1-800-Flowers, fell off the vine, brand extensions and projects such as her segmented weddings, wellness and, now, pet products have been an important part of Stewart's brand recovery.

- *She embraced new media.* Martha's brand has always been a multiplatform player, with a strong presence on radio, TV, and print; it has also been a pioneer of social media throughout her ups and downs. Her blogs alone (she has 11 niche blogs) provide a multitude of ways for her fan base to be engaged and build a user relationship.
- *She changed her style.* Before Martha Stewart's brand got shaken, her brand projected a tight, formal tone in much of her communication. The events around her conviction and prison time opened up her style, and they added not only a degree of self-deprecation and humility but also a lighter, more humorous side. This is reflected in all her media, but especially in social dialogue channels.

Although she never went to jail, Arianna Huffington also faced a lot of challenges with her brand and never gave up. Let's take a look at her story.

The Arianna Huffington Brand Turnaround Story

Michael Vick and Martha Stewart fell from brand glory as a result of bad choices or legal problems. In both cases, resilience and drive were instrumental in their journeys back. In Arianna Huffington's case, there was no conviction or addiction, the enemy of her brand might be called loss, or rejection. Arianna Huffington has had her share of rejection, but through resiliency and drive she has successfully turned a brand from down and out into a $315 million payday.

Huffington was born in Athens, Greece. Her parents, Elli and Konstantinos Stassinopoulos, divorced when she was 11. Adrianna credits her resiliency and journalist's pluck to her girlhood in Athens and the inspiration she received from both of her parents (her father was a journalist).

From there, Huffington moved to England and attended Girton College, Cambridge, where she earned her degree in economics. At Cambridge, she was the president of the Cambridge Union Society, the university's debate club. After being embarrassed in a televised debate with the late author and commentator William F. Buckley Jr., Huffington says, "What I learned was that no one else pays as much attention to humiliations and defeats as we do. I may have thought my career was over, but others were not as focused on one devastating evening."[7] Ultimately she became the president of the Cambridge Union debate team, and, as a result, she became a frequent guest on several British television shows.

At 23, she published her first book, *The Female Woman*, about the changing roles of women, which was translated into 11 languages. Since then she has written 12 more on varying subjects, from self-help and the power of Greek mythology to political satire and biographies. Despite the success of her first book, when she tried to find a publisher for her next one, she received 36 rejections. Running out of funds, Huffington approached a bank for a loan. That book, *After Reason*, about political leadership, would be published five years later. She says this first major defeat changed her career path.

After a 10-year relationship with the late *London Times* columnist Bernard Levin, Arianna moved to New York City in the early 1980s. She married Michael Huffington in 1986, and moved to Washington where her husband pursued a political career. They later established residency in Santa Barbara, California, in order for him to run in 1992 as a Republican for a seat in the U.S. House of Representatives, which he won. Arianna campaigned for her husband, courting religious conservatives and arguing for smaller government and a reduction in welfare. In 1994, Michael narrowly lost the race for the U.S. Senate seat to California to incumbent Dianne Feinstein. Michael and Arianna Huffington divorced in 1997.

In the late 1990s, after her divorce, Arianna began her own political transition from conservative to liberal. She later explained, "I left the Republican Party [because] my views of the role of government changed. I used to think that the private sector would solve many of the major problems we are facing—poverty, inequality. And then I saw firsthand that this wasn't going to happen."[8] She campaigned as an independent in an unsuccessful bid for the governorship of California in the 2003 recall election. Voters did not support her. She dropped out of the race before the election, but her name remained on the ballot. Nevertheless, she was declared a big loser, garnering less than .55 percent of the vote.

Today, Huffington has a string of published works, including a biography of opera star Maria Callas, one of Pablo Picasso that was adapted into a movie, and the 2003 *New York Times* bestseller *Pigs at the Trough: How Corporate Greed and Political Corruption Are Undermining America*. She had also authored several articles for the *National Review* and other noted publications and was a regular media contributor. Two years later, Huffington reported on the 1996 presidential elections for Comedy Central.

How Huffington Did It. In Huffington's words, she quickly dusted herself off and regrouped.

In 2003, through a friend Huffington met Kenneth Lerer, a former AOL executive and technology bright mind. After their friendship developed and many conversations later, they realized something was missing in [traditional] media. The conversation was moving online. There were a lot of voices and opinion, but no platform for them. The pair grew to know each other better over the next year and hatched an idea: a liberal version of the *Drudge Report*.

On May 9, 2005, the Huffington Post was born. The launch was greeted by many ill-wishers, Huffington writes in her book *Fearless*. In an article in the *LA Weekly*—the headline read: "Why Arianna's Blog Blows"—Nikki Finke claimed: "This website venture is the sort of failure that is simply unsurvivable."[9] In a *New York Times* article, the authors stated, "Few, including Mr. Lerer, ever thought it could be a legitimate business." Even Huffington's partner Lerer had his doubts. He voiced, "Blogging, after all, was done by loners in their basement."[10]

Today, the Huffington Post attracts more than 15 million page views per week and boasts a team of more than 3,000 content contributors from hardcore journalists to politicians, thought leaders, and entertainers. Plans under the AOL umbrella include expansion in key markets such as New York and Chicago and a deeper global presence.

So how does a brand that's hit some big bumps along the way, with a mob of critics, a dented 180-degree political change, and flip-flopping brand image build a news organization that a publicly traded company scoops up for millions of dollars land the founder on the *Forbes* list of the most influential women in media?

Whether one agrees with Huffington politics or her editorial flavor, there is no doubt she has turned around a floundering personal brand into an influential media empire.

The Huffington brand turned around because Huffington did these things:

- *She was absolutely fearless.* Arianna's mother instilled the idea that failure was not something to be afraid of. It was not the opposite of success. It was a stepping-stone to success. From the early days of Arianna's journey, she had no fear of failure. Perseverance is everything. She didn't give up. Everybody has failures, but successful people keep on going.
- *She would not allow critics to rain on her parade.* A huge part of building a confident brand and presence is to not let doubters and critics' opinions affect you. Often critics are motivated by jealousy, and many have no grounds, credentials, or authority on the subject. Arianna has had many loud naysayers and negative critics, from the 36 publishers that rejected her book idea, to the voters in California who rejected her bid for the governorship, to the *Los Angeles Times* writer who panned her "baby," the Huffington Post. They all tried to knock her out of the game. Had she listened to them, she would not be where she is today.
- *She built a strong network.* Arianna runs in circles of fame, movers and shakers, and celebrities, but she was not born into this place. Her relentless networking and connection mindset created this result. Today, she has an A-list address book of CEOs, entertainers, athletes,

and world leaders. She earned these relationships with a poise and drive over the years, and she strategically leveraged them to build her brand.

- *She built a public and visible platform.* From Huffington's days in college, she had something to say. . . and said it. When she started writing, giving speeches, and appearing on national TV and radio shows, her personality was larger than life. Her distinctive voice, accent, and spunk helped to create recognition, but personal and commercial brands cannot expect to be welcomed into any market's mind without many visible platforms from which to tell their story.

You Don't Have to Be Famous to Turn Yourself Around

Let's take a look at someone whose name you won't recognize from the media. Troy Evans is a speaker who attends the annual conference for NSA—the National Speakers Association. The story of how he turned around his personal brand is remarkable.

Troy Evans Brand Turnaround Story

Troy Evans was a former bank robber. Yes, you read that correctly. He had committed many terrible crimes, too many to list, actually. He was eventually convicted of five armed bank robberies, in three states, over a six-month crime spree, and he was sentenced to 13 years in the Federal Correctional Complex in Florence, Colorado.

Evans served seven years of his sentence. While incarcerated, though, he made the best possible use out of his time, earning two degrees and making the Dean's List with a 4.0 grade point average.

Evans had no money and limited access to the outside world. His brand—if you could call it one—was that of a dangerous, convicted inmate. Although Federal Pell Grants for the incarcerated had been eliminated, he set out to secure funding on his own through scholarships, grants, and foundation assistance.

After months of submitting applications, writing essays, begging, pleading, and getting daily rejections, Evans received a call from Robert Henry, then a humorist associated with the National Speakers Association. They soon met, and Evans's dedication to change and resilience convinced Robert and the NSA to award Troy his first scholarship. (This was one of many he earned totaling more than $40,000.)

The success of his educational pursuits brought new challenges for Evans. Jealous, angry reactions from other prisoners resulted in threats, daily fights, and almost deadly confrontations. Some wardens penalized Evans for his educational efforts and persistent requests for library and phone privileges. One warden in particular had it in for Evans—he moved Troy from his cell to "the hole," a 9-by-6-foot dark box shared with a severely disturbed inmate, for 60 days. The prisoner was nearly broken.

When Evans got out of the box, the warden transferred him to FCI (Federal Corrections Institution) Englewood, known as the nastiest prison in the Federal Bureau of Prisons. After three months, he was summoned to the records office and told there had been an error in his sentence: he should not have been sentenced to 13 years; he should have been sentenced to eight, and he was going home in 10 days.

Today, Evans dedicates himself to helping financial institutions minimize their risk of robbery. Capitalizing on his personal experience, he has built a successful brand as a speaker and bank security consultant; he has also authored two books.

Evans was not a star brand when he began his transformation. He was a regular kid, played sports, and was a good student. He wasn't a trouble-maker until he reached his teens when he began stealing from everyone, including his family, and hanging out with other teens with dangerous values and destructive habits.

The story of Evans's turnaround from bank robber to consultant to financial institutions and corporations around the world is inspirational. His resurrection epitomizes the core challenges brands face that hit bottom often.

How Evans Did It. The day Troy Evans was sentenced, he knew he needed to break the chains that put him in the prison and start his recovery.

His transformation was not fast. His disillusionment with his old way of life came with the realization that he was not as tough as he thought he was and that he could easily be killed in prison. The single moment of truth came when he accepted responsibility for his behavior, character, and crimes and recognized that he would have to radically change, reinvent himself, and get an education.

Out of prison and building a professional brand, Evans continues to break the chains of defeat. Today, he welcomes change and self-improvement as his brand has truly turned around. He is a regular guest and contributor on national media, adding insight to news stories about bank robberies, how criminals think, and security issues. He's also been cast in a pilot for a reality TV show about trust, and a movie about his life is in production.

Evans turned his brand around by doing these things:

- Welcoming change
- Leveraging what he knows
- Taking full responsibility for himself
- Being completely honest
- Being resilient
- Employing a multi-touchpoint tool kit

Troy Evans's story is one of an individual brand on a journey of change and recovery. But turnaround business, organization, and product brands travel similar paths on the road to redemption. Of course, returning a business brand to glory extends far beyond a one-person effort like Troy's; it can involve many stakeholders and thousands of teams across multiple locations around the world.

Turnaround Takeaways

Passion, talent, self-confidence, and the resilience to weather the storms of the brand's own making or that fate throws at them are essential qualities for turning around a brand or an individual life. The following are things you need to embrace and do to achieve turnaround success:

- Don't give up.
- Be honest and transparent.
- Walk your talk.
- Watch the company you keep—it really matters.
- If necessary, eat crow.
- Make sure the individual and the brand are in alignment—it fuels success.
- Keep moving forward.
- Start recovery as soon as possible.
- Experiment every day.
- Be absolutely fearless.
- Network every day.
- Don't let critics slow you down.
- Find highly visible platforms.
- Work to control your destiny; what's past is past.

Chapter 6

Game Changer 3: Lead Strong

This chapter is about bounce-back brand leadership. It's no cakewalk navigating any brand, but when an unexpected crisis, a series of stumbles in product launches, a bizarre accident, or questionable behavior is causing a negative impact on business, the organization, and people's lives—the job suddenly gets a whole lot tougher.

The media and public may be watching your every move, the team and your partners may be jumping ship, but you, as leader, not only must maintain calm and confidence but also have to figure out how to turn the corner and get back in the game quickly.

While many great leaders attribute their brand turnaround successes to the supporting cast and a solid team effort, the fact is that only one person can drive the car, make quick decisive turns, dodge flying objects, and, if necessary, slam on the brakes. I've spent nearly 30 years inside boardrooms, sitting in on committee planning meetings, and observing brands, and there is no doubt in my mind there is a good reason why you will not spot a statue of even one committee in any local park. The deadliest brand battles and brand transformations are never won without intentional, passionate, and strong individual leaders.

What It Takes to Lead a Brand Out of the Fire

In this chapter we will look at some brands that experienced significant bumps on their journey to—or back to—full brand greatness. Some lived through a series of setbacks, others suffered one big blow; some were the result of public outrage and lawsuits, and some were unpopular franchises with low-performing financials. Although the reasons for their problems were unique, their revivals shared something in common: effective—even great—leaders who led them back to glory.

Brand turnaround leaders may not necessarily be CEOs—they could be a variety of people who step up to lead the company out of a dark period, including chief marketing officers, professionals, or entrepreneurs. Their exploits are often recorded as case studies in business books—their battle stories become industry lore and we do well to heed the lessons that can be learned from their tales. Their followers may describe them with words like *evangelist*, *conductor*, or *commando*. The role brand turnaround leaders have is profound and often affects not only the organization but also the public.

A typical day for one of these turnaround leaders may include dealing with unreasonable media first thing in the morning, fighting with opposing lawyers in the courtroom later that morning, terminating mediocre managers at lunch, rallying the troops in the afternoon, and determining how best to solve the 500-pound problem that is drowning the brand at night. Brand leaders take big risks; they make unpopular choices; and sometimes they have to sacrifice personnel, other brands, and their personal lives in the process.

Leadership Qualities

In evaluating the leaders of many brands that are returned to their glory, it becomes apparent that many character traits commonly described in writings on leadership often show up in their biographies, in news stories, and on their websites. It makes sense that they would, because these traits—the seven leadership qualities in the following list—are critical to leaders who must charge ahead to make significant change and build value for their suffering brands:

1. *Resilience and toughness.* The ability to fight on while under fire
2. *Candor.* The strength to speak the truth
3. *Charisma.* The ability to inspire, empower, and excite
4. *Humility.* The innate modesty that allows brand leaders to value others' worth more than their own
5. *Gratitude.* The willingness to show appreciation toward all stakeholders
6. *Creativity.* The ability of leaders to use their imagination to solve problems
7. *Generosity.* The willingness to share the rewards—"if we all work hard, we all win"

When we study these leaders, we realize that there is another list of common characteristics shared by great leaders. The difference between the previous list and the list that follows is that these traits don't always make their way into corporate publicity materials; in fact, they are sometimes thought of as leadership taboos or even flaws.

At best, this is an unrealistic portrait of brand turnaround leaders; at worst, it is a bit hypocritical. In my real-life business experience, I not only have witnessed turnaround titans who have human foibles but also have seen how some of these less-than-perfect traits have been essential to their success.

Management consultant Anthony F. Smith said it best in his book, *The Taboos of Leadership*: "Most people don't understand the difficulty of the leader's job. While it is popular to embrace the idea of 'servant style or the leader with a big heart,' the truth is that effective leaders are often conflicted and behave in ways that are very human."[1]

Smith also believes most people are not comfortable discussing the darker side of leadership, but it exists and contributes to their successes. The truth is that leaders have these traits:

1. *Politic.* Leaders *do* play politics, and they take it very seriously.
2. *Single-mindedness.* Although leaders strive for work-life balance, their work is their life.
3. *Self-centeredness.* This trait is only dangerous in followers, not in leaders.[2]

I agree with him and would go further:

4. *Humanness.* True turnaround champs are *very* human.

Leaders possess a mix of flaws, issues, and oddities along with their high-performing transformative powers. Therefore, among leaders' common, but rarely discussed, personality traits, I would include impatience, hot-temperedness, insecurity, hyperactivity, and scattered management. (Another of these traits is arrogance. It sounds strange, I know, since we just cited humility as a trait common to leaders, but there are exceptions to every rule, and this is one of them.) That sounds like a few other brilliant minds we know: Donald Trump, Barack Obama, Ted Turner, Michael Bloomberg, LeBron James, and Rudy Giuliani have all been called arrogant at some time in their careers.

Brands on the hot seat require a leader who has strong convictions and who doesn't waffle. Leaders cannot fear failure, and they must be willing to make wrong decisions. Their nerves and skin must be tough, and they cannot let pressure and criticism from an impatient society and business world rattle them. Brand turnaround must also involve creativity, resourcefulness, and the ability for wrongness every now and then.

There is no cookie-cutter mold for turnaround bosses and top dogs. In fact, leaders seem to be a very diverse pack. There is a new breed and a new generation of leaders like Facebook's Mark Zuckerberg. He's young and cocky, and he bucks just about every stereotype of a typical CEO running a multibillion-dollar enterprise. From his hoodie, jeans, and flip-flops to his odd declaration that he will only eat what he hunts, his leadership style is not something you usually find in business books on leadership. Zuckerberg has had his share of brand bumps, including a legal one with his former partners and with public opinion over privacy issues.

Today's brand turnaround leaders can be young or old, Rhodes scholars, or college dropouts; they are male and female, from all races and ethnic backgrounds. They have thick skin, crazy hearts, and interesting rituals.

Here are some stories of some impressive brand leaders and a few of the traits that helped contribute to their success.

Mark Cuban and the Dallas Mavericks: Relentless Competitors

A very passionate leader who knows how to turn his bad-boy behavior into goodwill and great publicity, Mark Cuban and his leadership are competitive, curious, and passionately entrepreneurial.

Cuban is a serial entrepreneur, whose first step into the business world was at the age of 12, when he sold garbage bags to pay for a pair of expensive basketball shoes. While in school, he held a variety of jobs, including bartender, disco dancing instructor, and party promoter. He paid for college by collecting and selling stamps and once gained almost $1,100 from starting a chain letter. Maybe that was viral marketing before we knew what to call it.

A self-made billionaire entrepreneur today, Cuban sold not one, but two technology start-ups at the height of their profitability and scored big. With a net worth of $2.4 billion and a spot high on *Forbes'* World's Richest People list, today Cuban owns a business empire that spans movie theatres and cable networks to mixed martial arts ventures and investigative journalism.

In March 2000, Cuban bought the Dallas Mavericks for $285 million. At the time, the team was one of the National Basketball Association's laughingstock franchises, with a lackluster fan base and a stadium full of empty seats; it was losing money and competing with other, aggressive entertainment choices. Under Cuban's uniquely brash, charismatic, energetic, occasionally obnoxious, hands-on leadership style the team has risen to be one of the NBA's elite. His ability to turn bad behavior into great branding seems to be a sport in itself.

On January 8, 2002, the NBA assessed a league-record $500,000 fine against Cuban for his remarks regarding referees. In a story published in the *Dallas Morning News*, Cuban was quoted as saying that "Ed Rush [head of officiating] might have been a great ref, but I wouldn't hire him to manage a Dairy Queen. His interest is not in the integrity of the game or improving the officiating."[3]

The stint generated news and a big fine, and Dairy Queen was upset. In an interview, Cuban told *60 Minutes* that he got the last laugh, and turned the episode into a million dollars worth of free publicity.[4]

"They challenged me to come and manage a Dairy Queen, saying it wasn't that easy. And so I got up at 6 a.m., learned how to make a Blizzard, learned how to make a dip cone and I still never got the dip thing right,"[5] says Cuban.

"By the time the doors opened, there was lines around the block and there were helicopters above. And it was a zoo, but it was a blast." That's just one of many highly publicized events around the Cuban renegade style. Which adds to the rebound brand he created for the Mavericks.

In less than a decade, he has built the team into one of the most loved and fan-winning franchises in NBA history. Today, the American Airline's Arena regularly sells out, merchandise sales rank in the league's top 10, and, in 2010, *Forbes* magazine reported that the value of the team had increased since Cuban bought it from $280 million to $438 million.[6] And in 2011, he got a championship under his belt, too.

Mark Cuban's brand-building leadership traits include the following things:

- *Uncensored authenticity.* If you are a rebel, own it. Cuban is notorious for public outbursts and getting fined by the NBA. Every time he's fined, he matches the fine with a donation to a charity—the word is that the matching tally is more than $1.6 million.
- *Accessibility.* It's no surprise that Cuban made his money in computers, as he has embraced twenty-first-century technology. He's a regular blogger, he broadcasts his e-mail at every Maverick game, he's inviting fans to tell him how to make the experience even better, he constantly posts messages on Twitter, and he is always available to speak to the media.
- *Competitive drive.* A winning spirit definitely has an edge in brand building. Sports and business are like peanut butter and jelly, and, to Cuban, the ultimate sport is business.
- *Inner trust.* Cuban believes his gut feeling before any focus group. He gets out and observes, listens, and talks to customers every day. Mark often sits in the $8 seats and carries on with fans.

Mike Jeffries and Abercrombie & Fitch: Style and Substance

A creative, visionary leader who is obsessed with youth and fashion and who protects the brand he has turned around, Mike Jeffries has a leadership style that is controlling, quirky, and superstitious.

Jeffries, the current chairman and CEO of Abercrombie & Fitch Co. (A&F), was born into retail. His father, the owner of a small chain of party-supply stores in Los Angeles, let him select all the merchandise for the toy departments when Jeffries was just 12. He studied economics at Claremont McKenna College and got an MBA at Columbia University.

After working with many top retailers, in 1980 Jeffries founded Alcott & Andrews, a fashion store for career women. The brand did well at first, but when the company expanded, it got in to trouble. By 1983, Alcott was bankrupt. Next, Jeffries took a merchandising job at Paul Harris, a struggling

Midwest women's chain that slipped into bankruptcy protection not long after he arrived. In 1992, he joined the Limited family of brands as CEO of Abercrombie & Fitch.

The Abercrombie & Fitch brand was founded in New York City in 1892 by David Abercrombie and Ezra Fitch. A&F was originally an elite sports outfitter that specialized in outdoor and hunting gear, which outfitted Teddy Roosevelt, Ernest Hemingway, and many other high-profile sportsmen and adventurers. The original A&F didn't adapt to a changing sports market, and it filed for Chapter 11 bankruptcy in 1976.

In 1978, Oshman's Sporting Goods, a Houston-based chain, bought the A&F name, trademark, and mailing list, and it opened a store in 1979 under the Abercrombie & Fitch name in Beverly Hills, California. The next few years the brand evolved and the number of stores expanded to 26, but industry analysts criticized the hodgepodge of merchandise; the updated, more contemporary brand never really took off.

In 1988, The Limited's family of apparel brands purchased Abercrombie & Fitch for $45 million in cash. Inventory was cleared out and a stronger emphasis was placed on apparel. When Michael Jeffries joined A&F as its president,[7] it was losing $25 million a year. Jeffries' mission was to reinvent the brand.[8] Nearly two decades later, Jeffries with his quirky, perfectionist, control-freak leadership style has transformed a brand on the brink, selling "fuddy-duddy clothes"[9] to a dominant lifestyle-based brand for young people who aspire to a sexy American style.

Leslee O'Neill, A&F's executive vice president of planning and allocation, remembering what the company was like before Jeffries got there, was quoted in Salon.com as saying, "We had old clothes that no one liked. . . . It was a mess, a total disaster."[10]

Shortly after Jeffries joined A&F, he identified renowned, edgy fashion photographer Bruce Weber as someone to bring the first dose of sex and aspiration to the brand. At the time Jeffries couldn't afford to hire Weber, so he purchased one image and put it in one of the store's windows. Once described as "neo-preppy" by *Women's Wear Daily*, A&F gained attention during the mid- to late 1990s in part because of its racy advertising created by famous, sexually charged fashion photographers. Its homoerotic fashion spreads rubbed parents the wrong way and set up what would be an ongoing contentious relationship between the brand and authority figures. Of course, this made the brand a huge hit with teens and young consumers.

The turnaround is a result of Jeffries' crystal-clear vision and execution. He has successfully created a culture around youth, sex, and style. The company's branded headquarters is unique, with bonfires, tin-structured buildings, and dance music blaring nonstop; its stores are erotically dramatic environments; and its marketing is always provocative.

A&F has grown in spite of constant public pounding from conservative consumers and the media that disagree with A&F's ways of doing things, especially when it comes to marketing. Beyond the reinvention of the brand, Jeffries and the A&F brand have prevailed in a string of high-profile controversies, including lawsuits about employment practices and finances, marketing backlash, boycotts, and brand extension failures.

The interesting side of so many of A&F's highly publicized controversies is that they make their critics furious, but the controversies actually make the brand stronger with its core audience, who love them. While all of the "scandals" involving the A&F brand over the years have played out in the press, the brand has remained wildly popular. That has gotten it in "trouble" with parents and "squares" over pushing the boundaries of acceptability, which has hardly been a detriment.

For example, in 1998, A&F removed a story titled "Drinking 101" from its back-to-school-themed *A&F Quarterly* magazine after advocacy groups like Mothers Against Drunk Driving (MADD) protested. In the wake of the controversy, the Associated Press noted that "maybe . . . [the article] should have been called 'Marketing 101.'"[11]

Later came criticism and lawsuits that accused A&F of racism in its hiring practices and for its "Look Policy,"[12] which dictates how store attendees must look (e.g., wear store colors; do not wear a hijab).[13] This put the brand's image in a negative light, but for the most part the controversy did not resonate with core consumers.

In 2011 the brand was criticized and earned a lot of publicity for selling the Ashley Push-up Triangle bikini top designed to give very young girls a busty lift. After the initial news reports, A&F renamed the triangle top item, put it on sale, and was back to business as usual.

Despite all the social challenges, the greatest threat to the brand came in 2008 with the economic crisis and the loss of disposable income. According to Gilbert Harrison, who wrote for the Training Management Association (TMA) in May 2009, most retailers caved in to discounting, Michael Jeffries did not slash prices and continued to charge full price for A&F's trendy garb. Harrison explained the rationale for this decision, which "[m]any questioned ... at the time. While A&F underperformed its peers in terms of comp store sales, the results were hardly disastrous because the retailer maintained gross margins. Perhaps more importantly, A&F customers were not trained to look for discounts [something that has troubled other brands]." In this way, Jeffries "successfully safeguarded its image as a premium brand."[14]

In February 2011, a *Wall Street Journal* headline announced that for the quarter ending January 29, "Abercrombie & Fitch 4Q Profit Almost Doubles on Sales." Nowadays, A&F operates more than 1,000 stores and posts revenues of more than $3 billion. Expansion continues, with A&F's sights set on increasing its global markets.

Mike Jeffries' brand-building leadership traits include these things:

- *Intensity.* Jeffries leads with a driven, demanding, obsessive-compulsive style. His management approach is very intentional and passionate. His extreme personality is evident throughout the brand. Merchandise selection has clarity. Its provocative marketing is bold and policed for strict consistency.
- *Authenticity.* Jeffries doesn't apologize for who he is or for what the brand stands for. He believes in his brand and does not waver from its essence to conform to consumers who are not his target market.

- *Decisiveness.* Jeffries has been called a micromanager. However, his nondelegation style has certainly contributed to the consistent brand and its communications. According to Benoit Denizet-Lewis in Salon.com, Jeffries is controlling and makes the final decision on every piece of merchandise to the displays; he purportedly even goes so far as to personally interview every model the company hires.[15]
- *Focus.* Throughout Jeffries' tour of duty with the company, there have been many lawsuits that he has opted to settle. He believes fighting them would be a distraction, and no one can afford distractions. The company is passionate about what it does, and believes spending time defending against them is counterproductive. In his view, being a popular company with a lot of money makes you a target.

Jeffries also demonstrates his commitment to the brand by doing the following:

- *Walking the walk.* Even though Jeffries is much older than the brand's target customers are, he reflects its core values—look, feel, and attitude. He's in great shape, he sports the merchandise, he wears flip-flops to board meetings, and he exudes a youthful, casual, hip style.
- *Talking the talk.* A&F hires good-looking people to work in its stores because good-looking people attract other good-looking people, and that's who the company markets to—cool, good-looking people. Jeffries admits A&F goes too far sometimes and pushes the envelope; it's called being authentic and relevant to one's target customer.

Robert Ehrlich and Pirate's Booty: Resilient

Pirate's Booty has had a lot of trials in its 25-year history, but rough seas have made this brand stronger under Robert Ehrlich's fun-spirited, adventurous, and adaptive leadership.

The tale begins when founder of Robert's American Gourmet, Robert Ehrlich, an ex-commodities trader, created Pirate's Booty in 1986 to market healthy snack foods. Pirate's Booty followed a short-lived stint when Ehrlich made salad dressing from his mother's kitchen. The change in the category came when Robert realized that salad dressings hang out in refrigerators for a long time while snack foods have an ongoing consumer consumption.

Ehrlich found out that cheese puffs had no cheese in them and most of the ingredients were unpronounceable chemicals and additives. In response, he developed a line of natural-ingredient products offering healthier options than those currently available. Targeting high-end consumers, the snack was a huge hit, at once "good for you" and, at the same time, delicious. Pirate's Booty made *Vanity Fair*'s "in" list of healthy foods.

Early on, Ehrlich's leadership navigated Pirate's Booty through some very choppy waters. Throughout the years, U.S. Food and Drug Administration (FDA) violations, bad publicity, customer complaints, and lawsuits have shaken the company and brand on its voyage to success.

In December 2001, *Good Housekeeping* conducted tests on Pirate's Booty and found that the snack contained three times the fat (8.5 grams of fat—not the 2.5 listed on the package—in a one-ounce serving) and calories listed on the label.[16] The same mislabeling applied to the entire line of products: Pirate's Booty, Veggie Booty, and Fruity Booty.

The one-time lively and trusted brand was now tarnished by the news of a deceptive labeling scandal. The brand name that had made the product memorable also set it up perfectly as the "booty" of jokes. Jay Leno mocked the brand on the *Tonight Show*, saying, "Here's a tip: If the snack you're eating contains the word 'booty,' you're probably not going to be losing much weight."[17]

Other media, including the Spokane *Spokesman-Review*, blasted the snack and questioned the brand's honesty. Headlines read: "Pirate's Booty Turns Out to Be Fool's Gold,"[18] and the *South Florida Sun-Sentinel* reported "Digging into Pirate's Booty Reveals Skullduggery."[19]

Manhattan journalist and mother, Meredith Berkman, headed up a $50 million class action lawsuit against Pirate's Booty for incorrect nutrition labeling. She made it a crusade, saying, "The specifics of this case are not about the fat, but the larger context is truth in labeling. . . . I don't want their money—any rewards will go to charity. I just want them to be accountable."[20]

The reaction from Pirate Booty's parent company, Robert's American Gourmet, was swift. Instead of making ludicrous excuses, it was contrite and sincere. The brand initiated a recall and amended all packaging. A message on the website read, "These changes have made Pirate's Booty a more consistent and better snack."[21] To legitimize the actions, the new fat levels and calorie count listed on the label were verified by *Good Housekeeping*.

Unfortunately, lightning can strike more than once, and it did for Pirate's Booty. In 2006 the company recalled 153 cases of Wheat Free Chaos Snack Mix after discovering packages that contained . . . wheat.

In 2007, a 19-state salmonella outbreak that sickened 60 people, mostly kids, initiated a nationwide recall of Pirate's Booty and other snacks because of the suspected contamination. The company immediately acted to remove all products from the market. In a *Forbes* magazine article, Ehrlich said the recall accounted for 12 percent of the company's $50 million in sales. Following the incident, under Ehrlich's leadership, the company instituted stricter testing measures. In the *New York Times Magazine* Consumed column, Ehrlich explained that the brand survived these incidents "partly because it reacted quickly and openly." He added, "[Consumers] are looking for trust and a unique experience."[22]

Despite the major brand bumps, Pirate's Booty has continued to grow and be a standout brand in grocery stores and restaurants. It has achieved this by clearly knowing its brand essence and executing on it every day. Pirate's does not spend a lot of money on traditional media; instead, it leverages its unique quirky persona and product offering by giving people something to talk about. When the fourth installment of the *Pirates of the Caribbean* movie opened in theaters in the summer of 2011, Pirate's Booty rode that ship with related promotions. Its customer touchpoints also reflect the fun brand: when you call their headquarters, guess who answers the phone? A pirate! Check out the company's website and see a shipload full of celebrities eating the snacks.

In 2009, sales of the brand topped $50 million. The brand turnaround is the result of Ehrlich's passion for better and healthier snack options backed by a consistently distinct creative and quirky brand persona.

These are among Robert Ehrlich's brand-building leadership traits:

- *An ability to adapt.* From the early days, Ehrlich was open to change as his entire business offering evolved from one product with a long refrigerator life to a brand-new category that was often purchased because it could be quickly consumed. When his brand started getting beaten up by a variety of operational and marketing issues, he led the company to many new, better ways of doing things, including more stringent product testing and setting higher standards for vendors, and improved customer communications.

- *Adventurousness.* Ehrlich is a lifelong explorer and learner. He spends four months a year on the road scouring gourmet markets worldwide and attending food trade shows to discover the next big snack hit.

- *Transparency.* Throughout all the brand bumps, Ehrlich has always been brutally honest about mistakes the company has made along the way. Ehrlich has not fired or demoted any employee, despite the screwups, nor has he switched any manufacturing from an offending plant. "You could spend all day blaming people," he says philosophically. "The reason people want to do business with us is because I don't do that. It's better for there to be a flow and to figure out a way to trust people."[23]

- *Fun-spiritedness.* The success and turnaround of Pirate's Booty reflects Ehrlich's sense of humor and creativity. From the beginning he knew the importance of standing out and being distinct in the very cluttered snack category. From the goofy, offbeat stories around each brand snack, to the characters—a pilot, Sigmund Freud, and a mischievous-looking pirate—the brands scream, "Good times" and, "Good for you."

Howard Schultz and Starbucks: Visionary

The leadership of Howard Schultz, the chairman and CEO of Starbucks, is optimistic, experimental, and compassionate.

Starbucks opened in Seattle in 1971. The original business was founded by friends Jerry Baldwin, Zev Siegl, and Gordon Bowker. All three loved coffee and decided to open a small shop to sell fresh-roasted gourmet beans and coffee accessories. While they encouraged customers to try the coffee, they did not sell coffee by the cup.

In 1981, a plastics salesman for Hammarplast named Howard Schultz entered the picture. Just a few years later he would begin his journey toward creating a billion-dollar global brand. Hammarplast made plastic drip-brewing thermoses that Starbucks used in its stores. Howard Schultz would become to Starbucks what Ray Kroc was to McDonald's, a salesperson who saw a great product and opportunity, and who then made history.

In 1982, Jerry Baldwin hired Schultz to head up marketing for the small coffee venture. That year Schultz traveled to Milan, Italy, to attend an international housewares show. The trip was an epiphany for Schultz, who was infatuated with and inspired by the coffee culture of old-world Italy. On that trip, he had his first caffe latte. Upon returning to the United States, he shared the idea with his boss, but Baldwin and his partners were not interested in being in the restaurant business and thought the idea would distract them from their core business. That did not stop Schultz, who convinced them to add a small espresso bar in the corner of one of the stores. Within a couple of months the store that was selling espresso was selling 300 percent more coffee than any of the other Starbucks stores. The impressive numbers still did not sway the Starbucks owners and, in 1986,

Schultz left to start his own coffee house. It was named The Daily, or Il Giornale, after Italy's largest newspaper.

In 1987, the owners of Starbucks Coffee Co. wanted out and decided to sell their business, along with the name. After more than 217 investor rejections, Schultz raised $3.7 million and bought the business. He did this by convincing investors that the company could open 125 outlets in the next five years. The new company led by Schultz would include Il Giornale and the six existing Starbucks. Eventually they would all be named Starbucks, but they would follow the coffee house concept.

From here Starbucks growth took off, expanding to other cities including Vancouver, British Columbia; Portland, Oregon; and Chicago, Illinois. By 1991, Starbucks started a mail-order catalog business and began licensing airport stores. In 1992, the company went public, and it grew at a phenomenal rate. The world had a whole new mindset about coffee.

By 1997, the number of Starbucks Coffee stores grew tenfold, with locations around the world. Brand extensions were next. Some worked, others didn't. But growth continued and, unlike many other household names, Starbucks earned this status largely through word of mouth and its branded coffee community experience. By 2004, Starbucks reached a record 1,344 stores worldwide.

In 2000, Howard Schultz stepped down as CEO; he remained chairman and global strategist. Jim Donald, who joined Starbucks in 2002 as president of the North American division became president and CEO in March 2005.

In 2007, though, the coffee brand started experiencing some serious growth pains, posting its worst annual performance in U.S. trading. Adding to the challenge was the recession and the resulting decline in consumer discretionary spending.

Later that year came the infamous "we messed up" memo in which Schultz lamented about the company's aggressive growth and watering down of the brand experience. He came to the realization that growth plans that he himself had sold to analysts and partners—the famous 40,000 stores—were commoditizing the Starbucks brand, and that the trend needed to be reversed and Starbucks had to return to its roots in quality coffee and good training. The Starbucks brand did not smell so good. Sales and the stock price were rocky, competition was more aggressive, and the future of the iconic brand uncertain.

This was followed by serious politicking, conversations with his close circle of supporters, and a great deal of thought. Donald is gone, and Schultz returns to bring back the soul of Starbucks. The recovery process would be grueling.

In 2008, the company announced plans to close 600 stores in the United States and lay off more than 12,000 employees, the most in its history. This was round one, more closings and layoffs continued as the company and brand rebuilt its core and following.

Starbucks' first Seattle store opened on March 30, 1971. The company celebrated its fortieth anniversary in 2011. Today, the coffee chain has more than 17,000 locations around the world.

Howard Schultz's brand-building leadership traits include being the following things:

- *A master storyteller.* Schultz mastered the art of storytelling early in his career when he was raising his first round of funding. He had the vision, but then he had to impart that vision to his investor prospects. He continues to use this storytelling trait to lead and inspire his teams and to take the brand story to the market. Whether his message is about the company's values or a new product, he paints pictures and uses metaphors to communicate to all of his audiences.
- *An experimenter.* From the early days of Starbucks to the turnaround times, Schultz has always been willing to try new ideas. Few would have thought that someone could build a big, global brand without advertising. Schultz put his money on alternative ways to build Starbucks. These included word of mouth derived from the great in-store experience and publicity about its unique offerings through social

media. The launch and learn has certainly paid off. According to *Ad Age*, in May 2011 Starbucks passed Burger King and Wendy's in sales, earning the number-three spot for restaurant chains. What is most compelling about this achievement is that Starbucks spends one-tenth of what each of the other top five leaders do.

- *A good listener.* Schultz has always been in tune to the customer insights and has welcomed their ideas. In 2008, Starbucks started the My Starbucks Idea online community dedicated to sharing and discussing ideas to better the Starbucks company, products, and experience. In addition to customers submitting ideas on how to make their Starbucks experience even better, they can vote on the top ideas. Many of today's new products have been a result of this initiative. In fact, the number-one suggestion was that Starbucks create a loyalty program. More than a million people are now carrying the Starbucks gold card and getting significant rewards.

- *A compassionate agent.* The son of a Brooklyn truck driver who raised his family in the housing projects, Schultz watched his father struggle through his career without health benefits or corporate kindness, and he never forgot the experience. Even in the toughest times for the brand, Schultz never dismisses the importance of being the conscience of the brand. From offering health insurance to employees to being a friend to the Earth and the communities the brand serves, these programs of kindness and compassion have not only built goodwill but also have had a major impact on the identity of the brand.

New Tools for Today's Leaders

In addition to the leadership qualities already mentioned, today's brand turnaround leaders must understand the new digital and social media environments. Leveraging these platforms and tools can add layers of new influence and exposure. They can serve as important means for monitoring how well your brand his doing and better managing your brand's recovery.

The power of these tools comes from the speed to market they facilitate, the ability to update information regularly, the visual impact of broadcast video and images, and the historic accessibility to content that search engines provide. When a brand in trouble has its plan, story, and strategy in place, search engine optimization—a web marketing technique to drive visitors to an Internet site—allows the broadest, fastest dissemination of its message. When a brand in trouble does not, these same tools can cause further damage.

Not all brand leaders need to become daily tweeters, have thousands of friends on Facebook, and maintain a blogging presence. Who should do so depends on the nature of the brand, the amount of time they have available, and the resources on hand.

Commercial brands need to have a strong presence online and integrate all aspects of digital marketing from the website to social media into their communications. Leaders do need to know the ins and outs of new media, social network technologies, and social communities in order to cover the basics of reputation management and to contribute to the company's online footprint at the appropriate times.

Reputation management basics for leadership include these things:

- Securing your name's web address; for example, mine is www.Karenpost.com
- Googling or binging yourself monthly to see what pops up
- Setting up search engine alerts to let you know where your name is showing up. If you find content that does not add to your leadership reputation, find its source and try to get the information removed.
- Posting and optimizing good content about yourself can dramatically improve the complexion of bad search results. No matter what, content is king.

These are some social media basics:

- Setting up your LinkedIn account and keeping it current with up-to-date professional information
- Setting up a Google profile account
- Setting up a Wikipedia page, if you have enough news, book, and film citations

If you do set up social media accounts and know that you will not be active, include that in your account information and profile.

To blog or not to blog? that is the question. More and more C-level leaders are starting to blog. Some just publish internal blogs; others choose to post on their company blog as contributors; still others, such as Whole Food's CEO John Mackey, publish independently under their own name, even though the company also has a blog. The answer depends on your circumstances, time available, resources, and nature of your brand. If you decide to blog, a well-done one on your brand can serve as another channel with which to stay connected to your stakeholders and disseminate timely information.

Turnaround Takeaways

Turnaround leaders are a unique breed of people. Here are some traits they share that help them in their rise to the top:

- An ability to detach from the disaster or an event without losing sight of lessons learned
- A focus on making things better—with no blaming of employees, vendors, or the media
- A clear vision of the future that addresses the triple bottom line: finance, society, and the environment
- An ability to leverage their own strengths and those of their teams

- A willingness to embrace new leadership tools, including social media and digital communications
- A willingness to take calculated risks and accept failing forward
- A willingness to "launch and learn," fueled by a respect for research and a belief in their own gut instincts
- A love of the game, which they play to win
- A willingness to mix, mingle, and listen to all the stakeholders

Chapter 7

Game Changer 4: Stay Relevant

The marketplace is full of contradictions and varied points of view on every subject and brand. That's why there is Ben and Jerry's Cherry Garcia and Blue Bell's vanilla, and why both are successful. The marketplace is also full of harmony. It comes from like-minded people (tribes), whose word of mouth (tribal force) can further a cause with their commitment and take a brand from the Dead Sea to riding the waves again.

Different Tribes Need Different Love

For a shaken brand that has lost its core buyers, the task is to find the buyers who will forgive and forget past missteps and love the brand just as much as before. Remember, buyers can be consumers of your product, of your cause, of your story, or all three. In the simplest terms, brands in recovery need to matter to the people who matter most (a group we will examine in further detail throughout the chapter). Therefore, it's important to accept the idea that if everyone likes your brand, you stand for nothing. Being relevant to your most influential buyers is critical to recovery.

The brands featured in this chapter have all faced different challenges: Harley-Davidson's new ownership let the quality decline and the brand story slide; Hush Puppies' flood of foreign competitors resulted from changes in government regulations promoting free trade; Barbie's brand involvement in a lawsuit with a serious competitor whacked away a big piece of its market share, they all experienced a big brand burn. Their recovery in large part resulted from their ability to rediscover their relevance to their buyers rather than an attempt to be everything to everybody.

The bigger the brand, the more complex the pool of diverse and needy stakeholders, no matter whether they are customers, prospects, employees, vendors, partners, or even the media. Add to that the explosion of thousands of new, segmented communication channels, and a brand in troubled waters has a monstrous ocean to conquer.

Identify Your Core Buyer

Companies and brands that have turned around the most horrific situations consistently identify and prioritize their most important consumers and then craft both strategic communications and relationship-building programs to that group. Because they have so many constituents and public fiduciary duties, and their communications in certain areas are regulated, this is especially true for large and publicly traded companies. In fact, it is one of the most difficult things a brand team must master.

Now let's take a look at how Harley-Davidson did it.

Harley-Davidson Brand Turnaround Story

The Harley-Davidson (H-D) Motor Co. was not an immediate success. In 1903, two Milwaukee youths, William Harley and Arthur Davidson, successfully developed a small engine that could be attached to a bicycle. But it was too weak to power the vehicle up even a small hill. It was scrapped.

By 1905, improved H-D engines were sold to do-it-yourself (DIY) bicycle builders, and in 1906, a small factory was built in Milwaukee where the H-D headquarters still stand. One hundred fifty motorcycles were produced in 1907. In 1921, a Harley-Davidson was the first bike to win a race with a speed averaging more than 100 miles per hour. By this time, Harley was selling almost 30,000 units a year. During World War II, Harley-Davidson supplied almost 100,000 bikes for the war effort, creating a respectable brand name for itself in the process.

One of its early brand downfalls occurred in 1947. A Hollister, California, motorcycle rally turned into a "big riot." *Life* magazine published a photo taken at the event of a drunken man surrounded by broken beer bottles sitting atop a Harley-Davidson motorcycle. Thus, "biker gangs" were born, and, for the next 30 years, Harley-Davidson's brand name became closely associated with this culture and the Hells Angels. Lee Marvin and his gang rode Harleys in the 1953 film, *The Wild One*, based loosely on the Hollister incident.

Hollywood was not the sole cause of Harley-Davidson's public relations nightmare. Even worse for the brand than a connection with biker culture was its connection to bad product. In 1969 H-D was bought by American Machine and Foundry (AMF), which throughout the 1970s slashed costs by cutting back on quality and laying off workers. Soon, much as what happened to the automobiles produced by the Big Three across the state of Michigan, Harley-Davidson became synonymous with low quality and high price. The brand name came to be mocked by riders of other bikes as "Hardly Ableson."[1] The brand became a punch line for the problems with American manufacturing. Serious riders began to switch to reliable Japanese-made bikes. Sales were so slow at one point that H-D considered bankruptcy.

In 1981, Vaughn Beals Jr., Willie Davidson, and 13 senior executives staged a coup and bought Harley-Davidson back from AMF. "The Eagle Soars Alone" became the rallying cry for the company. Among other efforts, they launched a two-year bike buyback program to generate needed cash flow and implemented a "Materials as Needed" (MAN) plan that reduced costs and significantly improved quality.

In 1983, the brand focused on making its customers proud, launching the Harley Owners Group. The acronym for the group, HOG, soon came to mean everything the brand stood for. By 1990, there were 90,000 HOG members. By 2000, there were more than 500,000. In 1988, Harley-Davison launched a traveling museum, taking H-D memorabilia and classic bikes across the United States to reinforce the rich iconography of the brand. To this day, one of the most important things Harley-Davidson has done is to celebrate itself as a way of congratulating consumers for the purchasing decision they have made. No opportunity to celebrate an anniversary or a milestone goes without serious fanfare from Milwaukee.

Even as the brand is reinforcing pride in ownership through the HOG program; a heavy showing at the famed Sturgis Motorcycle Rally in Sturgis, South Dakota, an annual racing and stunt event begun in 1938;[2] and other campaigns, it is continually distinguishing its product through technical advances. While its bike's styling remains true to the H-D aesthetic, starting in the 1990s its components were updated to meet the modern rider's demands.

The recession that began in 2008 was not kind to Harley-Davidson: sales have been soft, dropping from a profit of $1 billion in 2006 to a $55 million loss in 2009 to a $146.5 million profit in 2010.[3] Its brand valuation—which Interbrand bases on financial performance, the role of the brand in purchasing decisions, and brand strength—has also fallen. Many industry insiders, however, believe the company will weather the downturn.

The Harley-Davidson brand remains proud and strong, which allows H-D loyalists and aficionados to keep their heads held high. It is a fighter brand, and it is aggressively battling to win back sales. The brand remains focused on its core buyer—baby boomers—and emerging new markets, including first-time buyers and younger consumers.

How Relevance Put Harley-Davidson Back on Track

Harley-Davidson has used a variety of strategies and tactics to remain relevant to its core buyers and build relevance among newer constituents.

To do this it has done the following things:

- *Expanded its outreach with new programs.* For HOG loyalists, in 2011 Harley-Davidson expanded its Fly & Ride program, which allows HOG members to rent motorcycles when away from home and also provides members with travel planning assistance and other services. About one-quarter of all 1,300 H-D dealerships participate.

- *Broadened its appeal to women.* Relevance shines through the brand in the way it is targeting women riders, who are one of the fastest-growing rider segments. Harley-Davidson's share of the woman rider market is an impressive 53 percent. Today, about 12 percent of H-D's sales are to women, 10 percent higher than the 1995 level of just 2 percent. H-D dealerships have also sponsored about 500 women-only events, and almost 30,000 women have participated.

  Model Marissa Miller has been the H-D spokeswoman since 2008. Harley-Davidson also has taken out ads in *Vanity Fair* magazine that feature celebrity female riders such as *The Biggest Loser* star Jillian Michaels and singer Jewel, and it has launched a microsite just for women. In 2010, it introduced a lighter bike with a lower seat.

- *Created special programs for first-timers.* In an effort to attract first-time buyers, Harley-Davidson has launched a rental program that allows potential customers to ride one of its bikes for a weekend and attend a "Fantasy Camp" for riders.

- *Went global.* Harley-Davidson is pushing into India, and as part of this effort it is using its messaging to educate Indian consumers on the importance of the brand; it has started chapters of the Harley Owners Group in New Delhi and Mumbai.

- *Cultivated its "rebel" image.* Harley-Davidson knows that while its image as a "biker gang" brand hurt it during the conformity-happy

1950s, it is a core value of the brand today. It directly participates in product placement efforts in films such as *The Green Hornet* and *Wolverine*, as well as in a TV series about a criminal biker gang, *Sons of Anarchy*.

- *Used Facebook as a research tool.* As Randy Sprenger, manager of electronic advertising and direct promotions for the brand, told *Adweek* in 2009, "One of the greatest advantages for social media is the voice of the customer. We'll post a question, such as, 'Are you in favor of darkening the bike out, blackening the bike out or shiny chrome?' We'll get customers to comment. It won't be unusual to receive 300 to 500 comments. It helps us learn what people are saying outside the walls of Harley."[4]

The H-D brand rebounded because it returned to relevance by doing these things:

- Creating operational incentives that drive cash and loyalty
- Creating multi-touchpoint experiences based on segmented values (e.g., women, boomers, first-time riders, and younger riders) that can transform into community relationships
- Creating PR-worthy annual events that become part of the brand heritage
- Learning from its newest customers' insights that will mold tomorrow's relevancy elements
- Expanding deeper into global markets by emphasizing the emotional appeal of the brand first and the functionality of the product second
- Leveraging product placement (in movies, TV shows, etc.) to core brand identity
- Tapping social media for building the community, creating two-way dialogue, and as a research tool

Keep Your Eye on Your Customer

How does a brand win a group of consumers and stay relevant? In times of crisis, how does it show sincere compassion and empathy to the consumer, project to its stockholders an attitude of confidence and calm, and, at the same time, avoid spoon-feeding potential plaintiffs' attorneys (who might sue the brand on behalf of injured clients for more money than most people can imagine)?

Audiences, adversaries, consumers, and influencers often have very competing agendas and needs. What's important to one party doesn't even earn a small blip on someone else's radar screen.

These are things that brands in recovery need to do:

- *Accept the fact that being loved by everyone means that you stand for nothing.* Everyone is not your customer or buyer—and will never be. The more you try to get everyone on your side, the more you'll alienate those who matter most.
- *Identify and prioritize their most important buyers and influencers.* I subscribe to the 80/20 theory, 80 percent of your brand love comes from 20 percent of your strongest brand ambassadors; pay attention to them, understand why they love you, and find others just like them.
- *Get into brand lovers' heads and hearts.* Hang out with them and listen. Find out what matters most to them: how you can solve their problems and provide emotional satisfaction through your brand.
- *Switch gears when needed by tailoring the messenger to the drilled-down segmented recipient.* This does not mean you need to change your set of core brand values, attributes, and identity based on every market segment; it means you adapt to your target audience, their sweet spots, and the filters that they sometimes use.

As you look to recover from any shake-up, the playing field is rarely fair or even. Often you carry the heavy weight of baggage around your neck and you are playing market catch-up because of major defections and loss of interest in your offering and brand.

Brand leaders must focus on the most meaningful aspects of their brand—the ones that make buyers loyal, love it, and want to tell their friends about it. The very essence of relevance is

- The magnet that attracts new buyers and attention
- The connection to common values and concerns
- A relationship to exchange shared interests
- A two-way dialogue that demonstrates you care (you can do this by educating buyers, treating them well, and never forgetting them)
- The application of your brand to their world and its needs
- A clear message that convincingly tells buyers "what's in it for them"

Let's take a look at a brand that was able to regain relevance after losing it: Hush Puppies.

Hush Puppies Brand Turnaround Story

The Hush Puppies brand has been around since 1958. The first shoe was created when Wolverine, parent company of Hush Puppies and manufacturers of work-related and casual footwear, was developing new methods for tanning pigskin for the U.S. military.

When the shoe was launched, it was described as the classic American style, which at the same time pioneered a new casual and relaxed fashion look that used an innovative shoe technology. Hush Puppies became the footwear phenomenon of the late 1950s and early 1960s. Wolverine soon took the brand international via licensing agreements. The parent company was eventually renamed Wolverine World Wide, Inc. in 1964. Between 1958 and 1965, the year Wolverine went public, sales of Hush Puppies nearly quintupled.

From the beginning, a basset hound served as the shoe's logo, earning status as the iconic symbol for the brand story. The Hush Puppies name and mascot were both dreamt up by the company's first sales manager, James Gaylord Muir. Originally, the agency representing the brand recommended the name Lasers. But when Muir was on a business trip to the South, he dined with one of his colleagues and the two ate hushpuppies, the traditional southern fried cornballs. When Muir asked about the name, he was told that farmers threw them at their hounds to "quiet the barking dogs." Muir saw a connection to his new product. "Barking dogs" in the vernacular of the day was an idiom for sore feet. Muir believed his new shoes were so comfortable that they could "quiet barking dogs."

Through the years, the brand grew in popularity, being the "in" comfortable and cool shoe for American families, who were shifting from a culture of conservative uniformity to a comfortable, casual way of life. Celebrities such as the Beatles and even the "Rat Pack" (Frank Sinatra, Dean Martin, Sammy Davis Jr., etc.) and Johnny Carson, at the height of their fame, worn them. Hush Puppies even claims their rubber soles saved the life of Rolling Stones guitarist Keith Richards when he accidentally touched his guitar against a mike at a 1965 concert. Richards was knocked unconscious, but medics believed that the crepe-soled Hush Puppies shoes he was wearing insulated him and saved his life.

By the late 1960s, Hush Puppies sales declined as it lost its appeal with younger buyers. Toward the end of the 1980s, the company seemed to slowly come back as sales increased, although, by 1990, 50 percent of U.S. shoe manufacturers had gone out of business. But the next decade sales again fell as inexpensive foreign imports and consumers' switch to athletic shoes for informal wear challenged the brand. In 1992, Rita Koselka noted in *Forbes* that, "among U.S. industries, few have been hit harder by foreign competition than shoemaking."[5] The brand bleeding didn't stop there. In 1989, Wolverine and Fred Goldston, a pigskin and cowhide broker, were charged with plotting the theft of cowhide from Southwest Hide Co.[6] Three years later, an impending jury verdict of more than $39.3 million, prompted Wolverine to settle the suit for $8.5 million. Thomas Gleason, CEO at that time, nevertheless insisted that Wolverine was innocent of the charges, "We were just the deep pockets around,"[7] he told *Forbes*'s Rita Koselka. Wolverine was also plagued with quality control and inventory problems in the late 1980s.

Then the music really stopped. Sales fell to less than 30,000 pairs in 1994, and the Hush Puppy brand wasn't cool at all. The parent company was thinking of phasing out the shoes.

How Relevance Put Hush Puppies Back on Track

Then through a combination of rejuvenated designs, savvy marketing, strict cost controls, and a healthy dose of good luck, Hush Puppies were showing up in all the right places.

As Malcolm Gladwell noted in his bestselling book *The Tipping Point* as well as in an earlier article he penned for the *New York Times* about Hush Puppies' reemergence, someplace along the way the "popularity" of the shoes reached a "tipping point" and the shoe was reborn.

In the article and book he pointed out that Hush Puppies was a dying brand until a few hipsters in New York City's East Village brought it back from the brink and into mainstream popularity without any advertising push. These were young people who had spent hours sifting through thrift-store bins. "And why did they do that?" asked Gladwell. "Because their definition of cool is doing something that nobody else is doing." Without increasing its ad budget, Hush Puppies saw its sales increase, and the footwear all of a sudden was cool again.

"Fashion was at the mercy of those kids, whoever they were, and it was a wonderful thing if the kids picked you, but a scary thing, too, because it meant that cool was something you could not control," Gladwell wrote. "You needed someone to find cool and tell you what it was." Part of what made Hush Puppies cool back then was the ability to say you were wearing the original design. There was authenticity in that, and to some extent exclusivity, because the trend was born from a relatively small group of people in an area known for its artsy vibe.

A relatively small number of young people began wearing the shoes because "no one else would wear them." The shoes became "hip in the clubs and bars of downtown Manhattan." Among the people wearing the shoes was Isaac Mizrahi, the clothing designer.

From there, a couple of prominent designers like John Bartlett and Anna Sui used the shoes in their collections. Designer Joel Fitzpatrick dedicated half his store to the line. Fitzpatrick's clientele included many celebrities like Paul Reubens (aka Pee-wee Herman), Sarah Jessica Parker, Ellen DeGeneres, Anjelica Huston, Susan Sarandon, and Sharon Stone. Word of mouth took over. And the brand was very cool once again.

In 1995, the company sold 430,000 pairs of classic Hush Puppies. The next year it sold four times that number, and that pattern continued. "In 1995, Hush Puppies won the prize for best accessory of the year at the Council of Fashion Designers awards dinner at Lincoln Center. . . ."[8]

Today Hush Puppies is a strong global brand that sells more than two million pairs of shoes annually, with licensing in 135 countries; 1,100 destination points worldwide; and 400 Hush Puppies shops. The brand plans to leverage this global strength (approximately 75 percent of sales are international) to increase sales in the United States.

From the early days of the brand, Hush Puppies has stood for simple, sensible, and casual comfort. The shoe's design is practical and has worked. As the brand has evolved, the company continues to innovate on its patented technologies that have provided product benefits such as its Worry-free suede waterproof, scuff, and stain-resistant technology and Bounce, its shock absorber.

After its surprising adoption by New York City's hipsters and fashionistas, the next step was to elevate the fashion sensibility of the brand, so Hush Puppies regularly tapped top designers to create special collections. For its fiftieth anniversary the company signed on high-profile designers and stylists such as Hollywood's Phillip Bloch and the United Kingdom's Rachel Fanconi, who created men's and women's shoes as part of Hush

Puppies' Guest Designer series. Throughout the years, they and others contributed not only their cachet to the brand, but also their distinctive eye for style as colors like Pepto-Bismol pink, Day-Glo green, and Blue suede shoes were added to the line.

A new divergence from the basic shoe line is a full range of footwear for men, women, and kids that includes boots, sandals, and other shoes aimed at the more athletic customers.

The Hush Puppies brand turned around because it did these things:

- *It recognized that the times were changing.* After a decade of corporate conformity, the world started seeing things the Hush Puppies way. In the mid-nineties, when major businesses like IBM and Ford relaxed their dress codes and embraced business casual and casual Fridays. Hush Puppies, the brand that invented casual, was there to congratulate the companies. It ran full-page ads in the *Wall Street Journal* and *USA Today* that recognized the fashion movement.

  Later Wolverine sent videotapes with tips for casual dressing at work to businesses throughout the United States, which helped to set the new fashion standard. By 1995, stores such as Barneys New York and Swell in California struggled to keep the shoes in stock.

- *It maintained its core identity.* Hush Puppies has developed a tight bond with its loyal customers not only with its product but also with a basset hound you can't help but love. This identity is recognized around the world, and its luster hasn't dimmed. Hush Puppies has maintained its well-known basset hound logo when other brands have been dumping their classic logos.

- *It went local while staying global.* With 75 percent of Hush Puppies' business coming from outside the United States, keeping things fresh and relevant in international markets is a priority. The company recently launched Hush Puppies Studio in various countries to achieve this goal. Unlike its usual outlets, these stores are more contemporary and trendy, and they include apparel. The company is planning to open nearly 100 stores across Asia Pacific this year, with its main focus being on lucrative markets such as China and India.

▨ *It cobranded with product placement.* The adage "you are the company you keep" holds strong for the Hush Puppies brand, and its product is often seen in entertainment hits like *Forest Gump* and the *Austin Powers* series of movies.

The Hush Puppies brand has rebounded and returned to relevance by doing these things:

▨ *Making operational improvements.* There's better product, more efficient systems to scale, and better communications.

▨ *Returning to core values and messaging.* Hush Puppies invented casual. When business instituted the shift to business casual, Hush Puppies aligned and seized the opportunity with a national ad blitz.

▨ *Mixing the old with the new.* Hush Puppies leveraged the heritage brand elements (e.g., nostalgia for the dog, iconic celebrities from past) with newer contemporary values (e.g., style, function, and branded technologies), creating a fresh image without eliminating the positive heritage elements.

▨ *Taking advantage of major historic milestones.* The brand used its fiftieth anniversary as the occasion to launch and reimagine its 1958 collection; it leveraged current touchpoints, including store events, publicity, and social media.

▨ *Extending the brand.* It introduced new, fashionable, and functional lines that are relevant to emerging global markets, women, athletes, and kids.

▨ *Cobranding with other brands.* It hired high-profile designers and publicized sightings of celebrities seen wearing Hush Puppies.

How Brands Lose Relevance

Gaining relevance doesn't automatically guarantee *sustaining* relevance. At any moment, your brand could begin to lose it. These things often happen:

- Brands grow, and with that comes bigger marketing departments, more audiences to cater to, and larger committees to appease. Suddenly brand relevance is so watered down that it's not serving the brand base or producing the outcome that everyone wants.
- Brand leaders can't see the big picture because they are caught up in the details. They don't recognize the problem because they are relying on old ways of researching and thinking.
- Brand leaders are reluctant to push out into new categories that they create, can own, and rule for fear of failure.

Tim Manners, branding expert and author of *Relevance*, believes marketers should give up the flashy practices and groupthink of the last 50 years, the demographics-driven strategies, fashion-obsessed images, and old-fashioned advertising. Today's customers don't care about those things. All they want to know is, "Why should I care? And what's in it for me?"

In *Brand Relevance: Making Competitors Irrelevant,* David Aaker explains how companies can keep their brand relevant through innovation and the creation of new categories or subcategories that they can "own" in the minds of consumers. Doing a good job at this not only moves one's brand ahead but it makes its competition irrelevant. Aaker believes companies waste money and resources by focusing on brand preference competition (e.g., "we're better than the competition") and should instead divert those resources to brand relevance and areas where there are not a lot of players.

Whatever the case, brands that want to come back need to start thinking more like their customers and not like people who are tasked with marketing projects. Being relevant can be the strongest bridge you have to the road back. And it's not enough to identify your relevance; you must also connect to your buyers in the most pertinent way, and do it often.

Relevant brands do these things:

- *They solve problems that matter.* What matters most to buyers comes from their system of beliefs (values), which can come from family, career, ego, and even peer pressure.
- *They bring emotional satisfaction to consumers.* This can run the gamut from happiness to pride to adventure.

The most potent brand relevance is fluid (ever-changing), fast (delivered when buyers need it), and concentrated (rich in meaningfulness). The famous Barbie is a brand that has exemplified all of these traits.

The Barbie Brand Turnaround Story

The inspiration for Barbie came as Ruth Handler, the wife of one of the cofounders of Mattel, watched her daughter Barbara play with paper dolls, and noticed that she often gave them adult roles. Realizing that there might be a gap in the market, Handler suggested the idea of an adult-bodied doll to her husband, Elliot, who didn't embrace the idea. Neither did Mattel's other directors.

While traveling in Europe, Ruth discovered a German adult-figured toy doll. The doll was exactly what Handler had in mind, so she purchased three of them. When she returned to the United States, Handler and an engineer reworked the design of the doll and named her Barbie, after her daughter. The new doll made its debut at the American International Toy Fair in New York on March 9, 1959. This date is also Barbie's official birthday.

Mattel sold about 350,000 Barbie dolls in the first year. By 2000, nearly a billion Barbie dolls had been sold in about 150 countries.

Barbie had become an icon, even immortalized by Andy Warhol, but by the 2000s, Barbie had lost her way. Little girls rushed to snap up the competing Bratz dolls, which were targeted at the hipper, young girl buyer. These dolls had a fresh, multicultural style, big eyes, and full lips. The unchanged Barbie seemed frumpy and outdated.

In 2001, Bratz dolls slowly began to eat into Barbie's market share, but when Bratz started outselling Barbie in the United Kingdom, Mattel mostly ignored the threat and went about business as usual. Barbie's sales peaked in 2002 at $1.52 billion worldwide.

The Barbie brand's initial reaction lacked distinctiveness (it ran like the rest) as it strayed from Barbie's core brand and focused on making Barbie more like Bratz. In an attempt to make Barbie more "edgy," Mattel toyed with the core wholesome brand promise. In 2004, a promotional stunt had Barbie dumping Ken after 43 years. The brand announced the breakup just two days before Valentine's Day. On the surface, it was an interesting PR stunt and earned Barbie millions of dollars of publicity at that time. On the other hand, it was unclear if the attempt was to be more relevant, sell more of the surfer-dude doll she dumped Ken for, or just elevate the brand awareness. Maybe it was some of all these things.

Despite this effort, in 2005, Barbie sales fell 30 percent in the United States and 18 percent worldwide—a shockingly large drop for an iconic product. The 40-something-year-old Barbie was struggling through a midlife crisis and losing her cool factor.

In December 2006, Mattel sued MGA Entertainment for $500 million, alleging that Carter Bryant, a former employee who designed MGA's Bratz dolls, came up with the idea while he was still working for Mattel in 2000 and secretly took the designs to MGA. The case has been litigating back and forth for over 10 years. Both sides have been a part of winning verdicts. As of this writing, the latest ruling came in April 2011 when U.S. District Court slapped Mattel, Inc. with $88 million in damages after tossing out its claims that rival MGA Entertainment stole the idea for its blockbuster Bratz dolls. This followed a jury verdict that also found Mattel guilty of misappropriation of trade secrets. This is not likely to be the end of it, as most believe Mattel will appeal.[9]

A New Perspective

In 2008, Mattel brought in a single strong leader, Richard Dickson, as the general manager of the Barbie brand. Dickson left Mattel in 2010; the brand seems to be staying the course he set.

When Dickson joined the brand, he immediately recognized that Barbie was 17 different shades of pink and that the brand used six logos. More than 1,000 brand licenses were outstanding. In a *CNN* interview, Dickson called it "brand goulash." Dickson slashed the Barbie brand back to its original core meaning.

He also mandated a mind shift. Barbie's supporting team took the brand too seriously. Instead of trying to control the world with their extreme brand police, they needed to celebrate Barbie and have fun.

Dickson eschewed traditional TV ads for more unique, publicity-generating tie-ins. He built Barbie a new pad on Malibu beach with help of top designer Jonathan Adler. He partnered Barbie with *Fashion Week*, where 40 designers, including Vera Wang, Betsey Johnson, Donna Karan, Calvin Klein, Carmen Marc Valvo, and Marchesa, all created special looks for everyone's favorite fashion icon. Barbie was hobnobbing with a very cool crowd, and the buzz was everywhere.

Barbie got her groove back by understanding these things:

- *Many friends keep the brand popular.* Barbie has always understood the value of many friends and segmenting the product line. Even when she was transitioning through her "finding herself again" years, Barbie has always had no shortage of personalities, characters, and friends who appeal to different careers, adventures, and pop culture events.
- *Barbie could learn from failure.* Not all efforts to rehabilitate Barbie's brand have been successful, but although she has stumbled, she's managed to get up. The website BarbieGirls.com, a meet-and-greet online world that attracted millions of users, struggled to convert the free site into an active source of revenue. The company closed the site in June 2010. And after two years and a major hoopla, Barbie's

Shanghai flagship store closed, too. While both were large invest-ments, the company claims that what it learned about both the online and Asian markets gave it valuable insight to apply to future projects.

▪ *Social media is valuable.* Barbie, of course, is very social. She's got a blog and is on Facebook and Twitter, too. And she's not just posting and tweeting discount messages and product stuff. She is a personal-ity. Barbie even tweets about her romances and adventures. One 2011 tweet reads: "Downloading 'True Whit' for my Kindle. Can't wait to dive into @whitneyEVEport's fab advice on my flight."[10] (That's Barbie tweeting about downloading the then recent Kindle edition of *True Whit: Designing a Life of Style, Beauty, and Fun* by Whitney Port and her plan to check out Port's Twitter site while Barbie's jetting off somewhere.) There was a time when the Barbie brand ignored con-sumer polling; today, it uses social media like Twitter to allow fans to determine Barbie and Ken's relationship.

It's also important to note that "telling the Barbie story" is a strong brand-building strategy for Barbie and her friends. Barbie has offered unique stories for three generations of doll lovers. In mid-2009, U.S. sales of Barbie made their first significant move up since 2006. Then, a year later, Barbie and Ken played a huge role in the movie *Toy Story 3*. The expo-sure resulted in a huge boost for the brand, with kids once again snapping up Barbies.

Six years after using Valentine's Day as an opportunity for Barbie and Ken to break up, the couple may be getting back together. In an effort to get the gossip mill cranking, Mattel has released a special 2011 Valentine's Barbie and Ken for the bargain price of $5 as a way to reintroduce the clas-sic characters to a new generation. The Valentine's Day tie-in includes a promotion with New York City's Magnolia Bakery as Ken gifts Barbie the iconic cupcakes.

Mattel has also remade Ken. After allowing the Ken doll to poke fun at itself in *Toy Story 3*, Mattel has leveraged this peak of exposure to give the now-50-year-old Ken a makeover so he appeals to modern girls. In addition, to appeal to an adult audience, Mattel produced a television-like reality show that aired on online media. The show, called *Genuine Ken: The Search for the Great American Boyfriend*, ran as an eight-part web series that culminated in a real guy winning the right to have the new Ken resemble him. The show debuted on Hulu.com and was cross-posted to the Barbie-branded YouTube channel. It received heavy social media support. *Genuine Ken* was a big hit with almost 25 million unique visitors in one month. The Barbie brand has done a good job of leveraging other webcast and broadcast channels to tell their stories.

The Barbie brand rebounded and returned to relevance by doing this things:

- Streamlining the branded assets, colors, logo, and licensing agreements
- Continuing to create new pop culture and multicultural products targeted at three generations of buyers
- Strategically partnering with like brands in entertainment, technology, and fashion
- Taking herself less seriously
  (Barbie is starting to have fun. Barbie has loosened the brand usage reins—no longer is every song parodist and artist laughing it up in *Saturday Night Live* skits worried about being sued.)
- Reducing its use of traditional media and, instead, turning to alternative awareness and branding methods such as product placement, publicity, and events
- Tapping social media for education, entertainment, and community building, as well as a research tool
- Balancing corporate talk with personalized girly gab and storytelling

Of course, as mentioned, a big part of bouncing back is redefining what matters to your brand.

The Six-Step "What Matters" Development Process

The list below highlights the basics of determining what matters to your brand, and it should serve as your guide. Start by framing what you know about your buyers, how the brand incident affects them, and what you still need them to learn. Then, address all of your key markets (e.g., prospects, customers, vendors, employees) and influencers (e.g., the media, trade and advocacy groups) using this process.

Based on your situation, you may want to add other elements. The process should be a mix of qualitative and quantitative research. If you have the resources, you may want to consider adding an outside research group to your team. If not, leverage the web, social media, customer feedback channels, and published research reports relevant to your markets.

Step 1—Gain Insight

By consumer segment, identify and prioritize these things:

- What their problem is; what their underserved needs are; what their desires are; what they care about
- Whether these issues existed before the brand incident occurred
- Whether their opinion about the brand has changed since the incident
- The reason(s) for any changes and new challenges

Walk in your buyers' shoes. Beyond demographics, even age, determine what values matter to your buyers:

- Creativity
- Expression
- Community
- Family
- Achievement
- Freedom
- Privacy
- Fun
- Responsibility
- Duty

- Status
- Adventure
- Sustainability
- Wisdom
- Spirituality
- Security

When you have these answers, determine how the brand can supply these needs.

Step 2—Innovate (New Solutions, Recycled Ideas, a Mix of Both)
Ask yourself how the brand offering can be improved:

- Purpose/meaning/function
- Design
- Technology

Step 3—Add Value
Ask yourself how the brand can add value:

- Tangibles/intangibles
- Pricing model
- Delivery method
- Extras that can deepen your brand's relevance:
  - Exclusivity
  - First mover
  - Personalization/customization

Step 4—Deliver an Amazing Experience
Ask yourself how consumer–brand interaction can be enhanced.

- Overall engagement with all senses
- The journey—before the purchase, during the transaction, and after the purchase
- The environment

- Extras that can deepen your brand's relevance:
  - Showing appreciation
  - Recognition
  - Reward

Step 5—Communicate

Examine how the brand's message and story are being conveyed:

- Persona—its language and look
- Strategic partners—with which to cobrand
- Outreach channels—external and internal
- Inbound feedback from all audiences
- Creative execution and tactics

Step 6—Invest and Immerse

Determine what resources are required to implement these new points of relevance, and then ask yourself if you should do these things:

- Reintroduce an existing brand offering and enhance its relevance
- Introduce a new (breakthrough) category and new brand
- Introduce new (highly segmented) brand-offering extensions

As you start formulating how you will heighten your relevance with your markets, answer these questions to further test your new ideas:

1. Are you current and contemporary?
2. Are you aligned with your business goals?
3. Is your message simple and straightforward? Is it easy to understand and remember?
4. Is there anything you can eliminate from the offering that makes another part of the offering even more powerful?
5. Are you distinctive?

6. Do you stand out above the market and the competition's noise?

With the answers to these questions in mind, you will be on your way to recapturing your brand's relevance.

Turnaround Takeaways

Staying relevant means brands have to do these things:

- Solve big problems with simple answers.
- Keep eyes and ears on the market, watch trends, converse, and listen.
- Walk in all of their stakeholder's shoes: customers, employees, investors, vendors, and even critics.
- Understand the buyers' value system.
- Identify strong segments of the top buyers' base.
- Don't want or attempt to please everyone.
- Be fluid and flexible.
- Be able to detach to the past if it's not working today.
- Be willing to launch, learn, and make mistakes.
- Find breakthrough ways to delivery, and communicate their relevance.

Chapter 8

Game Changer 5: Keep Improving

B ad things happen to good companies and to people every day. Whether it's a mean-spirited attack on your data by hackers, which Sony Play-Station experienced, or complacency and economic factors like those experienced by the Ford Motor brand and Marks & Spencer, the U.K.-based retailer, these incidents negatively mark a brand. Sometimes the black eye fades away quickly, and other times it causes serious internal damage with consequences that may last for years. Fast or slow, though, brand bounce-back only happens with some changes for the better.

Rethink, Recycle, and Reinvent

In the previous chapters, we looked at how taking responsibility, having conviction, exhibiting strong leadership, and being relevant are necessary Game Changers in the turnaround of brands. While all of these things are essential, this next action not only adds to the value and essence of a brand but also can present the greatest opportunity to shift the story away from past setbacks to the present and future prospects. Brands that have turned around—individuals, companies, products, and causes—have done so in large part because they did a lot of things better, they evolved and innovated, and they didn't stop there. Whether the improvements and changes were incremental or radical and revolutionary, most were integrated not only into the products and marketing strategy but also into the culture of the organization and its operations.

Ironically, some of history's worst brand beatings—Xerox and Ford are good examples—actually triggered the most meaningful improvements. Sometimes it takes a near-death experience for the innovation adrenaline to kick in. When a brand sees its sales drop 30 to 40 percent, the once fuzzy concept of "need to change" suddenly gets very clear. Or when a competitor gets so aggressive it drags a brand name through the mud, the wake-up alarm comes through loud and clear.

These grand aha moments can be the result of dysfunction (e.g., product recalls), short life-cycle trends (e.g., low-cost copycats), or adversarial relationships (e.g., special interest groups waging public wars and questioning a brand's intentions). No matter what the cause, though, the solution is to innovate and improve.

The act of innovation is often associated with technological and scientific breakthroughs; however, innovation is not limited to a category, a budget, or even a market—innovation is just a new way of doing something. Brands like Sharper Image, Circuit City, and Linens 'n Things failed in their original brick-and-mortar incarnations. All filed bankruptcy and were liquidated. A short time later, they were reborn with new owners as online-only businesses. Condé Nast's *Gourmet* magazine published its last issue in 2009, a victim of declining advertising sales and readers' shifting food interests. The Gourmet brand, however, will continue with books, television programs, and online properties.

Call it strategic rethinking, recycling of old ideas, or downright reinvention, it all boils down to making improvements and not stopping there.

Brands that bounce back understand that getting better is much bigger than just a rebound strategy; it's a source of growth and offers protection from being commoditized—the worst place a brand can go.

When meaningful innovation and improvement happen, brands in trouble often find new momentum and the fuel to take them the distance in their recovery.

Don't Wait for a Global Meltdown: Heed the Warning Signals

Red flags, flashing lights, and signs of brand decline are present every day in businesses around the world. Sales may be plummeting, labor costs may be out of control, or at least one competitor may be celebrating an innovative breakthrough. For big brands, this can mean posting millions—even billions—of dollars worth of losses. For smaller companies the same thing happens, but there are fewer zeros in the loss column. Whether the losses are large or small, these companies plug along, don't make any hard or radical changes, and convince themselves that things will get better soon.

Now, add this to the mix: consumer preferences change—what the brand had, consumers no longer want. Add a big, fat recession that paralyzes credit and lending, and that freezes spending. Suddenly, the brand that a short time ago was seeing warning lights is sinking in quicksand.

Let's take a look at a brand that managed to pull itself out of the quicksand.

The Ford Motor Company Turnaround Story

One of America's biggest brands lived through this nightmare. Its historic losses did not just appear suddenly one day. They were building while core pieces of the company's brand were dying. Complacency and failure to adapt to a changing consumer and world almost killed it.

Remarkably, Ford, its leaders, and every one of its team members shifted gears and pulled off an incredible brand turnaround.

For nearly a century, the Ford Motor Co. was synonymous with American corporate success and pioneering industrial manufacturing. Ford builds millions of vehicles every year and is ranked among the top five automakers in the world.

Throughout Ford's history, the company has experienced numerous challenges, scandals, and recoveries. During fuel shortages that strangled world economies in the 1970s, Ford, like other Detroit automakers, was caught flat-footed without the kinds of fuel-efficient cars the market demanded. Japanese brands saw their chance and opened the door to the U.S. marketplace. In the 1970s, engine fires in Ford's Pinto brand resulted in 27 reported deaths. Many say this was the reason Lee Iacocca, president of Ford at the time, was dismissed.

Thirty years later, after a decade of making highly profitable sport utility vehicles (SUVs), Ford again faced a marketplace it hadn't anticipated and for which it had no appropriate products. For decades Ford had competed by pushing technological innovation, but with its reliance on the SUV, the brand regressed.

These challenges were small compared to Ford's greatest challenge, which came 102 years after its founding. In 2005, Wall Street classified Ford bonds as "junk." In 2006, Ford's chairman William Clay "Bill" Ford Jr. asserted, "Bankruptcy is not an option."[1] That same year, Ford announced a $12.7 billion loss, the largest in the brand's history. At the North American International Auto Show, Bill Ford announced a plan to return Ford to its former glory. He called the plan "The Way Forward." The plan consisted of layoffs and financial restructuring, as well as a shake-up of the product line to, as *MSNBC* noted, "focus on building vehicles with new hybrid gasoline-electric engines and other environmental innovations, bringing out 250,000 hybrids by the end of the decade. Ford will also focus on smaller cars and bring out bolder designs."[2]

That year Alan Mulally was named CEO. He was not a car guy; he was not even a Detroit guy—he drove a Lexus—but he had an impressive record of success with Boeing. When he accepted the opportunity, he knew that things were bad, but he had no idea that the biggest crisis in automotive history was right around the corner.

In 2007, the auto industry fell victim to a global financial meltdown. Fuel prices and unemployment were rising; interest in gas-sucking SUVs, the core product of the U.S. automaker, declined; and a credit crunch threw the entire industry into the ditch. Things got so bad in November 2008— when Ford posted a $14.6 billion loss, which was even larger than its 2007 loss—that year all three automakers went to Congress to ask for help. Their $25 billion bailout request was turned down.

Later in 2008, with the change of administration in Washington, General Motors (GM) and Chrysler took TARP [Troubled Asset Relief Program] "bailout" funds, but Ford decided to fix the company without the help of the government.[3] At the time, it was running out of cash, had a mishmash of brands, and was experiencing many unresolved issues, among them labor costs and low productivity that needed rethinking.

By 2010, the company roared past earnings forecasts and posted its best first-quarter profit since 1998. It earned $2.6 billion, up 22 percent from a year earlier. Business experts call the turnaround at Ford Motor Co. nothing short of phenomenal, and they mostly attribute it to Alan Mulally and his reinvention of an American brand.

How Ford Bounced Back

After nearly driving off a cliff, Ford improved its brand by doing these things:

- *Rethinking how it did everything.* This meant bringing in a fresh perspective. The top leadership came from a different industry, with no ties to ways of doing things done in the past. They recognized that starting from scratch on all improvements was too costly and time consuming, and focused on being more operationally efficient by building multiple models and small SUVs on the same platform, thus lowering the fixed cost of each vehicle rolled off the assembly line. They also looked at resurrecting or recycling old ideas like the Taurus, which in its heyday was a top-selling car, which they did. In 2011, sales were strong, and plans are in the works to refresh the Taurus body style again in 2013.

■ *Focusing on innovative new vehicles.* At the same time as the company looked to the past, it was exploring new designs for the future. This energized the brand and helped it reintroduce itself to a whole new generation who had come to see Ford as stodgy. In 2011, Ford announced 10 fuel-efficient, smaller cars—it offered consumers the choices of gas-only, hybrid, or electric-only. Led by the all-new Ford Focus, the new vehicle lineup demonstrates how Ford is transforming its product range for a high-tech, fuel-efficient future.

■ *Concentrating on doing less but doing it better.* Ford was trying to do too much and had lost its focus. The "good" had become the enemy of the "great." Over the years, Ford not only had expanded its product line but also had bought several other car companies (Volvo, Jaguar, Land Rover, and others). The reinvented company now has a single focus—the Ford brand. It has sold all the other companies and even eliminated the Mercury lineup, a brand that Ford had been producing for more than 50 years.

■ *Retooling and reestablishing brand identity.* Now that Ford has all its "cars in row," it has a compelling feel-good, comeback-kid story and brand-new, next-generation product line to take to the market. Its advertising is fresh and energetic. One campaign takes a reverse spin on the tough grilling that goes on in press conferences, but Ford uses real, first-time customers at the center of the mock news conference. It has also introduced Doug, a puppet who appears in unexpected places, from the web to press conferences.

Social media also has been another important driving force for Ford. In 2008, Ford brought on Scott Monty to head its global digital communications. Under his leadership the brand has done an amazing job. In social media circles, Ford encourages a variety of Ford staffers, both at the corporate level and on local levels, to have a voice. Their efforts have humanized the big corporate brand, making it accessible, authentic, and transparent. The strategy has been coined Zero to 60 social media and integrates web properties, with promotions, videos, contests, and advertising. Ford's highly effective social machine has built one of the largest, most active consumer brand communities on the net. *Fast Company* magazine named Ford in its 50 Most Innovative companies for its advertising and marketing. The brand drives conversation with blogs, multiple Facebook pages (the Mustang brand alone has more than 1,293,719 fans), thousands of videos on YouTube that mention Ford, and more than 12 different Twitter accounts.

Monty has also earned a nice personal brand as a "web-celeb," appearing at conferences and advocating smart social media around the world.

Don't Hide from Critics; Learn from Them

Critics are like mosquitoes. They are everywhere and can be a terrible distraction. And many folks, including me, don't often think about their positive purpose. We focus on their annoying characteristics. It turns out that mosquitoes are important in our ecosystem; they are an important source of food for other creatures like bats, and some even pollinate plants.

Critics also have two sides: the bad side forces brands to waste precious resources. In some ways worse than time-consuming and expensive lawsuits, critical opinions can stay in the public's mind and wear down a brand's confidence. And that's unfortunate. It's human to want everyone's acceptance and support, but the reality is that everyone will *never* love your brand. Think about it in the same way as politics. A candidate can win by a landslide—in the 1936 presidential election, Franklin D. Roosevelt won 60.8 percent of the vote, still 36.5 percent did not support him and voted for Alf Landon. The truth about critics is that some are clueless and don't, and won't, ever understand your brand or position; some hold unreasonable ideas and opinions that just don't matter; and some are jealous or envious—competitors, media, and others—who just don't want you to succeed.

Then there are critics who actually bring some value. They may fundamentally disagree with your brand and disparage your efforts, but you still can learn a lot from them. You should pay attention to them, learn from their noise, and extract the opportunities their criticism implies to move your brand forward. Take a look at how McDonald's handled its critics.

The largest fast-food chain in the world, McDonald's serves 58 million people a day worldwide. The company's very name is so iconic that it sometimes is used as a stand-in for the entire fast-food industry. You might think that a brand as globally prominent as McDonald's would be immune to criticism at this point, but no matter how successful a company is, nobody is invulnerable.

The McDonald's Brand Turnaround Story

Established in 1940, McDonald's did for hamburgers what Ford did for automobiles. The company's 1948 innovation—"Speedee Service System"—streamlined food service and laid out processes still used in today's fast-food industry.

Merriam-Webster began including the word *McJob* in its dictionaries in 2003, which it defines as "a low-paying job that requires little skill and provides little opportunity for advancement." McDonald's creative response to this was to own it. Recent job recruiting literature has referred to McDonald's employment as "not bad for a 'McJob.'" One of the brand's greatest strengths is its alumni. Estimates vary, but they range from one out of every eight to one out of every ten Americans has worked at McDonald's at some time in their lives.

Over the years, McDonald's has faced many brand road bumps; it is also a constant target of animal rights, food, and culture activists. Recently, San Francisco lawmakers moved to outlaw the toys included with Happy Meals, saying Happy Meals contribute to childhood obesity and the toys entice the children.

Supersized Brand

On other hand, McDonald's understands branding like almost no other company. One of its greatest brand challenges came in 2004 with the release of the blockbuster documentary *Super Size Me*. The film features the director, Morgan Spurlock, spending a month eating only at McDonald's and focused on his declining health and weight gain during that period.

McDonald's is accustomed to responding to criticism, but the Spurlock attack was different. It targeted the brand as a whole. *Super Size Me* didn't demand that McDonald's take action to change its product; it more or less demanded it cease to exist. In fact, the film ends with the question, "Who do you want to see go first, you or them?" and a cartoon tombstone for Ronald McDonald. Regardless of how Spurlock's experiment was rigged, it expressed in entertaining fashion a growing sentiment toward fast food. As a documentary it was unusually popular at the theaters. A month after its release, the documentary was already the fifth best performing ever.

McDonald's recognized the power and momentum that *Super Size Me* was building. It hit the sweet spot of the brewing McDonald's backlash.

But instead of ignoring the furor, which would certainly have grown by doing so, the brand doused the fire by agreeing to change. Within six months it committed to eliminating its "Super Size" option, taking much of the wind out of the sails of its criticism.

McDonald's committed to a healthier menu, including salads. It began giving out pedometers. The devices, which measure how many steps a wearer has taken, are part of a campaign to shake up the company's image as a provider of unhealthy, high-fat, high-sugar food and encourage customers to take more exercise. However, health campaigners said the fat and sugar content of some of McDonald's food was so great that a typical person would need to walk more than five and a half hours to burn off a meal. Stung by criticism that its fast food is contributing to the obesity epidemic, and following threats of legal action from overweight Americans, the chain revamped its menus. "Adult Happy Meals" came with fitness information backed up by Oprah Winfrey's fitness guru Bob Greene. It was such a PR win that U.S. Department of Health and Human Services secretary Tommy Thompson commended the brand for "taking a lead role by helping educate its customers on this seriously important health issue."[4] In 2004,

McDonald's amplified its image by hiring impossible-to-hate model super mom Heidi Klum as a spokesperson.

Maybe the greatest brand win of McDonald's campaign was its appeal to Spurlock's own ego. To prove that his film had been more than a stunt, Spurlock added an epilogue to the DVD version of the film that claimed the film led to McDonald's discontinuing the Super Size and introducing a healthier menu. While this served to prove that Spurlock's efforts had had an impact, it also certified, by the critic himself, that McDonald's had changed for the better. In a sense, this neutralized the film's message for the future.

Of course, many laughed at McDonald's efforts. But most of these were the same people who were already against the brand before the film. McDonald's correctly recognized that its brand did not need to win over all of its critics, only the ones who were undecided.

While the entire health issue has not gone away, the Spurlock incident has brought a lot of positive change and improvement to the brand, even winning over Michelle Obama, when in July 2011, it announced it would shrink the portion of fries and offer a side of fruit or vegetable with its Happy Meals.[5] In an appeal to the nutrition conscious parent, its current website touts, "It started with you. Moms and dads are trying hard to get their kids to be more nutrition-minded. We listened. That's why our popular Happy Meals will have fewer calories and include a side of fruit. It's why our Chicken McNuggets now have less sodium. And why our national communications to kids will champion their well-being."[6] Today McDonald's is viewed as more in tune with societal trends and values than it was before the movie was released.

How McDonald's Bounced Back

McDonald's got millions around the globe to start "Lovin' it" again by turning a highly publicized brand hit into an opportunity to be a better fit with the changing demands of hungry consumers. It accomplished this by doing these things:

- *Retooling its product.* In May 2011, McDonald's continued to adjust to consumer tastes as it debuted its healthy menu "Made Just for You" platform. McCafé beverages, chicken-based options, and salads have all been placed under the "Made Just for You" banner. McDonald's has also used the First Taste Event in New York City to announce the addition of two new "Made Just for You" items: the Mango Pineapple Real Fruit Smoothie and the Asian Salad. McDonald's development team says the company is actively balancing flavor with the healthy attributes of each new menu item, exhibiting a more adult-focused strategy.

- *Reinventing the experience.* McDonald's Corp. is ramping up the remodeling of its 14,000 U.S. restaurants to make them cozier destinations. Spending more than $1 billion, the corporation expects about 600 restaurants to get a face-lift this year. The fast-food giant is changing the way its restaurants look inside and out so that customers will see them as a place where they can linger longer and, therefore, spend more money. The remodeled restaurants will replace bright reds and yellows with subtle colors and will feature flat-screen TVs, lounge chairs, and electric fireplaces. The chain is also adding free Wi-Fi in most of its U.S. restaurants.

Improvement Awareness Campaign

McDonald's knows that continually improving the brand is not enough; the market needs to be aware of the brand's progress. In addition to traditional media, which McDonald's continues to keep fresh and well segmented into diverse markets, the brand has been an active player in the new social media environments. In fact, it was named in the top three of restaurant brands by Social Media Index, a division of software firm Vitrue, Inc. The ranking is based on the number of mentions on social networking sites like Twitter and Facebook, photo-sharing sites like Flickr, check-ins on location-based services, and inclusion on blogs.

In 2010, when McDonald's named Rick Wion its first-ever director of social media, he knew his marching orders were threefold. He needed to build the business, manage customer problems, and beef up outreach to target groups such as mom bloggers.

McDonald's is considered a fun and social brand, so it is no surprise that social media efforts have taken on an important marketing, communication, customer satisfaction, and turnaround role for the brand. The success in humanizing the brand and keeping customers informed of brand improvements is the result of these things:

- Monitoring the new social channels for over a year before they jumped in to participate and actively listened before they spoke
- Scheduling a diverse team to serve the social programs (The team includes PR, customer service, and product development people who can address different areas of the brand. This also allows them to build subpersonalities—for example, competent, exciting, child friendly, nutritious, good value—online.)
- Recognizing that tools and applications are evolving every day and their efforts need to stay fluid and open to new ways of doing things

Times Change: Don't Stand Still

Nostalgia is sound strategy for many brands. Comfort foods and household products like Uncle Ben's rice or Arm & Hammer Baking Soda are great examples of brands that depend on brand loyalty to keep growing with generations of consumers. Today, popular brands like Nike and Adidas have launched highly successful retro-designed shoes, which tap into a history of style and winners.

These nostalgic brand offerings take consumers back in time to a place filled with good memories and sentimental experiences. Fifty or sixty years after they first appeared, these brands are able to transfer legacy identities into trust, and they make classic cool and retro hip. When this phenomenon works, it's powerful, but there is a fine line between leveraging the past and being stuck in time, like a tacky, light-blue leisure suit.

The brands just mentioned operate in narrow categories: food and sporting apparel. Their retro products are specific to their category. And, for that reason, it works. However, brands that span many categories such as department stores can't afford to stand still; they've got be current and moving ahead of the next big thing.

While legacy brand attributes are important and have appeal, the world is quickly changing, and to stay relevant, a brand needs to keep pace, especially if a core segment of its market is aging and may be moving on to other products. Beauty and lifestyle brands are two current examples of this trend. Trends come and go, technologies and innovations redefine careers and family roles, and social values change. The British retailer Marks & Spencer is a lesson on how a legacy brand on top for decades took a big dip because it didn't keep up with change.

The Marks & Spencer Brand Turnaround Story

Marks & Spencer (M&S)—colloquially known as M&S, Marks and Sparks, and Marks—is a British brand with a rich and regal history of dressing and feeding customers worldwide for more than 125 years.

The company was founded by a partnership between Michael Marks, a refugee who came to England from Poland to escape anti-Jewish repression,[7] and Thomas Spencer, a cashier from Yorkshire. On Marks's arrival in England, he worked for a company in Leeds, West Yorkshire that employed refugees. In 1884, he met Isaac Dewhurst, the owner of a Leeds warehouse, who inspired him to open his own stall in Kirkgate Market in Leeds. In 1894, Thomas Spencer, a friend of Dewhurst's, invested in Marks's business. They opened their first store, in partnership, in Manchester.

They called their new stores Penny Bazaar, and in addition to the catchy name, they added the words "admission free" to encourage customers to browse without any obligation to buy. While this is the norm now, it was unheard of then. By the turn of the century, Marks and Spencer's business rapidly grew by acquiring other small markets, and soon it was Britain's homegrown retail empire, selling clothing, food, and housewares. Both founders died before the 1920s, and, after a legal battle, Michael Marks's son, Simon, gained control of the company.

By the early twentieth century, Marks & Spencer became a national institution. It was unapologetically British, symbolizing quality, and as much a British icon as polo matches and scones and cream.

Marks & Spencer was also known as a business innovator. It was the first retailer to open its own scientific research laboratory to develop and test new fabrics. Soon the company opened Marks & Spencer's café bars, which offered low-cost food service; over time, these cafés evolved into cafeterias, another progressive idea. In 1959, Marks & Spencer became the first retailer to introduce a no-smoking rule, and, in 1961 it banned dogs—unusual in Europe—with the exception of guide dogs. And, in 1970, it introduced the first food "sell-by" date labeling system to ensure freshness.

In the early years, M&S pioneered some unique business practices. It sold only British-made goods, under its private label St Michael; had a no-quibble refund policy and accepted any return, no matter when the item was purchased; had no fitting rooms (it does now); did not accept credit cards (it now does); and remained closed on Sundays (it is now open that day)—all of which, at the time, added to the distinctiveness of its brand.

The 1980s were a very profitable period for Marks & Spencer. In 1986, it introduced a furniture department into its stores, and, in 1988, it became the first British retailer to make a pretax profit of £1 billion. It also opened a flagship store in Hong Kong. In 1999, the company launched its website, offering online shopping 24 hours a day, 7 days a week (24/7) and a number of new private label brands of clothing.

Marks & Spencer was a beloved brand that the British were proud of and other countries enthusiastically supported. By the 1980s, it had expanded to new service categories (e.g., a finance division), opened stores in other countries, and was evolving its brand to appeal less to a traditional, middle-class consumer who wanted high value for the price and more to one who was modern, upscale, and fashion-minded.

Fast-forward to the new millennium: after almost 115 years of strong customer loyalty, shareholder success, and £1 billion profits, in 1999 sales started to plunge dramatically—more than 40 percent in one year. In 2001, the iconic retailer reported record declines and a mere £145 million profit.

The Marks & Spencer brand was hit hard as a result of changing customer preferences and expectations about choice, style, and services. During this period, M&S was commonly described as old-fashioned, overpriced, boring, and drab.

The next few years brought major changes to the Marks & Spencer culture and operations with new leadership, new products, a younger, hipper attitude, and a fresh brand identity.

After struggling for almost a decade, Marks & Spencer is back in its glory. It has more than 21 million people visiting its stores each week; sales figures are up; expansion is back on track; and, most of all, there is a revived admiration for the brand. New generations are discovering relevance in product offering and experience, and mature customers are coming back to what had once been their favorite store.

How Marks & Spencer Bounced Back

Here are some of the strategies the company employed:

- *It simplified things.* In the late 1990s, the private label St Michael brand was discontinued in favor of Marks & Spencer. The company shuttered money-losing stores in Europe, and it spun off or sold poor performers like clothing retailer Brooks Brothers and Kings Super Markets Inc.
- *It brought in fresh minds.* A younger, hipper management team replaced many senior managers as well as board members, whose long tenure incited comparisons to the British civil service.

- *It broke tradition.* After 125 years of doing things one way, it changed many policies—for example, credit cards would be accepted and stores would be open on Sundays—and added the kind of goods its customers wanted, more than 400 outside brands.
- *It gave itself a visual makeover.* From the logo ("Your M&S") to its ads, from its website to its store design and interiors and the type of in-store promotions it held, everything was reinvented to make M&S appear fresh, modern, and energized.
- *It aligned with other fashion notables.* High-profile celebrities helped bring the new brand to the market. Ads and TV spots included Twiggy (who first appeared in 1967, returning later in 1995 and 2005), David Jason, Erin O'Connor, David Beckham, Antonio Banderas, and Claudia Schiffer.
- *Even its food marketing was given a sexy edge.* Its "This is not just food, this is M&S food" campaign created a stir from fans. The spots feature slow-motion, close-up footage of various food products, described by Dervla Kirwan in a sultry voiceover of various enticing instrumental songs—most notably Fleetwood Mac's "Albatross." Some critics called it "food porn."
- *It made sustainability a new important value.* To demonstrate it is a good steward of the planet Earth, Marks & Spencer launched "Plan A," a five-year, 100-commitment ecological plan, with the goal of becoming the world's most sustainable major retailer. To accomplish this, the company is working with customers, suppliers, and employees to combat climate change, reduce waste, use sustainable raw materials, trade ethically, and help everyone lead healthier lifestyles.
- *It began collaborating.* For years Marks & Spencer had the reputation of being a big brand, one that was bureaucratic and ignored its customers' desires (a kind of M&S-knows-best attitude). Although the crisis years were tough, many believe that without that alarm bell, M&S would not have changed. Among other operational initiatives

in 2009 M&S got very serious about better collaboration with customers and employees in an effort to improve ideas, obtain feedback, and understand its customers and employees' complaints and how to respond to them.

If There's a Problem, Fix It

In the old days, criticism of brands was controlled or limited by the critics' resources. If a critic didn't have a PR force or money to buy advertising, its antibrand views often went unheard and unnoticed, saving many brands from high-profile public attacks and potential brand hits.

Social media has changed the playing field, which both helps and hinders many brands. The easy-entry, low-cost, high-volume, and viral nature of social media can put a bright spotlight on an issue quickly and with little cost. Consumer brands have been pummeled in social media attacks; for example, Pampers was, for allegedly causing diaper rash. So have business brands, like Dell, which saw its customer service operation hung out to dry by a blogger. These companies have felt the ramifications of this new communication environment on their brands.

In the early days of social media, when the user base was small and limited to early adopters, brands often sat on the sidelines watching, convinced that these voices represented a small group and therefore were not a problem. That may have been the case then, but today such a posting can be a serious challenge. Not only is it low cost and fast to post antibrand opinions, but with time these opinions and posts grow like weeds, getting indexed by search engines and ultimately building a war chest full of content that can be picked up by the media and seen easily by millions around the world. Unless brands are looking to retire early, these waves of antibrand sentiment cannot be ignored.

Let's take a look at how one specialty chemical company handled this problem.

Albemarle Corporation Brand Turnaround

In the late 1990s, global environmental advocacy groups started waging a heavy attack on chemical companies over the safety and sustainability of their products. Broadcast news, editorials, and online media put a lot of heat on the industry as a whole as well as on specific companies.

This pounding hit many legacy products that consumers used daily. One category that came under attack was fire and flame retardants, which are found in consumer products like electronics, furniture, and automobiles. They have saved millions of lives and protect property. The Albemarle Corporation, a specialty chemicals maker and leading provider of flame-retardants, was one of the companies targeted. Albemarle has been around for more than 100 years, pioneering and bringing to market a range of products that address a variety of consumer and business needs.

The company invests millions in safety research and development, and while it believes its products are safe and that fire safety remains a global priority, it also realizes that societal and business values toward protecting the environment have heightened. It knows that negative public opinion can damage years of earned goodwill and product acceptance in the marketplace.

Rather than digging in its heels and fight the public backlash, Albemarle set out to develop new and improved products at the same time as it worked to better communications with environmental groups, soccer moms, and the industry. In 2011, it launched a companywide green alternative brand called Earthwise. The eco-initiative is demonstrating the shared interests of sustainability and safety. Through new technologies, educational, and advocacy efforts, it hopes to change perceptions and offer consumers and businesses many more eco-friendly choices.

The new environmental technology and improvement initiative has been well received. The company is posting record earnings, and growth in flame retardants continues to be one of its strongest business units. To support the new face and reinvention of fire safety solutions as a greener alternative, the company has invested significantly in internal communications, as employee knowledge and a culture of sustainability are key to introducing a changed product, social media, online education, and advocacy programs, all of which are new to the chemical industry.

Rethink How You Think

In all of the brand turnarounds in the chapter, clear, constant change and improvement has been a must. Several of the brands that experienced some of the hardest meltdowns were those that blindly focused on the bottom line and reducing costs while the customer was neglected and their changing needs ignored.

Whether yours is a megacompany or a small business, there are many ways you can improve and reinvent your brand and move it toward recovery. To get your innovative juices flowing, here are 15 questions to get you started:

1. How has my market evolved?
2. What are my customers' new values: the environment, safety, privacy, something else?
3. How do my customers align with my core brand essence?
4. What are their new needs, desires, and sweet spots?
5. What can be dropped from my brand so that other aspects can stand out better?
6. Have I set up the right conversation and collaboration channels to take in new ideas from customers, employees, and vendors?
7. Is the tradition in my brand nostalgic or really just out of date?
8. What can be recycled or refreshed?
9. How does sustainability fit in?
10. Are there opportunities for niche market segmentation brand extensions?
11. If resources are no object, what problem can I solve?

Once you spot improvement platforms, ask yourself:

12. How will I package and deliver this?
13. How can I make it even more distinct?
14. How can I best take this message to the market?
15. How will I know it is working?

Turnaround Takeaways

The world does not stop changing, and brands need to keep on improving. Meaningful rethinking, recycling, and reinventing take doing these things:

- When you see a red flag, take action; you may not have a second chance.
- Bring in outside noncategory or industry experts to lead.
- Don't be married to any idea, product, or service.
- Focus on scalable improvements.
- Concentrate on doing less, and doing it better.
- Don't hide from critics; learn from them.
- Don't be afraid of failure.
- Be willing to kill traditions.
- Be aware that *visibility* of improvements is just as important as the improvement.
- Leverage new and social media for communication and research.

Chapter 9

Game Changer 6: Build Equity

I t's raining brand bombs. In spring 2011, the head of the International Monetary Fund (IMF) and, until then, potential candidate for president of France, Dominique Strauss-Kahn, faced multiple charges resulting from an alleged sexual assault on an employee at a New York City hotel. The city prosecutor later dropped the charges, but his brand certainly got a little dinged up. Also, Arnold Schwarzenegger was revealed to have had a love child, and Rupert Murdoch's British tabloid, the *News of the World* closes after a phone-hacking scandal returned to the news.

Ouch. And what's most intriguing about these falls from grace is that they potentially affect not only the three brands at the center of each scandal but also many other people and brands, including Strauss-Kahn's political party, Schwarzenegger's next movie franchise, and the investors in Murdoch's next business deal.

Brands, whether commercial, nonprofit, or individual, frequently find themselves in the doghouse. They mess up, hang out with the wrong company, or sometimes simply fall victim to bad luck.

Is there a lifesaver that can save and turnaround these latest brand disasters? It's too soon to tell. Just as the verdict is still out on the long-term impact of Tiger Woods's sexual indiscretions; Lindsay Lohan's bouts with the law, the result of drug and alcohol-related problems; AIG's financial meltdown, caused by the 2008 collapse of the housing market, which led to losses in the credit default swaps—a type of insurance policy—it issued to large mortgage holders; Sony PlayStation's data hack, caused by a security breach that left the network down for days; Mel Gibson's volatile temper, alleged domestic abuse, alcohol abuse, and instances of hate speech toward a number of groups; and charges that Avon bribed foreign officials. If history is any indicator, and if these brands follow the course of many of their predecessors, there is hope. If they've done their jobs right to begin with and have relentlessly built up their brands' equity long before they needed it, they have a leg up. And, of course, maintaining the brand from there on is crucial.

Brand equity accrues over time and is the result of marketing, communication, and experiences associated with a brand name. If you look at the greatest brand turnarounds—and we've examined some of them here—you will notice a common commitment to growing the brands' equity. They do this by optimizing connectivity, consistency, and transparency. They make sure they do these things:

- Converse, engage, and build trust with all constituents, customers, employees, and partners
- Deliver on their promises
- Are authentic
- Stay in the front of consumers' minds with consistent messaging
- Have an open and honest dialogue with all stakeholders in good times and in bad

With the advent of new online media and social networking, in more recent brand turnarounds, you will also see the increased value of—and need for making—digital friends and fans, and for maintaining strong relationships long before a brand bump comes along.

Consider Bill Clinton. His situation when he was U.S. president was at least somewhat comparable to Arnold Schwarzenegger's. Clinton made some very bad judgments and they became very public. Yet today, he has certainly become a strong brand again. In fact, in an early 2011 *Wall Street Journal/ NBC News* poll, Clinton is the most popular politician in the world—55 percent of the people polled held positive opinions of the former president.

Thus far, we have looked at many brands that stumbled and tumbled and then came back. Now, we'll explore just how brands relentlessly build and store brand equity, and the critical role that has played in their turnarounds.

Why Brand Equity Matters

Brand equity is a social and emotional currency.

For some, it's an important line item on a balance sheet before a proposed acquisition or sale. For others, such as large public companies, it can represent a formula component in the highly publicized "Best Global Brand Report," an annual value assessment by Interbrand, a leading brand consulting firm. For all brands, no matter their size or type, brand equity is the net balance of positive worth and value versus negative behavior and risk.

Brand equity can also be a badge of honor a brand earns from doing good deeds, behaving likeably, and creating a notable public profile through social media buzz, publicity, advertising, and word of mouth. No matter how it's built, brand equity comes directly from consumers' opinions: from their satisfaction with the product and/or experience, awareness level, positive associations with popular values, and familarity with the brand's distinctive attributes.

Having brand equity is like having cash in the bank that a brand can save and spend if and when a storm hits. However, it's important to remember to make deposits in all channels—one savings account in one bank won't be sufficient.

Building brand equity through sound brand management and communications as we once knew it is so passé. The days of buying your way into the hearts and minds of the market are last decade, at best, and the concept that you can control every piece of information is pure fantasy. Today, brands that successfully turn around do so because they have mastered the art and science of listening, learning, and leveraging relationships and insight to acquire more mental brand assets (social capital and emotional stock) than liabilities (mishandled situations and armies of critics).

Brand Equity Can Serve as Psychological Fuel

When trouble strikes, brand equity propels a brand quickly past its misstep even before the public finishes reading the news article about the incident.

For example, in early 2011, a Southwest Airlines plane was forced to make an emergency landing because a three-foot hole tore open its fuselage. A few days after the incident, Southwest—one of the most beloved brands in America with a "skyful" of brand equity—announced that it was grounding 81 planes for inspection. While this was not Southwest's first incident—in 2009, the carrier was fined more than $7 million for maintenance violations—Southwest did not experience any great customer defection or see its business plummet. The brand had built up enough equity to handle such hits.

Similarly, Nike, one of America's most iconic brands, has taken many brand-shaking shots, but it just keeps jogging forward. In Nike's case, its brand creation myth is an important part of its power. Founded by Bill Bowerman, University of Oregon track coach, and Philip Knight, CEO of Blue Ribbon Sports, in 1964, the company became Nike Inc. in 1978.

Nike understood the importance of brand equity from the start. In 1971, Blue Ribbon Sports began using the Nike "swoosh" to differentiate its product, and the company registered the mark in 1974. Through a combination of technological innovation and partnering with professional athletes, Nike claimed around 50 percent of the athletic shoe market in 1980. In 1985, the brand would launch its most successful partnership of all time with the Michael Jordan "Air Jordan" shoe. In 1988, Nike told America to "Just Do It," which became one of the most legendary taglines of all time. Today, Nike's robust legacy has become a world unto itself—Nike dominates that many athletic and apparel categories. The brand not only markets new, technologically advanced products (such as the Nike + iPod shoes, which measure one's workout progress in terms of distance and pace), but also deftly manages a nostalgia market for new, though retro-designed, Dunk shoes.

The Nike brand for all of its successes has also had its share of challenges. During the 1990s, Nike's use of child labor in Pakistan and Cambodia came under fire. Protests from student groups followed. Although Nike admitted that they "blew it," they insisted that they had only done so inadvertently. [1]

In 1997, a *New York Times* report on labor conditions in Nike's factories in Vietnam exposed oppressive working conditions and the presence of harmful materials.[2] Nike swiftly responded. Phil Knight committed to joining the Fair Labor Association and to enacting air quality tests in its factories to meet standards of the Occupational Safety and Health Administration (OSHA). In May 1998, Nike raised the minimum age of its footwear factory workers to 18.[3] While this was a victory for labor rights, it was also a brand victory for Nike as headlines across the nation noted the brand's caring move. A *New York Times* headline read "Nike Pledges to End Child Labor and Apply U.S. Rules Abroad."[4]

In a 1998 address to the National Press Club, Knight openly acknowledged Nike's guilt, and committed to doing better, saying, "It has been said that Nike has single-handedly lowered the human-rights standards for the sole purpose of maximizing profits. . . . The Nike product has become synonymous with slave wages, forced overtime and arbitrary abuse. I truly believe that the American consumer does not want to buy products made in abusive conditions."[5] Since these incidents, Nike has offered to open all of its factories to inspection, as long as competitors do the same. The brand has received praise from labor rights groups for the offer.

Nike handled the criticism well; however, this issue will likely be an ongoing challenge for the company. But as with Southwest Airlines, does the average consumer (whose closets, cars, and lockers are filled with Nike products) defect over this kind of news and start buying another brand? Did sales and market share plummet after these reports?

Despite these brand bumps, Nike's annual revenues have increased from $6.4 billion in 1996 to nearly $19 billion in 2010, according to the company's annual reports.

Brand Equity Can Serve as a Teflon Shield

Brand equity can repel brand hits and sometimes make it seem as if they never happened; in a worst-case scenario, there may be minor dings.

Ronald Reagan earned the sobriquet, the "Teflon President," because the staff scandals that surrounded him had no effect on the president's popularity. Had the nickname not already been used, President Clinton would surely have been given it. Charges and character dings just would not stick to him. For this reason, he earned the title "Comeback Kid," even as he campaigned for the presidency the first time around. Clinton was an equity builder from his earliest days. He seemed naturally endowed with intangible assets that many brands could learn from, among them:

- *Charismatic communications and collaborative leadership style.* These made him a magnet for followers and constituents.
- *Political skills as ambassador, coalition builder, and confident leader.* These served to attract a cross-section of admirers and fans, even among those who did not agree with his positions.
- *Ability to build and maintain high-profile bipartisan relationships.* One of Clinton's keys has always been his ability to straddle separate, otherwise uncooperative groups.

Much to people's surprise, after Clinton's impeachment, his brand just got stronger, and, after he left office, his commitment to being a philanthropic leader, heading up global relief and charitable projects around the world, and his involvement in issues of public concern have all further enhanced his brand.

The Source of Brand Equity

Brand equity stems from advocacy, admiration, and credibility forces, all of which might be summarized as a brand's *fan base and history*. How much equity a brand has can be judged by the number of years a brand has been in the marketplace with a solid and honorable reputation, and these things:

- The number of loyal fans, friends, and supporters a brand has
- The level of their passion and conviction toward the brand
- The volume of their voices
- The power of their connections
- Their willingness to refer others to the brand
- The demonstrated willingness of fans, friends, and supporters to buy what you are selling—your product, your message, or your cause, now and in the future

Having brand equity boils down to this: at the moment of choice between buying a brand, doing business with it, or jumping on the band-wagon for a cause, does the cumulative amount of public admiration, respect, loyalty, and perceived value of the brand sway the scale to "Yes, I'm with you," or in the case of a troubled brand, does it lead the public to say, "I'll give you the benefit of the doubt"?

Think of brand equity as your growing principal on a piece of property. You make payments by doing good, being honest, and delivering on your promises. You reduce your value and equity by withdrawing capital to cover costly mistakes or to compensate for not showing up at all.

When a brand has a strong supply of equity, consumers are often more forgiving of mistakes, bad behavior, and shortcomings. Brand followers and supporters grasp onto the positive perceptions they've had about a brand and often quickly forget (or, at least forgive) a misstep.

Pitfalls and Opportunities

Before we delve into what has worked to build brand equity or how brand equity has helped specific brands turnaround, let's take a quick look at six things brands must keep in mind as they strive to build equity. The state of the branding environment is complex and poses many new challenges for brands, but that same complicated maze of messaging is filled with great opportunities for turnaround brands that need to protect and build brand equity. Here are a few:

1. *Message noise and overload.* J. Walker Smith, executive chairman of The Futures Company, told *USA Today* in 2005 that consumers encounter from 3,500 to 5,000 marketing messages per day versus 500 to 2,000 in the 1970s. No doubt that number has grown substantially since then; just this morning my inbox had more than 1,000 e-mails with banner ads, branded signatures, and other marketing noise.

   The flip side of all the noise and clutter is that consumers and the media welcome comeback kids, new products, and innovations that can benefit them. If a brand returns and has solid intrigue from a new or improved offering, a dose of humility, and newsworthy elements, it can break through. Does your brand have what it takes to break through all this clutter?

2. *Shrinking attention spans.* "It used to be that the most valuable thing on the planet was time, and now the most valuable thing on the planet is attention,"[6] says John Greening, associate professor at Northwestern University's journalism school and a former executive vice president at ad agency DDB Chicago. In his study of America's attention span and TV commercials, Greening concluded that attention spans are shrinking but marketers are adjusting. A 15-second ad is more common today than a 30- or 60-second spot was a few decades ago. Nielsen

research agrees; advertisers used almost 5.5 million 15-second TV commercials in 2009, a 70 percent jump in five years.

While all brands, whether or not in turnaround, don't use TV to build their story, this trend toward a limited attention span is important for anyone with a message to note because it implies two things: (1) your messaging has to be direct and concise, and (2) consumers also have short memory spans. Can your message be boiled down to one sentence?

3. *Millions of voices and channels.* No matter how you do the math, the number of public voices, opinions, and news sources has gone through the stratosphere. Combine online, print, broadcast, word of mouth, and social networks, and the volume and reach are endless. Not many can afford to—or should—invest in every outlet. That would result in a lot of wasted messaging, talking to markets who don't give a darn about your brand. Brand leaders that build equity well focus on the biggest rivers—the outlets that touch the largest population of their target markets—and they don't expend time, money, or energy on outlets that are small or irrelevant creeks.

To achieve brand equity, a brand has to connect with the largest *targeted* channels. Do your branded messages connect and leverage the most relevant outreach channels?

4. *The viral effect.* Just like a bad strain of the flu, the viral effect is a normal condition in today's branding environments. On the Internet, by word of mouth, and even through traditional media channels, what starts as a rumor, piece of content, a video, or an image quickly finds itself *everywhere*. The viral effect can be the brass ring for brands seeking awareness. In 2008, Justin Bieber's mom posted videos of Bieber singing at a local competition on YouTube. Soon Atlanta-based talent manager Scott Samuel "Scooter" Braun discovered him, and a brand was born. It has been reported that as of 2011, Bieber is worth more than $100 million. In May 2011, his video "Baby" held the all-time number-one spot on YouTube, with over 500 million views.

The viral effect can also be a brand's biggest nightmare—for example, when brand kamikazes fire off malicious or brand-degrading messages and suddenly millions of people are exposed to it. Many high-profile brands have experienced the downside of the viral effect, including

- Apple ("iPod's Dirty Secret"), where two young filmmakers posted a video on their personal website—and later on YouTube—airing their frustrations with Apple when it was slow to respond to a battery issue
- Domino's Pizza ("Boogergate"), the stomach-turning YouTube video showing employees tampering with the food
- Sony's alleged service and product decline became a viral sensation when a customer produced and posted a song parody called "How to Kill a Brand" (Xbox 360) based on The Fray's hit "How to Save a Life."

Each was viewed by millions 'round the world. Brands seeking more equity need to monitor and tap into viral strategies. Are your branded messages ready to travel on the fast track?

5. *Permanence of online content.* Today what goes online stays online for many years. (Forever?) This means the content, images, text, and video you and others post may live beyond you and your brand. The good news is that with smart content optimization you can add to your brand's visibility daily and build a lasting footprint. The downside is that if your brand gets shaken and you don't handle the situation right, that sad story can linger for decades. *Sometimes* inaccurate postings will be removed, if you request it.

   To achieve brand equity, brands must regularly monitor and leverage content surrounding their brands and related topics. Have you established means to monitor your brand online? And are you taking full advantage of content permanence through search engine optimization strategies?

6. *Appetite for sensation, high drama, and controversy.* What bleeds leads in many news and information outlets, both online and offline. Con-

sumers love scandals, and the media loves it when consumers want to see it on their broadcast and print properties.

To achieve brand equity, brands must be prepared and armed to respond to publicized brand bumps and events. Are you ready for TV cameras and photographers swarming like pests at your offices after a brand bump?

Given these factors, to formulate your turnaround and build more brand equity through connectivity, consistency, and transparency, you must remain vigilant.

Turnaround Equity-Building Framework

Here are some strategies to get your turnaround going:

1. *Monitor the situation carefully and often.* Make use of free tools such as Google Alerts, in order to follow coverage and posts on any subject. Also, set up topic watch searches with utilities in social media networks. For instance, Twitter lets you set up custom subject searches and will track activity on any keyword. There are many paid services that provide more filter results (see the Resources at the end of the book).

2. *Develop a strategy for responding to bumps:*
   - Your tone—Will you play offence or defense or just lay low?
   - Your story—Do you have a detailed version, a very boiled down one of only a couple of sentences, and a one- or two-word version that encapsulates it?
   - Your symbols—Are logos and graphic marks and your style of photography and type treatment consistent? Do they reflect the identity of the brand?
   - Your voices—Who are the messengers? Many brands include a team that includes the CEO and subject brand ambassadors.
   - Your road map and schedule—Where will you be, and when?

3. *Know how you will showcase your brand:*
   - Find the highest-traffic social avenues.
   - Repurpose the strongest shows and stories (content, messages, and events).
   - Leverage offline and online venues together to make for a stronger army.
   - Get help from friends, vendors, and industry advocates.

Brand equity has propelled many brand turnarounds, and many of those brands have gone on to build even greater equity through connectivity, transparency, and consistency.

Connecting to Your Customer through Engagement and Dialogue

The importance of listening to your customers—and learning from them—is a truism, and it's never truer than when your brand is in trouble. The next turnaround is an example of how listening to and having conversations with both loyal customers and critics has had a positive impact on the brand.

Pampers Brand Turnaround Story

Since 1961 Pampers diapers and its related baby products have been part of the Procter & Gamble Company (P&G). Pampers leads the disposable diaper category, which is just a slice of Pampers' brand. Disposable diaper sales are projected to reach $26.6 billion by 2012. Pampers spent a total of $41.4 million on advertising in 2009. In recent years Pampers has expanded its core brand from absorbent offerings to a full range of baby development products. This increase in scope adds to the brand's equity as more products are developed, marketed, and consumed. Pampers enjoys a 40-plus-year history, strong name recognition, and a community of loyal customers. It has built a reputation of innovation starting with the first disposable diaper to eliminating safety pins to its latest technology that reduces bulk, is more absorbent, and is more environmentally sustainable.

In March 2010, Pampers launched the Dry Max line, an upgrade of its Cruisers and Swaddlers products. Pampers hailed it as the biggest innovation in 25 years: by incorporating the absorbent material directly into the diaper rather than suspending it in a pulpy mass, the diapers were 20 percent thinner and, according to Pampers, the "driest diaper ever."

By April, parents started complaining that the diapers were causing severe diaper rash. One mother who contacted the company and was dissatisfied with its response launched a Facebook page that garnered 11,000 friends by May. More Facebook pages launched. Parenting websites and chat rooms also went wild with moms who used loaded language such as "chemical burns," "wounds," "sores," and "blood" to recount Dry Max "horror" stories. [7]

Forbes's Trevor Butterworth aptly described the situation: "some who were unhappy with the change took to Facebook to protest the new design, and once the idea the diapers caused 'chemical burns' was put into play, people began to report seeing chemical burns. And then the media started to report the reports of chemical burns."[8]

In May of that year, two class action lawsuits were filed against P&G, and the Consumer Product Safety Commission (CPSC) and Health Canada announced they were launching an investigation into Dry Max. Several dozen Dry Max Pampers lawsuits have been filed against Procter & Gamble over the problems. All federal complaints have been consolidated in the U.S. District Court in Cincinnati and are pending resolution.

On May 6, P&G issued a news release in which Jodi Allen, vice president for Pampers, said, "To date, there have been in excess of two billion diaper changes using the new product, with only a handful of rash complaints, none of which were shown to be caused by the type of materials in our product. In fact, we have received fewer than two complaints about diaper rash for every one million diapers sold, which is average for our business. The majority of our consumers are telling us that they prefer the Dry Max product over the ones it replaced because it is 20% thinner than before."[9]

On May 20, in a stepped-up counteroffensive concerning Pampers Dry Max diapers, Procter & Gamble flew mommy bloggers from around the country to Cincinnati where it hosted an event to answer questions and took its guests on a tour of the company. P&G even brought back the same, trusted, now-retired company scientist who, three decades earlier, had disproved rumors that P&G's Bounce fabric softener sheets caused clothes dryers to catch fire. It also "diverted 40 to 50 employees to marketing and research duties on Dry Max full time, extended its Pampers phone line from five to seven days a week, and consulted with more than a dozen outside experts."[10]

In June, the company launched an "early and often" advertising strategy to deflect negative attention, which included increased Internet advertising expenditures and issuing more coupons for Dry Max diapers. By July, Pampers had lost about 3 percentage points of diaper market share in the United States to Kimberly-Clark.

Internal review of the Dry Max launch identified lack of transparency as the trigger for the negative onslaught. Because of distribution issues, Dry Max was available in certain markets prior to the official launch, and instead of using new packaging in these markets, Pampers simply put the new diapers in the old packaging, which caused suspicious moms to start blogging about it.

On September 2, the CPSC and Health Canada announced that "they have found no cause linking Pampers Dry Max diapers and reports of diaper rash and other skin conditions."[11]

Despite investigations by the U.S. Consumer Product Safety Commission and parents' complaints about diaper rash via outraged mommy bloggers and Facebookers, the *Wall Street Journal* reported that Pampers Dry Max had increased market share. Sanford Bernstein analyst Ali Dibadj, cited by the *Journal*, commented that the brand "does not seem to be suffering from this public relations threat, so far."[12]

Pampers brand rebounded because of its predebacle brand equity and its follow-on initiatives, which included these things:

- *Remaining confident in the storm.* There is no question that the negative publicity and social media buzz about Dry Max was real. Pampers took the situation seriously, but it also knew that it had done the research and testing and had a product that met its brand's standards for quality and safety.

- *Increasing its response team.* When the negative rumbling about the new diaper designs started, Pampers bumped up its response team in order to listen to the feedback, move forward, and keep its loyal base informed of the latest related developments.

- *Reaching out and holding a dialogue.* The brand responded to media inquiries with interviews and by sharing testing results and the research that went into the new product. The communications team along with Jodi Allen, vice president for Pampers, contacted the unhappy bloggers, listened to their concerns, and answered their questions.

- *Finding the misstep and apologizing for it.* Pampers was surprised that the new product in the old packaging caused the backlash it did. It noted in several interviews that putting an improved product in older packaging is standard practice in the industry. It will definitely know better next time. However, once it got engaged in the online conversations, it used the social voices of its loyal brand ambassadors and mommy bloggers, in addition to its representatives' apologies, to soften some of the burn.

- *Continuing to build brand equity.* Following the social media brouhaha and associated bad publicity, Pampers continued its efforts to stay connected and grow its fan base. Its website Pampers Village, which launched three years prior to the incident, is robust with helpful content for parenting; its blogs and forums are updated regularly with advice from its team of medical, science, and parent advisors; nonprofit partners like UNICEF and their own social media programs— boasting over 700,000 fans on Facebook alone—are abuzz with conversation and brand admiration.

Lessons Learned

The Dry Max brand bump can teach all brands a bit about the complex new world of social media and how a few unhappy customers can quickly pour gasoline on a small, contained fire and ignite a huge blaze. The proportion of unhappy people posting negative messages was actually a microdot of the total customer base. All brands and improved products will have critics. That being said, brands cannot underestimate the noise and media attention that can come from even an isolated group.

When the new and improved product was shipped in old packaging, transparency was low. Letting consumers know about any changes in advance would have made the relationship more open and might have prevented some of the hostility and complaints. Fortunately, the Pampers brand had the goodwill of millions of parents who have trusted the name for years, were ready to support the new technology, and remained loyal.

Transparency: The New Trust

There has been a lot of talk about transparency ever since online and social media began emerging as such important, impactful channels for brands. Transparency adds to the trust consumers have with a brand, which translates to brand equity, as every strong relationship contributes to the public's admiration and bond with a brand.

Lack of transparency can turn into a major brand bump, as it gives consumers a reason to publicly punish the brand for what is deemed to be careless, deceptive, and inconsiderate behavior. Whether it's the Pampers ordeal, or Wal-Mart enlisting a team of paid bloggers to comment on products, or brands that offer rebates that contain so many provisions that the chance of actually getting one in this lifetime is next to none, the impact on consumers when discovered can devastate a brand. Consumers feel—correctly in some cases, incorrectly in others—that the brand is trying to pull something over on them, is being dishonest, is trying to hide something, or is being greedy. Sometimes they feel a combination of these things.

Brands in a turnaround position need to weave transparency into all parts of their culture and marketing. All brands can score points with consumers by practicing these things:

- *Full disclosure.* Paying bloggers, celebrities, and expert advisors to make recommendations needs to be disclosed.
- *Truth in labeling.* A brand's labels need to be honest and explicit about the product's ingredients, where it is manufactured, its nutritional data, potential side effects and risks, and so on. All the facts need to be clearly presented.
- *Using disclaimers openly.* Whether the disclaimer is for a brand's contest rules, policies and procedures, or for health warnings, it should be readable (not in 2-point type size) and easy to understand.
- *Truth in advertising.* When dishonest claims, misleading communications, and incomplete disclosures are made, the brand is asking for trouble. For example, in spring 2011, the *Wall Street Journal* reported that US Airways and Continental were fined more than $160,000 by the Department of Transportation for failing to include fuel surcharges in ticket prices on their websites.[13]
- *Owning up to mistakes.* Consumers are forgiving and understand that the people who represent brands are human and can make mistakes. What is not forgiven is when brands won't admit their errors or that they could have done something better when the public believes otherwise.

Maintaining a Consistent Visible Presence

Unlike Pampers, many brands do not have the luxury of 40-plus years of thriving brand equity.

The next brand we will look at was popular with one generation in the 1970s and 1980s, and had to rebuild its equity 15 years later. Through aggressive and even controversial moves, the brand has regained an awareness and identity through consistent and frequent messaging.

Candie's Brand Turnaround Story

Candie's was a very sexy shoe brand that was hot and then was not. Candie's was first designed and marketed by Charles Cole, the father of shoe designer and retailer Kenneth Cole, in the early 1980s through his company El Greco. The first Candie's shoe, known as the "slide," was a sexy, high-heeled "mule" that took off when Olivia Newton-John wore tight pants and high-heeled shoes similar to the Candie's in the movie *Grease*. By the mid-eighties more than 14 million pairs of slides were sold—one out of four American women owned a pair.

Charles Cole sold a 60 percent majority interest in El Greco to a U.K. firm in 1986. Sales dropped from a peak of $130 million in 1984 to $29 million in 1991, as the price for Candie's footwear increased and marketing for the brand steadily decreased.

Neil Cole, another son of Charles Cole, had played an integral role in the first success of the Candie's brand and saw an opportunity to revive it when 1970s fashions returned to the stores. Neil Cole's firm purchased the shoe company in June 1991. Later the company went public.

The brand was on a path to revival in the mid-1990s with a multimillion-dollar ad campaign that reflected women's increased independence 15 years after the shoe's original launch. One popular television commercial featured two women traveling across the country in scenes reminiscent of the women's adventure movie *Thelma and Louise*. After further brand extensions and licensing agreements, the company was acquired in 1993 by the Iconix Brand Group.

In 1996, with the company on sound financial footing, Neil Cole orchestrated an even bigger full-scale resurgence of the Candie's slide shoe through collaboration with well-known fashion designers such as Betsey Johnson, Nicole Miller, and Anna Sui. This time, marketing the brand to young women required a brand-new plan, as research showed that only 30 percent of this target was familiar with Candie's.

How Brand Equity Put Candie's Back on Track

Since the new target market was clueless to history of the hot and sexy Candie's brand, the company invested in a major ad campaigns with sexy, super-celebrity talent to help spread the sultry buzz.

It knew that no matter how great a product is, if the market does not hear it and see it in a compelling way, they forget it. Candie's used bold advertising in national media. From the first ad, the message was bold and provocative. Jenny McCarthy, former *Playboy* centerfold and TV personality, appeared prominently in fashion and lifestyle publications with not much on other than the shoes. These edgy and controversial ad campaigns coincided with the launch of the *Jenny McCarthy Show* on MTV.

The Candie's/McCarthy ads generated a lot of talk, but they were rejected by many. This slight controversy just increased the brand profile and persona. *Vogue* and *Cosmopolitan* said no thank-you to an ad showing McCarthy ogling a plumber's butt. Equally racy celebrity ads with other celebrities followed. The "Anywhere You Dare" ad campaign with former child star Alyssa Milano was banned, as were ads featuring Carmen Electra and Dennis Rodman. Criticism and praise was loud, but history repeated itself as Candie's regained popularity.

These moves also crafted Candie's comeback image as a fearless, sexually charged brand with strong ties to the "it and in" girls of pop culture. All of these high-profiled rejections made the brand even more loved and sweeter to loyalists, earning Candie's lots of free publicity in both broadcast and print channels. Through the years, in its marketing, the brand would continue leveraging top celebrities, including Fergie, Britney Spears, the Dixie Chicks, and most recently Vanessa Hudgens, former *High School Musical* sweetheart.

In the early 2000s, with its brand now well reestablished and back, Candie's began a semimoral, but not always uncontroversial, reformation. In 2001, the brand started a foundation to influence youth culture about preventing teen pregnancy. The program was designed to increase awareness and provide young girls with information so they could make the right decisions. It included events, national advertising, online social engagement, and, again, high-profile celebrity involvement.

One of its efforts was the launch of an "abstinence" app featuring a crying baby that represented an "insta-dose of parenthood!"[14] When you click on an image of a baby, the loop begins and a pink logo pops up telling you to "Pause Before You Play." Among other celebrities, the campaign features Bristol Palin and Mike "The Situation" Sorrentino in a "spontaneous'" conversation backstage at *Dancing with the Stars* about abstinence and safe sex. According to the head of Candie's Neil Cole, the video was viewed nearly one million times in just three days on YouTube.

While the initiatives earned lots of publicity and attention, many critics were in a huff about Bristol Palin earning more than $260,000 for her contributions to the campaign. Related pregnancy prevention charities got $35,000. The company defends its payment to Palin, saying that her ads and the reporting about her PSAs reached one billion people and, they say, that number is growing. They also noted that the Candie's Foundation gives only a small amount to other groups that work directly to help prevent teen pregnancy, because the foundation believes it can reach more people through endorsements and advertising.

Cole, the company's CEO, has explained in media interviews, "The primary purpose of the foundation is to educate American teens. . . . We talk to millions of teenagers through celebrity and media about how they shouldn't have babies. A clinic may deal with hundreds of people; we are trying to change culture." [15] A survey by YPulse, a youth media research firm, polled one thousand 14- to 19-year-olds in January 2011. It showed that 57 percent of respondents said Bristol's PSA got their attention, compared with 27 percent for a noncelebrity announcement.[16]

In 2005, Candie's scored a major deal with Kohl's department stores in which the retailer was granted exclusive rights to sell all Candie's merchandise *except* shoes in its more than 1,000 stores in the United States.

Today the brand is back, as popular as ever and associated with the young, sexy, and active junior markets exclusively in Kohl's stores. The brand continues to expand in global markets through licensing agreements.

The Candie's brand rebounded because Candie's rebuilt its brand equity by doing these things:

- *Leveraging and updating its earlier brand identity.* Candie's bought exposure with paid ads; earned fashion credibility by associating the brand with top celebrities; and it kept its name in the news by making itself relevant by leading change and campaigning for sexual responsibility, reducing teen pregnancy through its educational foundation.
- *Being consistent.* Candie's never strayed from its playful and sexy image. Its classic pink logo and naughty girl persona is seen in high-profile fashion magazines, such as *Vogue* and *Cosmo*, and on its website and social media sites. This style consistency and color is apparent in its fully integrated marketing programs that include outdoor, online, in-store signage, and direct mail campaigns.
- *Maximizing celebrity cobranding.* Candie's engagement of top pop culture celebrities, such as its recent choice, Vanessa Hudgens, has been another strong and consistent branding asset.
- *Focusing on exclusive relationships* Candie's partnerships with Kohl's provides entrée into more than 1,000 retail stores and co-op marketing opportunities.
- *Courting and translating controversy into visibility and publicity.* Candie's has never been shy about a little rule breaking and controversy. From its racy ads to the stir about Bristol Palin, it knows that this attention just builds more equity in the core customer.

Turnaround Takeaways

There is no perfect formula for which media choose or what methods to use to build brand equity for the future or how to use it to help bounce back from an incident—that depends on many factors such as the brand's offering, audience, and resources. Nevertheless, the following are all ways to add to a brand's equity and are worth addressing, especially if your brand is working through a comeback.

- *Recognize the new warehouse of weapons and use them.* From social media networks like Facebook, Twitter, YouTube, and LinkedIn to self-published microsites and blogs, social media have given the public new voices and power that can turn up the volume on a bad situation in a matter of minutes; brands know this. They also know that same communication pipeline can reverse the negative sentiment just as fast.

  They also tap into thousands of diverse and highly targeted media channels, both on and offline. At the same time, they don't neglect traditional media.
- *Maximize partner and friend support.* For a commercial or nonprofit brand, this can be a strategic partner with a strong brand; for an individual brand, this can be a likable or sympathetic spouse or family member.
- *Employ authoritative stand-ins for the brand.* These non-human symbols communicate your credibility, professionalism, and expertise in your category. For some brands, a graphic standard and a high production quality are used; for others, it can be evidence of achievement, awards, industry recognition, and honors.
- *Use social proof.* Social proof is any kind of evidence that indicates others like what you are doing. This can be a testimonial from customers, widgets on your website that show social love from Facebook and Twitter, or logos of big media outlets that have covered your brand. All of these will further your credibility.

Brand equity is a social and emotional currency that brands need to have stored up before they need it. Brands earn it and keep it by

- Doing good deeds, behaving likeably, and creating a notable public profile
- Establishing easy methods for stakeholders to converse, provide feedback, and get help
- Maintaining a visible presence on social media channels with dedicated resources for marketing and research
- Balancing online dialogue with promotion and nonselling relationship building
- Valuing honest and transparent relationships with all stakeholders
- Leveraging third-party publicity and word of mouth
- Understanding the power and permanence of the web content
- Speaking the truth

Chapter 10

Game Changer 7: Own Your Distinction

When it comes to branding, if you run like the rest, are indistinct, or don't own your unique place in your customers' minds, your brand will likely become the equivalent of road kill.

Today, global economies offer so many choices, many of which provide value and solve problems. In an environment of so many options, blending in just ensures a brand's place as a price-driven commodity, which is a tough zone to play in and win. When buying decisions are based solely on price, margins shrink, and what was, or might have been, a brand is just another commodity. Loyalty is nonexistent, and defections are common. As a result, brands lacking individuality typically spend a lot more on marketing, because consumers can't identify why their product is any different or better than their competitors'.

Standout Brands Play Smarter

Distinctive brands find their marketing dollars are more effective because their investment links their product in the consumers' minds to recognizable and often proprietary innovations, compelling stories that are organic to the product and uniquely theirs, or a bold, breakaway campaign that people can't forget.

Clearly, creating a solid distinction is a pivotal strategy in successful brand building. The successful companies, organizations, and professionals that embrace this discipline are easy to spot: Their distinction is lodged in our brains. Ironically, for turnaround brands the other six Game Changers become easier to manage and get traction because they were built on a clear foundation of their distinction. Indeed, many brands that successfully turn around or survive a brand bump have done so faster because they have had a strong identity that includes unique attributes and brand assets.

The brands in this chapter own their space. They clearly know who they are, and they tout their distinctiveness to every corner of their identity. Although they have experienced a bump, the strategy, discipline, and practice of brand distinction have aided their journey back. Sure, a competitor could have jumped in the game, but it would have had some serious catching up to do to overcome the mental equity that these brands have accumulated.

Brand distinction can come from a brand's offering, persona, or experience. In most cases, it's a combination of these things. For healthy brands or brands in recovery, true distinction serves as a bright flag that flies high above competitors' territory through good times and tough times.

Brand Distinction and Recovery

Brands in comeback mode are in a challenging position, as they are often fighting time and have limited resources. More important, they are playing catch-up and have the extra challenge of winning back the hearts and minds of fans and supporters.

Being distinct and owning a unique place is not going to turn a brand around by itself, but it is an engine of persuasive power that can speed things up and keep you on track while other parts of your game are improving.

Call it positioning or imprinting a brain tattoo (i.e., one's unique set of assets and propositions), every brand needs a mental marker that consumers can't get out of their minds and that sets it apart from all the other choices. In the oceans of sameness and "me-too" offerings, it is essential that turnaround brands dominate and own their points of distinction.

Turnaround brands must make up ground by quickly and efficiently earning back the trust, the credibility, and the authority they once had in their customers' minds. This means getting the attention of the consumer, standing out from competing players, being a positive memory, and proving the worth of the brand's value so the market lets it back in the game. Distinctiveness makes this possible, because it

- Eliminates confusion
- Gives more bang for the marketing buck by allowing marketers to focus on the brand's distinctive attributes
- Demonstrates another layer of value and relevance, often resulting in a premium price
- Gives consumers something extra to hold on to that makes it difficult to let the brand go

In the clutter of today's marketplace, all brands, whether they are a product, company, service, individual, or a cause, are competing for money, time, attention, and support. Being distinct, memorable, and unique is often the deciding factor in the ultimate buying decision.

It's been reported that the average grocery store has 40,000 SKUs (stock-keeping units) or products to select from; the typical department store has more than 50,000. Whatever your category is, consumer or business-to-business, there are likely many excellent and viable options for the buyer.

Consumers and buyers keep score as they rationalize their purchases, investments, and public support. Women especially have been known to rationalize even a completely emotional decision.[1] Rationalizing is the story the buyers tell themselves to give them a reason to buy. Brand distinction, unique attributes, character features, and distinct selling propositions provide these reasons. They represent extra value and extra points. When consumers or followers decide what to buy, support, or advocate, these reasons translate into "is the brand worth it to me?" questions.

Loyalty expert Jill Griffin who authored *Taming the Search-and-Switch Customer* and several other books on customer loyalty and customer win-back calls it the "Worth It Test." She recommends that brands answer these five important questions both internally and with their customers to grade their brand distinction:

1. Does our brand provide real substantive differences that are important to the customer?
2. Does the brand provide convincing proof of these differences?
3. Can we easily articulate the brand's differences?
4. Do employees exemplify the brand differences through word and deed?
5. Relative to the price difference, does the brand deliver substantially more value than our best competitor?

Here are two more internal questions:

1. Does our messaging and communication exemplify the brand differences?
2. Is our brand distinction easy to copy, or are the barriers of entry strong?

No doubt you didn't answer yes to all of these questions. Being distinct is not easy. And so many brands default to the notion that offering quality and loving customers is the ticket to distinction. They alone are not. Ninety-five percent of brands out there make those claims. Sure, quality and loving the customer are important, but distinct brands drill those concepts down deep and provide unique actions and evidence to prove them.

Finding real brand distinction takes these things:

- *Courage.* Most leading brands that are distinct were pioneers. This means creating ideas that are absolutely foreign and even odd to some people. It also means not letting naysayers and critics slow you down. That's scary for a lot of companies.
- *Long-term commitment over short-term results.* Stellar brand distinction does not happen overnight. It requires consistent building of the brand's platform and the strength not to waver or water it down to appease short-term revenue goals.
- *Integration.* A single ad campaign will not save a brand from drowning, nor will one unique product feature. Brand recovery and distinction victory come from a total integration of the brand in all touchpoints, media outlets, and so on. This requires operational and marketing discipline.

When it comes to building brand distinctiveness, there is no difference between healthy brands and brands in trouble. The principles are the same. Brands in trouble just don't have the luxury of time and, many times, the resources needed to demonstrate their distinction.

To be distinct in a meaningful way, the brand has to do these things:

- *It has to truly stand out.* The brand must look different, sound different, and act different than others.
- *It has to have legs.* The brand must be extended and woven into multiple consumer touchpoints.
- *It has to be relevant to the primary buyer.* Consumers must see the brand as fulfilling their needs and values.
- *It has to have strong barriers to entry.* This will make it difficult for competitors to copy the brand.

Geek Squad Brand Distinction Story

One of my favorite brand stories is Geek Squad. Its rise and journey should inspire every small start-up with a good idea. Geek Squad was started in 1994 by Robert Stephens, a former computer science major who dropped out of college with $200 and a bicycle. He turned a side job repairing personal computers into a global business-to-business and direct-to-consumer brand.

Within a year Stephens had two employees and 15 freelance agents, and $100,000 in billings. Clients included 3M and Cargill. Fast-forward: Best Buy does a two-year trial run with Stephens's company, putting a handful of Geek Squad agents inside one of its stores. Geek Squad soon expands to several major markets, and, in 2003, Best Buy acquires Geek Squad, with its 62 agents and almost $3 million in revenue. Stephens stays on as "founder and chief inspector." Today, Geek Squad has approximately 20,000 employees in 1,038 Best Buy stores and seven stand-alone Geek Squad locations.

Geek Squad's unique and distinct persona started in the very early days when Stephens was sending employees dressed in nerdy "uniforms" (consisting of too-short dark pants and white socks) to fix computer glitches at local companies or homes. Today the Geek Squad brand represents a modern-day team of special agents focused on helping people who are facing a range of gadget and technology challenges.

In an article titled "Geek Squad: Best Buy's Corporate Mythology," Kerri Susan Smith pointed out that from the beginning "Geek Squad had a cohesive and appealing mythology that worked with customers using computers at home. . . . Geek Squad's approach was reassuringly intimate: 'Of course it's confusing, but we'll be right there to rescue you.' [And] marketed itself effectively through stories that had characters. [For example,] employees would be called 'intelligence agents'. . . . 'counter intelligence agents' would help customers in the store, from behind the counter, etc. . ."[2]

Yet, despite all their success, the Geek Squad has made some missteps and experienced a few brand bruises.

A Question of Integrity

In 2006, Geek Squad was sued for allegedly using pirated copies of proprietary repair software. The lawsuit filed by Austin-based Winternals claimed that employees of Geek Squad continued using Winternals' proprietary software after the commercial licensing agreement with the retailer ended. Best Buy and Geek Squad were accused of copyright infringement, circumvention of copyright infringement systems, and misappropriation of trade secrets, commonly thought of as pirating.[3]

Negative publicity and online coverage like this can sting a brand's credibility and raise questions of integrity and trustworthiness. A settlement was eventually reached, and Winternals created a three-year agreement with Best Buy, allowing Geek Squad employees to lawfully use the software company's licensed programs.

Geek Squad handled the incident and got back to doing what it does well. Its strong identity as a leader in the gadget service and repair business and its team of badge-carrying professionals has overridden the issue.

A Question of Values

Different values correlate to different brand impressions. Geek Squad is a perfect example of this phenomenon. It has been praised for its help in identifying and convicting child pornographers in several states. Its technicians found the material on personal home computers they were repairing, and they called police. While this generated positive publicity for the company, some didn't see it that way. Some online communities, techno types, privacy advocates, and journalists, for example, as late as 2008, Violet Blue, a *Forbes* "Web Celeb" and one of *Wired* magazine's "Faces of Innovation," continued to hammer the brand.[4] Critics question the principles and ethics of a technology company that does not honor an important American value: privacy. Geek Squad's CEO has been grilled about this subject at several large technology conferences. With poise and confidence, Stephens defends his company's actions and then questions the bloggers who have attacked his brand, asking if they are bound by the same standards and integrity journalists were once held to.

The very nature of Geek Squad's business makes it a prime target for an online brand bashing, warranted or not. It seems to be managing the attacks and keeping its brand strong by building on its distinction and leadership position in the gadget fix-it space.

Both of these situations could cause brand dissention and be viewed as small dents. But a strong brand with shining-armor distinction keeps growing and moving forward.

Thus, Geek Squad has built its unique brand through these things:

- *Humor.* From its fresh-orange color scheme (for years, technology was conservative and mostly blue) to the quirky and unexpected brand characters, who show up in their signature Geekmobiles, the brand takes the edge off what could be a stressful situation.
- *Harmony.* Although the brand was bought by Best Buy, it has maintained its unique identity; at the same time, it comfortably cohabitates in the stores under its original brand, showing—in this case—that two brands can be better than one.
- *Helpfulness.* Geek Squad makes its living providing technology configuration and repair services through Best Buy stores everywhere; Geek Squad's YouTube channel includes hundreds of videos that show people how to do it themselves. It isn't trying to sell you services—at least, not at that point—it is simply being helpful.
- *Availability.* Geek Squad is the first national 24/7 task force dedicated to solving people's technology challenges.

Geek Squad's Brand Ownership

Geek Squad employs a wide range of techniques to ensure that its unique approach to gadget fixing and repair and brand resonates on touchpoints:

- *Package.* The look and feel is consistent—black-and-orange, quirky, and fun. Geek Squad's look is unmistakable, from the agents' badges and nerdy uniforms (even the bottom of the agents' black shoes are stamped with the Geek Squad logo, so it leaves marks in the mud) to the on-the-go Geekmobiles.
- *Culture.* The once-gimmicky story evolved into a complete way of doing business and building relationships with employees and customers. Stephens refers to his team as a closed social network with lots of dialogue.
- *Reach.* The Best Buy deal put the brand in the right place: millions of consumers buy all sorts of things, from gadgets to computers to home theaters, at Best Buy, and many of them need help on how to use the equipment as well as with setting it up and repairing it. On the other hand, anyone—not just Best Buy customers—can purchase the Geek Squad's services.
- *Communications.* As you would expect, the Geek Squad is involved in social media and has a team of public defenders responding to feedback and service issues.

Last, but not least, it makes its brand hard to copy.

Brand Distinction as Bounce Back Booster

Unlike Geek Squad, whose bumps did not have great impact on its earnings, the companies we are going to look at now not only experienced bad press but also had their sales take a hit. All recovered as the result of a variety of actions ranging from operational changes to product innovation and design and stepped-up marketing. But there's no doubt in any of these cases that strong brand distinction played an important role in their return to glory.

SunChips Brand Distinction Story

SunChips, a product of Frito-Lay, was launched in 1991 to meet a specific consumer demand for healthy alternatives to traditional snack foods. But not until sales were flatter than the chips did the company recognize that its core customers were also very interested in sustainability and good stewardship of the planet in the products they purchased. Soon after, the brand promise and distinction reflected that sentiment, and SunChips was repositioned as a healthy and eco-responsible brand.

The product seemed to deliver on all of those promises and the healthy-for-you, a good-for-the-earth practices became a hallmark of the brand's distinction. The snacks contain nutritious ingredients, 18 grams of whole grain, and some extra fiber for good measure; furthering the brand's distinction, much of it was produced in plants that used solar energy instead of fossil fuel.

Furthering Its Distinction, SunChips Stumbles

This story kept on growing. In the spring of 2009, Frito-Lay told its fans that SunChips would now be packaged in a new biodegradable bag made from plant material that was completely compostable. The original bags, made from polymers such as polypropylene and polyethylene, weren't recyclable. In fact, Frito-Lay's research predicted it could take more than 100 years for the original bags to decompose.

The new packaging was launched with a lot of promotional noise around Earth Day. But that noise was nothing compared to the noise from rattled customers. The new bags, when crinkled, were obnoxiously loud. So loud, in fact, that consumers were not shy about making a bigger rumble. News coverage about the problematic packaging followed; chatter on social media sites was everywhere; there even were Facebook pages complaining, "Sorry But I Can't Hear You Over This SunChips Bag" that gathered more than 44,000 fans.

The bag malfunction and ensuing bad press led SunChips' sales to decline by more than 11 percent in a span of 52 weeks, and Frito-Lay soon reverted to its non-eco-friendly packaging.

It seems that consumers were willing to deal with small annoyances for the sake of the environment, but the bag issue crossed the green line. Frito-Lay didn't crumble the brand's good intentions after the incident. SunChips soon announced that it had developed a "quieter compostable bag," which used a rubbery adhesive between the bag's layers to soften noise.

Just when Frito-Lay thought the packaging mess was behind them. CBS's *Early Show* aired a segment featuring Bob Markovich of *Consumer Reports*, who claimed that the bags did not decompose in 13 weeks as the company claimed. Markovich said his team placed SunChips bags in a home compost pile and tended the pile for three months, only to find at the end of the process that the bag had hardly changed. Frito-Lay responded to the segment by stating that it partnered with an independent laboratory to evaluate how well the packaging composted and received third-party certification from the Biodegradable Products Institute.

While the packaging snafu was a bump for the brand, the company nevertheless earned points from the market when it listened to its customers, responded to the issue, and was transparent about the problem and solution.

Efforts from the healthy and green repositioning have paid off. In an interview with *BrandWeek.com*, Gannon Jones, the vice president of marketing for Frito-Lay, said that its environmentally friendly campaign struck a chord with consumers, as sales saw a significant jump after the start of the campaign. SunChips came to be viewed as different from its competitors. The Frito-Lay product has rooted its brand in environmental causes as well as health-forward thinking. "This strategy has paid off handsomely," says Jones, "as SunChip sales are up 17.6 percent, totaling $201.8 million for the 52 weeks ending June 15, per IRI (Industrial Research Institute)."[5]

Their distinction is clear, the trend toward sustainability and healthy choices continues to grow, and more than 500,000 Facebook fans still love 'em.

SunChips Repositions and Rebounds

When SunChips decided to reposition as the "good for the planet, good for you" snack, it clearly carved out its spot on the green grass and did an excellent job of taking this story to all of its touchpoints, namely:

- *A healthy product.* SunChips, made with whole-grain ingredients, contain 30 percent fewer calories than potato chips.
- *Healthy partners.* SunChips has also partnered with other health-promoting brands, such as the 34,000 Subway shops worldwide, and it has participated with eco-supporting nonprofit organizations such as *National Geographic* to give away grants of $20,000 each to five people who come up with the best ideas to make their communities greener. It has also joined forces with Earth911.com as a major sponsor of the 2010 Earth Day Twitter contest which offered prizes for tips on reducing, reusing, and recycling waste.
- *Green values, processes, and practice.* The brand has made a major commitment to green practices and manufacturing and to paying attention to the full life of the product packaging, from compostable packaging to solar energy and providing education to consumers on eco-practices. In 2011, the brand donated $1 to environmental education funds for each person who went to SunChips' Facebook page and clicked the "Like" button.

Next, we come to a company that lost its fizz. The confection brand went kaput when the government banned one of its sweetening agents. Its strong distinction was a key ingredient in its comeback.

Fizzies Brand Distinction Story

Fizzies were introduced to the market in 1957 by Emerson Drug Company (whose signature product at the time was Bromo-Seltzer, an effervescent headache remedy). They are fun tablets that, when dropped into a glass of water, fizz and dissolve, creating sweet-flavored, bubbly drinks that kids love.

In 1962, the Emerson Drug Company was acquired by Warner-Lambert Co., which sold the product nationally. Available in seven flavors, sales exploded both nationally and internationally, achieving more than double the sales volume of its chief competitor, Kool-Aid. According to a spokesperson for the company, even the government purchased them for troops during the Vietnam conflict to flavor poor-tasting water.[6]

In 1968, the U.S. Food and Drug Administration banned cyclamates (artificial sweeteners), which were used to bond Fizzies ingredients. Production of the tablets ceased, and Fizzies went off the market. In 1995, the original makers reformulated Fizzies using aspartame (Nutrasweet), and Fizzies were back on the market until 1996, when the company filed for bankruptcy.

In 2005, the Fizzies trademark was bought by Amerilab Technologies, which sweetened it with sucralose (also used in Splenda). Fizzies have taken off again; this time focused on distribution through the independent confectionery channel. Fizzies are carried by more than 25 major confectionery distributors, hundreds of independent retailers, and numerous catalogs and websites. The product has been referenced in the Food Network's *Unwrapped* series, in movies (e.g., *Animal House*), and by comedians (Red and Rover, among others).

How Fizzies Got Its Zip Back

Fizzies sells to candy channel retailers. The obvious market for Fizzies is the independent store frequented by baby boomers. But, as it learned the hard way in 1996, this strategy is not enough to bring the brand back; the company had to expand its thinking and reach. It has done so by creating these things:

- *A distinct experience and product.* To stay true to the sentiment and unique character of the brand, the company has spent a lot of time promoting the distinct experience and nature of the product. "The pop fizz sensation is a very cool thing for grandparents, parents, kids, and kids at heart," explained Chris Rodengen, Sales and Marketing Coordinator for the company. "We often hear from . . . baby-boomer[s] stories about the positive experience of sharing Fizzies with their grandkids. They remember having contests with their friends to see who could keep the fizzing tablet in their mouth the longest, and kids enjoy making their own beverage and watching it fizz. It's old meets new. And it's distinctly Fizzies, and other confections like Snickers or Milky Way bar can't touch that." [7]

- *A distinct mix—healthy, innovative, and fun.* Fizzies have no fat; one tablet has only five calories and 100 percent of the Vitamin C people need. Because they use an artificial sweetener, they can be eaten by people on diets or with diabetes. With the growing media attention to the negative effects of obesity, soda pop, and corn syrup, the company has recognized that a healthier and more affordable alternative to soda represents a big opportunity.

- *A breakaway category.* Fizzies is now being promoted as more than a candy. Fizzies have begun to be incorporated in many different treats. Independent retailers have experimented with using Fizzies as an ingredient. Crush it, bake it, top it, or fizz it. Fizzies have been incorporated into sundaes, ice cream cones, milk shakes, rice crispy bars, sugar cookies, and cupcakes. All of these concoctions add to the feeling that Fizzies is not just a product but an experience. Fizzies have also been found in a variety of unique gift baskets.

  The company is currently developing more convenient packaging and configurations to meet the needs of schools, some of which have already expressed interest in carrying the product as a soda alternative, which opens a new market for Fizzies. In some schools, kids have even used the candy in science experiments.

- *A unique delivery system.* One of Fizzies most influential marketing efforts stresses Fizzies' portability. Fizzies can be enjoyed anywhere there is water and easily fits into backpacks and water bottles, which positions it nicely in the big on-the-go market. Camping, picnics, field trips, walking, and bicycling represent a few of the many options.

The Fizzies brand has rebounded because Fizzies is a unique standout-in-a-crowd brand. Its unique candy/beverage offer is quirky and fun. The brand leverages its distinction on all touchpoints, from its packaging, website, social media story about the secret formulas at the Fizzies Factory to the endless new Fizzies concoctions for adults and kids.

Brand distinction applies to all kinds of brands—commercial, cause-related, individual. Distinction is vital for all.

Brand Distinction and the Individual Brand

Pee-wee Herman is an individual brand who got into trouble and has recovered. His unique style of comedy launched his career in the late 1980s and early 1990s; then, one day, it suddenly changed.

Pee-wee Herman Brand Distinction Story

The actor/comic Paul Reubens began his career in the 1970s doing an "improv" act that was intended for adult audiences. In 1980, he developed a stage show, *The Pee-wee Herman Show*, which was filmed and aired on HBO in 1981. The character in that show, Pee-wee Herman, went on to become Reubens' brand. Later, he toned down the act for children and became a very successful star in the Emmy-winning *Pee-wee's Playhouse* from 1986 to 1991. His 1985 film, *Pee-wee's Big Adventure*, is now iconic.

On July 28, 1991 all that ended. The *Orlando [Florida] Sentinel* headline read, "TV Star Pee-wee Herman Arrested at Adult Theater."[8] Herman had been arrested for obscene behavior in an X-rated theater by an undercover cop. That Pee-wee was a children's favorite made his arrest all the more damaging. Had he simply been a movie star, the incident probably would have subsided quickly. But Pee-wee's status as a children's star, combined with his clownishness, immediately lent his image a dangerous clown vibe. A story in the *Sarasota (Florida) Herald-Tribune* ran under the headline "Pee-wee's Problem: What To Tell Kids?"[9] A movie in development was canceled as was his TV show.

Paul Reubens' response was to poke fun at what had happened to him. His first appearance after his arrest was at the 1991 *MTV Video Music Awards*, where he asked, "Heard any good jokes lately?" The actor/comic appeared as the Pee-wee Herman character only intermittently during the next two decades. Reubens did play some roles as other characters, for example, in movies such as *Blow*, with Johnny Depp.

When you have talent, time can be a healer, and it appears that Pee-wee Herman is back. In June 2010, Reubens did an interview with the *New York Times* in which he talked about a new movie. In August of that year, he went as Pee-wee to the Sturgis Motorcycle Rally , where he tried to lead the largest ever "Tequila" dance. (Pee-wee's dance on toe-point to the pop tune "Tequila" was a highlight of *Pee-wee's Big Adventure*.) *The Pee-wee Herman Show* opened on Broadway in November 2010 and aired on HBO in March 2011. In January 2011, Herman appeared on *Saturday Night Live*.

Paul Reubens is a gifted actor and comedian. He built a unique brand that is so strong that most people don't even know his real name; he's just Pee-wee. Even his star on Hollywood's Walk of Fame reads "Pee-wee Herman." From his signature laugh, to the bow tie and goofy suit, Pee-wee Herman is a distinct brand through and through. Check out his website (http://www.peewee.com/); it reeks of the iconic quirky star's brand. Were it not for his established, consistent, and distinct identity, his future would have looked very different.

Action Plan to Develop Brand Distinction

Whatever type of brand yours is, consider how you can maximize its unique features or what you can add to it to make it stand apart from all others. There are two parts to distinction planning. First, you need to identify your opportunities for difference. Distinction can be developed and leveraged with these things:

- Distinct brand niches or specialties
- Distinct brand personality or characteristics
- Distinct brand physical and size stature
- Distinct brand look and feel
- Distinct brand innovations
- Distinct brand campaigns
- Distinct combinations
- Distinct delivery methods
- Distinct pricing
- Distinct policies
- Distinct locations
- Distinct processes
- Distinct materials
- Distinct formula
- Distinct brand stories
  - Things you have exclusively—for example, a collection of rare bird eggs
  - Things you have done exclusively—for example, broken records or made history
  - Things you *don't* have: calories, toxic ingredients, and so on
  - Things you did first—for example, sent your product to the moon
  - Things you do differently—for example, don't have assigned seats on a plane

Second, you must own your distinction, transforming a single idea into clear title to your turf. This can be done by doing these things:

- Articulating your distinctions in a simple, concise way
- Creating patterns of social, industry, and credibility proof in all your touchpoints—for example, having social proof (e.g., the number of

"likes" on Facebook) and industry proof (e.g., an award, credibility proof, or certification)

- Effectively translating your distinction to market segments within your fan base
- Leveraging symbols and messages (e.g., taglines, icons, graphic marks, coined phrases) in internal and public communications

Turnaround Takeaways

Distinction alone will not save a brand from a bad situation, but it will accelerate the process by giving buyers something to hold onto that translates into value. Super brands not only identify their points of difference but also weave them into the total brand experience by doing these things:

- Pushing beyond quality of product and love for customers (everyone says that!)
- Identifying truly unique services, products, and character traits
- Communicating the distinction in clear, memorable, and remarkable ways
- Making sure these unique characteristics matter to the buyer
- Setting up barriers to copy the distinctions
- Leveraging all the senses, media, and touchpoints

Afterword

Returning home and to glory is the ultimate reward for every brand that has fallen out of favor.

As I finished writing this book, I realized how inspired I was by all the brands that turned around, didn't give up, and found the fortitude and relentless spirit to come back.

Driving change for brands in trouble is a tough journey and really one that never stops. There are always quick turns, bumps, potholes, and even flying objects—all scary, and many dangerous—that a brand must confront.

People, competition, the press, and even employees will sometimes be heartless and unreasonable.

Jobs will be on the line, egos will get beaten up, millions of dollars will fly out the window, and your new label may be big loser.

Stay the course. Put on your superhuman cape every day, and don't stop believing.

Brands gone bad get written off. They are declared unsalvageable, clinically dead. And yet every year, a pack of them return. I can explain some; others will forever remain a mystery.

Who would have thought that Exxon, the poster child for environmental catastrophes in the late 1980s would be toppled from that dubious honor by an even bigger disaster? Who, in the eighties would have believed Exxon would be the most profitable company in the United States and number two in the world in 2010 as reported in the *Fortune 500 Annual Report*?

Many wrote Chris Brown off and said his career was over after his conviction for felony assault and making criminal threats against his girlfriend. He was sentenced to five years' probation, abuse counseling, and community service. His talent, timing, and tenacity resurrected his battered brand. His anger issues and post-meltdown antics were dismissed by his fans, and his *F.A.M.E.* album went to number one on *Billboard*, selling more than 270,000 copies in the first week.

Both Exxon and Brown had naysayers; both returned to glory.

As I studied brands that faced death and defeat, I realized more than ever that for many the transformation was public and that many took the roads we've just examined. Others found their way through good luck and a deep-rooted network of friends and supporters who helped pull them out of the mud.

Brand turnarounds never really end. There will always be temptations, vices, challenges, and surprises. Throw in a few crazy characters and you have the recipe for many more brand turnaround stories.

If and when your brand gets hit by outside forces and uncontrollable situations, or if the bad or weak in you and/or your brand explodes, remember, there is life after a disaster and brand meltdown.

Take a deep breath and apply the seven game-changing strategies. Know that time heals and believe it is your time.

1. Take responsibility.
2. Don't give up.
3. Lead strong.
4. Be relevant.
5. Keep improving.
6. Build equity.
7. Own your distinction.

If you are one of the lucky ones who dodged the bad luck and misfortune, apply the seven game-changing strategies and you will live a longer, healthier brand life.

It's an honor and joy for me to be in your brand universe. I congratulate you and your commitment to continue to learn and advance your brand and achieve your goals. If you need more help reach out through my website www.brandingdiva.com and visit my blog at www.brandturnaround.com, where I will continue to post updates on brands gone bad and their recovery. If you know of an interesting brand turnaround, please share the stories, shoot me an e-mail, or post it as a comment.

Brand on!

Resources

Brand turnarounds can be tough. Having trusted resources to add to your arsenal can certainly help with your efforts to excel. The following are some of my favorite resources that I recommend. They are companies and tools that provide brand-related services and knowledge, experts who have advised me, and other books and online publications from which I've gained a lot. This list is also posted and updated on my blog found at www.brand turnaround.com.

Crisis Communications and Media Training Experts

Denis Calabrese, Deniscalabrese@aol.com
Frank Robertson, Frank Robertson Media,
    http://www.frankrobertsonmedia.com/
Merrie Spaeth, Spaeth Communications, Inc.,
    http://www.spaethcom.com

Customer Loyalty and Winback Expert

Jill Griffin, The Griffin Group, http://www.loyaltysolutions.com

Marketing, Branding Insight Websites and Blogs

Nicole Armstrong, http://www.morethanalogoblog.com/
Brandchannel, http://www.brandchannel.com
Cool News of the Day, http://www.reveries.com/
Seth Godin, http://sethgodin.typepad.com/
Martin Lindstrom, http://www.martinlindstrom.com/

MarketingProfs.com, http://www.MarketingProfs.com
MarketingSherpa, http://www.marketingsherpa.com
Marketing Virtual Library, http://www.KnowThis.com
John Moore, http://www.brandautopsy.com
Online marketing, http://www.copyblogger.com/
Andy Sernovitz, http://www.damniwish.com/, http://gaspedal.com/blog
David Taylor, http://www.wheresthesausage.typepad.com

Online Brand Monitoring Services

NetBase, http://www.Netbase.com
Radian 6, http://www.radian6.com

Research Experts and Brand Value Ranking Reports

The Blackbaud Index of Online Giving, http://www.blackbaud.com/
Brand Keys, http://www.brandkeys.com/
Millward Brown Optimor, http://www.millwardbrown.com
Top 100 Global Brands Report, http://interbrand.com
YouGov, http://today.yougov.com

Storytelling Coach

Doug Stevenson, http://www.dougstevenson.com

Trend Websites and Blogs

Springwise, http://www.springwise.com
Ubercool, http://www.ubercool.com

Recommended Reading

Branding

Aaker, David A. *Brand Relevance: Making Competitors Irrelevant.* Jossey-Bass, 2011.

Gobé, Marc. *Emotional Branding: The New Paradigm for Connecting Brands to People.* Allworth Press, 2001.

Kelly, Francis, and Barry Silverman. *The Breakaway Brand: How Great Brands Stand Out.* McGraw-Hill, 2005.

Lindstrom, Martin. *Brandwashed,* Crown Business (September 20, 2011).

Lindstrom, Martin. *Brand Sense.* Free Press, 2010.

Lindstrom, Martin. *Buyology,* reprint ed. Crown Business, 2010.

Manners, Tim. *Relevance: Making Stuff That Matters.* Portfolio Hardcover, 2008.

Murry, Brian H. *Defending the Brand: Aggressive Strategies for Protecting Your Brand in the Online Arena.* AMACOM, 2003.

Trout, Jack. *Differentiate or Die: Survival in Our Era of Killer Competition.* Wiley, 2001.

Change

Balasco, James, and Ralph Stayer. *Flight of the Buffalo: Soaring to Excellence, Learning to Let Employees Lead.* Warner Books, 1994.

Godin, Seth. *Linchpin: Are You Indispensable?* Portfolio Trade, 2011.

Godin, Seth. *Pock the Box.* The Domino Project (March 1, 2011).

Heath, Chip, and Dan Heath. *Switch: How to Change Things When Change Is Hard.* Crown Business, 2010.

Pink, Daniel H. *Drive: The Surprising Truth about What Motivates Us.* Riverhead Hardcover, 2009.

Ressler, Cali, and Jody Thompson. *Why Work Sucks and How to Fix It: The Results-Only Revolution.* Portfolio Hardcover, 2008.

Emotional Wellness

Hyatt, Carole, and Linda Gottlieb. *When Smart People Fail: Rebuilding Yourself for Success.* Penguin Books, 1993.

Loehr, James E. *Stress for Success.* Crown Business, 1998.

Rosner, Bob. *Working Wounded: Advice that Adds Insight to Injury.* Faces Publishing Company, 1998.

Leadership

Healey, Joe. *Radical Trust: How Today's Great Leaders Convert People to Partners.* Wiley, 2007.

Smith, Anthony F. *The Taboos of Leadership.* Jossey-Bass, 2007.

Loyalty

Griffin, Jill. *Customer Loyalty: How to Earn It, How to Keep It.* Jossey-Bass, 2002.

Griffin, Jill. *Taming the Search-and-Switch Customer.* Jossey-Bass, 2009.

Word of Mouth/Trust

Brogan, Chris, and Julien Smith. *Trust Agents: Using the Web to Build Influence, Improve Reputation, and Earn Trust.* Wiley, 2009.

Sernovitz, Andy. *Word of Mouth Marketing: How Smart Companies Get People Talking,* rev. ed. Kaplan Press, 2009.

Diversity Marketing

Godin, Seth. *We are All Weird.* The Domino Project, 2011.

Notes

Chapter 1

1. Willie Pietersen, *Reinventing Strategy: Using Strategic Learning to Create and Sustain Breakthrough Performance*, New York: John Wiley & Sons, Inc., 2002, 180.

2. Steven Greenhouse, "Nike Shoe Plant in Vietnam Is Called Unsafe for Workers," *New York Times*, November 08, 1997, http://www.nytimes.com/1997/11/08/business/nike-shoe-plant-in-vietnam-is-called-unsafe-for-workers.html?pagewanted=4 http://www.nytimes.com/1997/11/08/business/nike-shoe-plant-in-vietnam-is-called-unsafe-for-workers.html.

3. "Domino's Inc.," FundingUniverse.com, accessed May 7, 2011, http://www.fundinguniverse.com/company-histories/Dominos-Inc-Company-History.html.

4. "Domino's Inc." http://www.fundinguniverse.com/company-histories/Dominos-Inc-Company-History.html.

5. Chris Matyszczyk, "Domino's apologizes for booger-sandwich video," Cnet News, April 15, 2009, http://news.cnet.com/8301-17852_3-10220787-71.html.

6. http://www.redcrossblood.org/learn-about-blood/blood-facts-and-statistics, accessed July 31, 2011.

7. www.blackbaud.com/files/graphs/bbindex-online.html, accessed July 31, 2011.

8. Phil Jackson, *The Last Season: A Team in Search of Its Soul*, New York: Penguin Press, 2004, 143.

9. "Pete Rose Gambling Scandal—Rose Admits Betting on Reds to Win Every Night," 411lowdown.com, accessed May 7, 2011, http://www.411lowdown.com/2007/03/14/pete-rose-gambling-scandal/.

10. ESPN NBA, "Kobe Bryant's Apology," September 2, 2004, http://sports.espn.go.com/nba/news/story?id=1872928, accessed July 31, 1011.

11. "NBA Nicknames," Kidzworld.com, accessed May 9, 2011, http://www.kidzworld.com/article/6449-nba-nicknames.

12. Kitty Bean Yancey, "Aruba: Caught in the Winds of a Mystery," *USA Today*, September 29, 2005, http://www.usatoday.com/travel/news/2005-09-29-arubaupdate_x.htm, accessed July 31, 2011.

Chapter 3

1. http://en.wikipedia.org/wiki/ValuJet_Flight_592, accessed August 8, 2011.

2. Reiches Baird, "Restructuring: Why Should a Company Change Its Name?" ReichesBaird.com, accessed May 26, 2011, http://www.riechesbaird.com/resources/res_at.aspx.

3. Bruce Horovitz, "What's in a Name? Company Survival," *USA Today.com*, September 29, 1997, http://pqasb.pqarchiver.com/USAToday/access/16378300.html?dids=16378300:16378300&FMT=ABS&FMTS=ABS:FT&type=current&date=Sep+29%2C+1997&author=Bruce+Horovitz&pub=USA+TODAY&desc=What%27s+in+a+name%3F+Company+survival&pqatl=google.

4. Associated Press, "ValuJet to Buy AirTran, Drop Its Name," *Augusta Chronicle*, July 24, 2011, http://chronicle.augusta.com/stories/1997/07/11/biz_211199.shtml.

5. http://www.sbnonline.com/2007/09/intensive-care-how-kim-cripe-built-an-executive-team-to-turn-around-children-x2019-s-hospital-of-orange-county/, accessed August 11, 2011.

6. http://www.choc.org/about/index.cfm, accessed August 11, 2011.

7. Daniel H. Pink, *Drive: The Surprising Truth About What Motivates Us,* New York: Riverhead Books, 2009.

8. Cali Ressler and Jody Thompson, *Why Work Sucks and How to Fix It: No Schedules, No Meetings, No Joke—the Simple Change That Can Make Your Job Terrific,* New York: Portfolio, 2008.

9. Jim Collins, *Good to Great: Why Some Companies Make the Leap... and Others Don't,* New York: Harper Business, 2001. And Jim Collins, *How the Mighty Fall: and Why Some Companies Never Give In,* New York: Jim Collins, 2009.

10. ABC News/Entertainment, "When Fame and Addiction Run in the Family," http://abcnews.go.com/Entertainment/CelebrityCafe/story?id=8248270&page=2, accessed August 11, 2011.

11. http://www.forbes.com/wealth/celebrities/list?ascend=true&sort =moneyRank, accessed August 11, 2011.

12. http://www.hollyworth.com/robert-downey-jr-net-worth, accessed August 11, 2011.

13. http://en.wikipedia.org/wiki/Kwame_Kilpatrick, accessed August 11, 2011.

14. Krissah Thompson, "With Detroit in Dire Straits, Mayor Invites Big Thinking," *Washington Post,* February 8, 2011, http://www.washington post.com/wp-dyn/content/article/2011/02/07/AR2011020705338. html, accessed August 11, 2011.

15. Kurt Badenhausen, "America's Most Miserable Cities," *Forbes,* January 29, 2008, http://www.forbes.com/2008/01/29/detroit-stockton-flint -biz-cz_kb_0130miserable.html, accessed August 1, 2011.

16. "January Sales Come in at Satisfactory Pace," February 1, 2011, http://www.autoobserver.com, accessed August 1, 2011.

17. Louis Aguilar "Cool Factor Lures the Young, Artsy to Detroit," *The Detroit News,* June 29. 2011, http://www.detnews.com/arti-cle/20110629/BIZ/106290366/Cool-factor-lures-the-young—artsy -to-Detroit, accessed August 8, 2011.

18. Christopher Baum, "Seven Steps to More Productive Positioning," *Destination Marketing Monthly*, March 19, 2008, http://www.destinationmarketing.org/DMAI_News/IssueView .asp?IssueID=58&CommType=DMM, accessed August 8, 2008.

19. Chris Jones, "What Happens in Reno a Victory for Las Vegas," *Gaming News*, August 16, 2006, http://www.casinocitytimes.com/ news/article/what-happens-in-reno-a-victory-for-las-vegas-160449, accessed August 1, 2011.

20. Nathan Skid, "Whole Foods Browses in Midtown," *Crain's Detroit Business*, April 3, 2011, http://www.crainsdetroit.com/ article/20110403/FREE/304039993/whole-foods-market-browses -in-midtown#.

21. Securities and Exchange Commission, Washington, D.C., Litigation Release No. 17465 / April 11, 2002, http://www.sec.gov/litigation/ litreleases/lr17465.htm, accessed August 8, 2011.

22. James Sterngold, "Man Opens Fire in Xerox Office, Killing 7," *New York Times*, November 3, 1999, http://www.nytimes.com/, accessed August 8, 2011.

23. Betsy Morris "The Accidental CEO: She Was Never Groomed To Be The Boss. But Anne Mulcahy Is Bringing Xerox Back From The Dead," CNNMoney, June 23, 2003, http://money.cnn.com/ magazines/fortune/fortune_archive/2003/06/23/344603/index.htm, accessed August 8, 2011.

24. Ibid.

25. "Xerox Chairman Mulcahy: Leading a Turnaround," *Wall Street Journal* online video, April 27, 2009, accessed August 8, 2011.

26. "Crisis Helped to Reshape Xerox in Positive Ways," Knowledge@ Wharton, November 16, 2005, http://knowledge.wharton.upenn.edu/ article.cfm?articleid=1319, accessed August 8, 2011.

27. Anne Mulcahy, "Leadership: Six Leadership Lessons That Work," Women's bix.us, undated, http://www.womensbiz.us/issues/may07/ leadership.asp, accessed August 8, 2011.

Chapter 4

1. Judith Rehak, "Tylenol made a hero of Johnson & Johnson: The recall that started them all," *New York Times*, March 23, 2002, http://www.nytimes.com/, accessed August 15, 2011.

2. Jerry Knight, *Washington Post*, October 11, 1982 as quoted in Tamara Kaplan, "The Tylenol Crisis: How Effective Public Relations Saved Johnson & Johnson," http://www.grif.com.au/Tylenol.79.0.html, accessed August 15, 2011.

3. Ann Landers, "Johnson & Johnson Handles Tylenol Crisis with Integrity," syndicated column, December 7, 1982, http://news.google.com/newspapers?id=hZpQAAAAIBAJ&sjid=pV0DAAAAIBAJ&pg=6604,6893244&dq=tylenol+johnson+and+johnson+package&hl=en, accessed August 15, 2011.

4. Tamar Lewin, "Tylenol Posts an Apparent Recovery," *New York Times*, December 25, 1982, http://www.nytimes.com/1982/12/25/business/tylenol-posts-an-apparent-recovery.html, accessed August 15, 2011.

5. Jeff Jarvis, "Dell lies. Dell sucks," June 21, 2005, http://www.buzzmachine.com/archives/cat_dell.html, accessed August 15, 2011.

6. Dell Hell, http://www.dell-hell.blogspot.com/, accessed August 15, 2011.

7. "Hanging Up On Dell?" *BusinessWeek*, October 10, 2005, http://www.businessweek.com/magazine/content/05_41/b3954102.htm, accessed August 15, 2011.

8. George W. Bush, "Text of Bush Speech," CBS News.com, February 11, 2009, http://www.cbsnews.com/stories/2003/05/01/iraq/main551946.shtml, accessed August 15, 2011.

9. Helene Cooper and Sheryl Gay Stolberg. "Obama Declares an End to Combat Mission in Iraq," *New York Times*, August 31, 2010, http://www.nytimes.com/2010/09/01/world/01military.html, accessed August 15, 2011.

10. "1938: 'Peace for our time'—Chamberlain" BBC Home, http://news.bbc.co.uk/onthisday/hi/dates/stories/september/30/newsid_3115000/3115476.stm, accessed August 15, 2011.

11. http://en.wikipedia.org/wiki/Deepwater_Horizon_oil_spill #Consequences.

12. "Gulf of Mexico Oil Spill (2010)," *New York Times*, updated April 25, 2011, http://topics.nytimes.com/top/reference/timestopics/subjects/o/oil_spills/gulf_of_mexico_2010/index.html, accessed August 15, 2011.

13. Ibid.

14. http://www.montblanc.com/products/11867.php, accessed August 15, 2011.

15. Erika Kinetz, "Montblanc's $25,000 Gandhi Pen Stirs Controversy," *USA Today*, updated October 2, 2009, http://www.usatoday.com/money/world/2009-10-02-mont-blanc-india_N.htm, accessed August 15, 2011.

16. "Anger at Montblanc's Gandhi Pen," BBC News, October 2, 2009, http://news.bbc.co.uk/2/mobile/business/8287754.stm, accessed August 15, 2011.

17. Emily Wax, "Consternation in India Over $23,000 Commemorative Gandhi Pen," *Washington Post*, October 3, 2009, http://www.washingtonpost.com/wp-dyn/content/article/2009/10/02/AR2009100203191.html, accessed August 15, 2011.

18. Ashby Jones, "The Lawsuit's in the Past, But Taco Bell is Still on the Offensive," Law Blog, April 20, 2011, http://blogs.wsj.com/law/2011/04/20/the-lawsuits-in-the-past-but-taco-bell-is-still-on-the-offensive/, accessed August 15, 2011.

19. Joanne Kaufman, "The Fall of Jimmy Swaggart," *PEOPLE Magazine*, March 7, 1988, http://www.people.com/people/archive/article/0,,20098413,00.html, accessed August 15, 2011.

20. Joanne Kaufman, "Scandals: No Apologies This Time," *Time Magazine U.S.*, October 28, 1991, http://www.time.com/time/magazine/article/0,9171,974120,00.html, accessed August 15, 2011.

21. Jeff Bailey, "JetBlue's C.E.O. Is 'Mortified' After Fliers Are Stranded," *New York Times*, February 19, 2007, http://www.nytimes.com/2007/02/19/business/19jetblue.html, accessed August 17, 2011.

22. Ibid.

23. Scott Mayerowitz, "Angry JetBlue Flight Attendant Flees Plane at JFK Airport via Emergency Slide," August 9, 2010, http://abcnews .go.com/US/jetblue-flight-attendant-steven-slater-arrested-flight-jfk/ story?id=11361298, accessed August 17, 2011.

24. Rachel Sklar, "David Letterman Blackmail Shocker: Host Confesses To Affairs After Extortion Attempt," *Mediaite*, October 2, 2009, http://www.mediaite.com/tv/david-letterman-blackmail-shocker-host-confesses-to-affairs-after-extortion-attempt/, accessed August 17, 2011.

25. Ibid.

26. Ibid.

27. Matea Gold and Scott Collins, "David Letterman affair Is No Joke," *Los Angeles Times*, October 3, 2009, http://www.latimes.com/ entertainment/news/la-et-letterman3-2009oct03,0,878590.story, accessed August 17, 2011.

28. "Professor Albert Mehrabian's Communication Model," Businessballs.com, accessed May 27, 2011.

29. Associated Press "Rangel Vows Not to Resign," August 10, 2010, http://www.wbur.org/2010/08/10/rangel-not-to-resign, accessed August 17, 2011.

30. Devlin Barrett, "Rangel Censured for Ethics Violations," *Wall Street Journal*, December 3, 2010, http://online.wsj.com/article/SB1000142405274 8703377504575651131359459018.html, accessed August 17, 2011.

31. Aixa Velez, "Edwards Mistress: I Am Not a Home Wrecker," April 29, 2010, http://www.nbcchicago.com/news/local/Reille-Hunter -Denies-Shes-a-Home-Wrecker—92421259.html#ixzz1VJeXp3FjNBC Chicago, accessed August 17, 2011.

32. Springboard, "Akio Toyoda Will Not Appear Before Congress," HubPages [undated], http://springboard.hubpages.com/hub/ Akio-Toyoda-Will-Not-Appear-Before-Congress, accessed August 17, 2011.

33. Stephen Evans, "A Spitzer in the Eye for Glaxo," BBC News, June 4, 2004, http://news.bbc.co.uk/2/hi/business/3778377.stm, accessed August 17, 2011.

34. Editorial, "After Eliot Spitzer," *New York Times*, March 13, 2008, http://www.nytimes.com/2008/03/13/opinion/13thu2.html, accessed August 17, 2011.

Chapter 5

1. "Michael Vick: Doing Time," 60 Minutes, CBS News, August 16, 2009, 5:00 PM, http://www.cbsnews.com/video/watch/?id=5245553n, accessed August 17, 2011.

2. Rosalind S. Helderman, "'Straight Arrow' Considers Health-Care Suit," *Washington Post*, December 8, 2010, http://www.washington post.com/wp-dyn/content/article/2010/12/07/AR2010120706982. html, accessed August 17, 2011.

3. "Martha's Mess . . . . An Insider Trading Scandal Tarnishes the Queen of Perfection." *Newsweek*, July 1, 2002.

4. "Martha's Last Laugh: After Prison, She's Thinner, Wealthier & Ready for Prime Time." *Newsweek*, March 7, 2005.

5. Brooks Barnes, "Show Skewers Martha Stewart, With Her Blessing," *New York Times*, August 10, 2008, http://www.nytimes.com/2008/08/11/business/media/11martha.html, accessed August 19, 2011.

6. Krysten Crawford, "Martha Ready to Do Time: Trendsetter Wants to Start 5-month Sentence Soon to Get this 'Nightmare' Over With," September 15, 2004, http://money.cnn.com/2004/09/15/news/news makers/martha/index.htm, accessed August 17, 2011.

7. Mary Vinnedge, "Arianna Huffington: Pushing the Limits," *Success*, [undated], http://www.successmagazine.com/arianna-huffington -pushing-the-limits/PARAMS/article/1184/channel/22#.

8. Chris Stanford, "10 Questions for Arianna Huffington," *Time Magazine U.S.*, July 3, 2008, http://www.time.com/time/magazine/

article/0,9171,1820145,00.html#ixzz1VVx6Z2IK, accessed August 19, 2011.

9. Nikki Finke, "Celebs to the Slaughter: Why Arianna's Blog Blows," *LA Weekly*, May 12, 2005, http://www.laweekly.com/2005-05-12/ news/celebs-to-the-slaughter/, accessed August 17, 2011.

10. David Carr and Jeremy W. Peters, "Big Personality and Behind-the-Scenes Executive Prove a Top Media Team," *New York Times*, February 7, 2011, http://www.nytimes.com/2011/02/08/business/ media/08huffington.html?pagewanted=all, accessed August 17, 2011.

Chapter 6

1. Anthony F. Smith, *The Taboos of Leadership: The 10 Secrets No One Will Tell You About Leaders and What They Really Think*, San Francisco: Jossey-Bass, 2007, jacket.

2. Ibid., inter alia. and interview with Karen Post, April 2011.

3. David Dukcevich, "Faces in the News," *Forbes*, January. 9, 2002, http://www.forbes.com/2002/01/09/0109facesam.html, accessed August 18, 2011.

4. Rebecca Leung, "Self-Made Maverick," *60 Minutes*, December 5, 2007, http://www.cbsnews.com/stories/2004/02/12/60minutes/ main599975.shtml, accessed August 20, 2011.

5. Ibid.

6. "NBA Team Valuations, #6 Dallas Mavericks," Forbes.com, undated, http://www.forbes.com/lists/2010/32/basketball-valuations-11 _Dallas-Mavericks_324736.html, accessed August 20, 2011.

7. "Michael S. Jeffries," Forbes.com, undated, http://people.forbes.com/ profile/michael-s-jeffries/520, accessed August 20, 2011.

8. "Flip-Flops, Torn Jeans—And Control," *BusinessWeek*, May 30, 2005, http://www.businessweek.com/magazine/content/05_22/b3935105 .htm, accessed August 20, 2011.

9. Benoit Denizet-Lewis, "The Man behind Abercrombie & Fitch," Salon.com, January 24, 2006, http://www.salon.com/life/feature/2006/01/24/jeffries, accessed August 20, 2011.

10. Ibid.

11. Mark Williams, "'Drinking 101' Controversy Helps Abercrombie & Fitch, Analysts Say," in *Seattle Times*, August 24, 1998, http://community.seattletimes.nwsource.com/archive/?date=19980824&slug=2768292, accessed August 20, 2011.

12. "Abercrombie to Pay $2.2 Million in 'Uniform' Suit," Consumeraffairs.com, August 11, 2003, http://www.consumeraffairs.com/news03/abercrombie.html., accessed August 20, 2011.

13. Jerry Higgins, "Abercrombie & Fitch's 'Look Policy': Jim Crow Gets a Corporate Makeover," Imagine 2050, July 8, 2011, http://imagine2050.newcomm.org/2011/07/08/abercrombie-fitch%E2%80%99s-%E2%80%9Clook-policy%E2%80%9D-jim-crow-gets-a-corporate-makeover/, accessed August 20, 2011.

14. Gilbert W. Harrison "Managing Retail to Outlast the Recession," TMA, May 14, 2009, http://www.turnaround.org/Publications/Articles.aspx?objectId=10954, accessed August 20, 2011.

15. Benoit Denizet-Lewis, "The Man Behind Abercrombie & Fitch."

16. Sally Squires, "Digging Into Pirate's Booty Reveals Skullduggery," *Washington Post*, February 24, 2002, viewed at http://articles.sun-sentinel.com/2002-02-24/health/0202210711_1_veggie-booty-pirate-s-booty-fruity-booty, accessed August 20, 2011.

17. Maggie Farley, "Mom Blows Whistle on 'Booty' Snack," *Los Angeles Times*, viewed at May 20, 2002, http://articles.sfgate.com/2002-05-20/news/17546005_1_meredith-berkman-fruity-booty-pirate-s-booty, accessed August 20, 2011.

18. Heather Lally, "Pirate's Booty Turns Out to Be Fool's Gold," *Spokesman Review*, March 12, 2002, http://news.google.com/newspapers?id=OCcSAAAAIBAJ&sjid=lfIDAAAAIBAJ&pg=5303,516023&dq=pirate%27s-booty&hl=en, accessed August 20, 2011.

19. Sally Squires. "Digging Into Pirate's Booty Reveals Skullduggery," *Washington Post*, February 24, 2002. http://articles.sfgate.com/2002 -05-20/news/17546005_1_meredith-berkman-fruity-booty-pirate-s -booty, viewed August 20, 2011.

20. Maggie Farley, "Mom Blows Whistle on 'Booty' Snack," *Los Angeles Times*.

21. *"Woman sues Pirate's Booty Maker for dlrs 50 Million Saying Snack Food Label Foiled Her Diet," AP Worldstream*, April 13, 2002, http:// www.3fatchicks.com/forum/weight-loss-news-archive/15424- woman-sues-pirates-booty-maker-dlrs-50-million-saying-snack- food-label-foiled.html, accessed August 20, 2011.

22. Rob Walker, "Consumed: Snack Mentality," *New York Times Magazine*, June 29, 2008, http://www.murketing.com/journal/?p=1339, accessed August 20, 2011.

23. Helen Coster, "Tainted Booty," *Forbes Magazine*, April 21, 2008, http://www.forbes.com/forbes/2008/0421/084.html, accessed August 20, 2011.

Chapter 7

1. Urban Dictionary, http://www.urbandictionary.com/define.php?term =Hardly-Ableson and The Motorcycle Bikers Dictionary, http://www .totalmotorcycle.com/dictionary/H.htm, accessed August 21, 2011.

2. http://en.wikipedia.org/wiki/Sturgis_Motorcycle_Rally, accessed August 21, 2011.

3. Rick Barrett, "Recession Takes Toll on Harley Dealers: Store Closings Place Number of U.S. Dealerships at About Same Level as 2002," Milwaukee Wisconsin, *Journal Sentinel*, http://www.jsonline.com/ business/114839684.html, accessed August 21, 2011.

4. Adweek staff, "How Harley-Davidson Drives Mobile Marketing, Facebook," April 29 2009, http://www.adweek.com/news/advertising -branding/how-harley-davidson-drives-mobile-marketing-facebook -105714, accessed August 21, 2011.

5. Koselka, Rita, "The Dog That Survived," *Forbes*, November 9, 1992, p. 82.

6. Read more: Wolverine World Wide Inc.—Company Profile, Information, Business Description, History, Background Information on Wolverine World Wide Inc. http://www.referenceforbusiness.com/history2/88/Wolverine-World-Wide-Inc.html, accessed August 21, 2011.

7. Read more: Wolverine World Wide Inc.—Company Profile, Information, Business Description, History, Background Information on Wolverine World Wide Inc. http://www.referenceforbusiness.com/history2/88/Wolverine-World-Wide-Inc.html#ixzz1VrykTAQA, accessed August 23, 2011.

8. Koselka, Rita, "The Dog That Survived," *Forbes*, November 9, 1992, op cit.

9. http://www.cfda.com/past-winners/, accessed August 23, 2011.

10. http://twitter.com/#!/BarbieStyle/status/35495695423111168, accessed August 23, 2011.

Chapter 8

1. Nick Beams, "Ford and GM Debt Reduced to Junk Bond Status," World Socialist website, May 9, 2005, http://www.wsws.org/articles/2005/may2005/gm-m09.shtml, accessed August 25, 2011.

2. Ibid.

3. Ian Swanson, "Rejecting Bailout Wins Political Capital for Ford," January 27, 2010, The Hill, http://thehill.com/homenews/administration/78211-rejecting-bailout-wins-political-capital-for-ford, accessed August 25, 2011.

4. *Associated Press*, "McDonald's Pushing Salads and Pedometers," April 15, 2004; Diet & Fitness MSNBC.com, http://msnbc.msn.com/id/4749559/, accessed August 25, 2011.

5. Agence France Presse, "Michelle Obama Happy with McDonald's Menu Shift," July 11, 2011, http://news.yahoo.com/michelle-obama

-happy-mcdonalds-menu-shift-171330772.html, accessed August 25, 2011.

6. http://www.mcdonalds.com/us/en/food/food_quality/nutrition_ choices.html, accessed August 25, 2011.

7. M&S People, http://marksintime.marksandspencer.com/People/ accessed August 25, 2011.

Chapter 9

1. Steve Boggan, "Nike Admits to Mistakes over Child Labour," *The Independent/Americas*, October 20, 2001, http://www.independent. co.uk/news/world/americas/nike-admits-to-mistakes-over-child -labour-631975.html, accessed August 25, 2011.

2. Steven Greenhouse, "Nike Shoe Plant in Vietnam Is Called Unsafe for Workers," *New York Times*, November 8, 1997, http://www. nytimes.com/1997/11/08/business/nike-shoe-plant-in-vietnam-is -called-unsafe-for-workers.html?src=pm, accessed August 25, 2011.

3. Eun Lee Koh, "Nike to Raise Minimum Age of Its Workers at Shoe Factories, 18, but 16 at Shops that Make Apparel," *San Francisco Chronicle*, May 13, 1998, e: http://www.sfgate.com/cgi-bin/article. cgi?f=/e/a/1998/05/13/NEWS10565.dtl#ixzz1W4LoCRsS, viewed August 25, 2011.

4. John H. Cushman Jr., "International Business: Nike Pledges to End Child Labor and Apply U.S. Rules Abroad," *New York Times*, May 13, 1998 http://query.nytimes.com/gst/fullpage.html?res=9C02E0DC14 30F930A25756C0A96E958260, accessed August 25, 2011.

5. E.J. Dionne, Jr., "A Victory over Nike: and a Win for Sweatshop Workers," viewed at http://findarticles.com/p/articles/mi_m1252/ is_n11_125/ai_n27538550/, accessed August 25, 2011.

6. "Advertisers Switching from 30- to 15-Second TV Spots," Advertising@Suite101, October 29, 2010, http://www.suite101.com/content/ advertisers-switching-from-30-to-15-second-tv-spots-a302033, accessed August 25, 2011.

7. Ben Popken, "New Dry Max Pampers Causing Rash, Burns, Sores, Boils?" The Consumerist, April 26, 2010, http://consumerist.com/2010/04/new-dry-max-pampers-causing-rash-burns-sores-boils.html, accessed August 26, 2011.

8. Trevor Butterworth, "Procter and Gamble has a Virtual 'War of the Worlds' Moment," Forbes.com, May 25, 2010, http://www.forbes.com/2010/05/25/war-of-the-worlds-marketing-opinions-columnists-trevor-butterworth.html, accessed August 26, 2011.

9. "Pampers Calls Rumors Completely False," May 6, 2010, http://www.pginvestor.com/phoenix.zhtml?c=104574&p=irol-newsArticle&ID=1423829, accessed August 26, 2011.

10. Dan Sewell, "P&G hosts bloggers in defense of Pampers Dry Max," May 20, 2010, http://finance.yahoo.com/news/PG-hosts-bloggers-in-defense-apf-3920454817.html?x=0, accessed August 26, 2011.

11. "CPSC and Health Canada Find No Cause Linking Pampers Dry Max to Diaper Rash," September 2, 2010, http://www.pampers.com/en_US/parenting-articles/pampers-dry-max-diapers/101465, accessed August 26, 2011.

12. Sheila Shayon, "Pampers Isn't Tossing Dry Max," June 15, 2010, http://www.brandchannel.com/home/post/2010/06/15/Pampers-Promotes-Dry-Max.aspx, accessed August 26, 2011.

13. Susan Carey, "U.S. Fines Continental, US Airways," *Wall Street Journal,* June 2, 2011, http://online.wsj.com/article/SB10001424052702303657404576361662241658484.html?KEYWORDS=us+airways+and+continental+fined, accessed August 26, 2011.

14. "Free Abstinence App from Sexy Candies Shoes," Feminists for Choice, January 19, 2011, http://feministsforchoice.com/free-abstinence-app-sexy-candies-shoes-2.htm, accessed August 26, 2011.

15. "Bristol Palin's Outrageous Payday," Daily Beast, April 6, 2011, http://www.thedailybeast.com/articles/2011/04/06/bristol-palins-big-teen-pregnancy-awareness-paycheck-raises-eyebrows.html, accessed August 26, 2011.

16. Ibid.

Chapter 10

1. Tracy, "Mary Kay and the Art of Rationalization," Pink Truth, May 4, 2011, http://www.pinktruth.com/2011/05/mary-kay-and-the-art-of -rationalization/, accessed August 26, 2011.

2. Kerri Susan Smith, "Geek Squad: Best Buy's Corporate Mythology," Knowledge @ W. P. Carey website, January 14, 2009, http://knowledge .wpcarey.asu.edu/article.cfm?articleid=1731, accessed August 26, 2011.

3. David Utter, "Winternals Picks a Fight with Geek Squad," Security Pro News, April 13, 2006, http://www.securitypronews.com/news/ securitynews/spn-45-20060413WinternalsPicksAFightWithGeek Squad.html, accessed August 26, 2011.

4. Violet Blue, "The Geek Squad's ongoing porn problem/Bloggers catch the tech service pilfering porn and it turns into a local PR disaster, while Violet Blue wonders 'Is nothing sacred?'" SFGate.com, February 21, 2008, http://articles.sfgate.com/2008-02-21/living/ 17119604_1_consumerist-hard-drive-customers, accessed August 26, 2011.

5. Brandweek.com, August 11, 2008, quoted in John Grubb, "Post #4: Sunchips' Marketing . . . Paying off," March 7, 2011, http://johngrubb .wordpress.com/2011/03/07/post-4-sunchips-marketing-paying-off/, accessed August 26, 2011.

6. Interview with Chris Rodengen, Sales and Marketing Coordinator, Amerilab Technologies, May 13, 2011.

7. Ibid.

8. "TV Star Pee-wee Herman Arrested at Adult Theater," *Orlando Sentinel,* July 28, 1991, http://articles.orlandosentinel.com/1991-07 -28/news/9107280441_1_pee-wee-herman-pee-wee-playhouse -reubens, accessed August 25, 2011.

9. David Grimes, "Pee-wee's Problem: What To Tell Kids?" *Sarasota (Florida) Herald-Tribune,* August 13, 1991, http://articles.sun-sentinel .com/1991-08-13/news/9101300884_1_pee-wee-herman-movie -theater-daddy, accessed August 26, 2011.

Index of Brands

Index

About the Author

Karen Post is an entrepreneur, branding authority, and author. Her first book, *Brain Tattoos: Creating Unique Brands That Stick in Your Customers' Minds,* was published in 2004.

Known to many as the "The Branding Diva" for over three decades she has been building memorable brands that sell product, advocate causes, create loyalty, and add value.

Since 2000, she has led Brain Tattoo Branding, a firm that provides creative and strategic services to start, grow, and manage brands. Karen is also a sought-after speaker who addresses global audiences, and she is proud to have been the first female American speaker to address the Saudi Arabian Airlines national conference in 2011.

Karen started her first business at age 22, and built two successful companies—an award-winning ad agency and a legal communications firm specializing in high-stakes litigation that she led for more than 20 years.

Throughout her career, her work has benefited diverse industries, from start-ups to Fortune 500 companies, including Albemarle, ACNielsen, Choice International, Cox Cable and Media, Saudi Arabian Airlines, Chevron, Johnson & Johnson, Bank of America, Xerox, Sara Lee, Pepsi, and Procter & Gamble along with many emerging businesses, trade associations, professional athletes, entertainers, and politicians.

Karen is a regular branding commentator on FOX TV and has been featured in other business and marketing print, broadcast, and online media outlets, including FOX, NBC, Bloomberg TV, CBS's *Early Show,* the *New York Times,* the *New York Post, Fast Company, Miami Herald,* the *Boston Globe, Financial Times, Entrepreneur, Success Magazine,* and *NPR.*

CPSIA information can be obtained
at www.ICGtesting.com
Printed in the USA
LVOW02*1402230916

505964LV00001B/1/P